Prisoners of War

True stories of evacuees: their lost childhood

by H V Nicholson

The Blitz began in September 1940 and for the first time since the beginning of the Second World War the civilian population of Britain experienced the terror of German bombs. Suddenly, the Government's evacuation scheme, which was started a year earlier and had been ignored by the majority of the population, began to make sense. Millions of people took refuge in the countryside, among them hundreds of thousands of children who were sent away from their homes, most of them to live with strangers. What happened to those children? Were they all looked after by kindly foster parents? Were they all given plenty to eat and tucked up in bed for the night with comforting words? That is the spin that has been put on the evacuation for 60 years. But, sadly, the truth is different. These are the true stories, told for the first time, of evacuees who lost their childhood. They were abused sexually, physically and mentally throughout the war. Some have lived with feelings of guilt and shame for 60 years. Others harbour bitter memories. All have survived to tell tales that are astounding in their frankness. They are also funny and full of compassion. They want to share them with you.

First published in 2000 by
Gordon Publishing, London
PO Box 23882, London SE15 2WN

Cover picture: The Imperial War Museum

Cover design: Leroy Playford

A catalogue record for this book is available from the British Library
ISBN No. 0 9538960 0 5

Printed and bound in Great Britain by Omnia Books Limited

Preface
by Dr Sebastian Kraemer

Each generation has to learn new and unpalatable facts about the care of children. The evacuation itself exposed the extent of child poverty that had hitherto been invisible to the better off. Later, in the 1960s we were forced to acknowledge the reality of "battered babies" and, perhaps even worse, in the 1980s child sexual abuse. Yet in the 1940s doctors were already beginning to understand that our attachment to those whom we love is the most precious resource we have, and its disruption a damaging wound that is not easily repaired later, if ever. The pioneering child psychiatrists John Bowlby (founder of the Department for Children and Parents at the Tavistock Clinic), Emanuel Miller (father of the doctor and theatre director Jonathan) and Donald Winnicott wrote to The Times to protest at the effect of evacuation on pre-school children but it was never published. Bowlby said in a letter to his wife in November 1939 "the letter to The Times seems to have been sabotaged, which is annoying". They did publish a well-argued letter in the British Medical Journal in December 1939, with little effect.

Children were sent miles away to live with strangers, while their parents stayed at home. The purpose was to protect the children from bombs. The result was that they were separated from their parents, whom they could daily imagine might be killed during an air raid, and placed in the care of people they did not know. As Susan Isaacs, the psychoanalyst who surveyed the effects on children evacuated to Cambridge, said: "In time of danger and uncertainty, individuals have even greater need for unity and for the reassurance provided by the familiar background of their lives. The evacuation might have been far less of a failure if it had been planned with more understanding of human nature, of the way in which ordinary parents and ordinary children feel and are likely to behave."

As is often stated many children had wonderful experiences, seeing the countryside for the first time in their lives and being cared for with kindness and love. This book is about those, not necessarily a minority, who were not so lucky. They were abused and neglected, and their stories have not been told before. These revelations of harsh treatment could perhaps not have been fully accepted until now, given the tendency of all generations until this one to minimise children's evidence, even to blame them for disclosing it. At this late stage we can see that narrative can still have some healing effect, however modest.

As the author warns us, a "strong stomach" is required to read these accounts. Ms Nicholson's primary task is not so much to explain why all this happened, but to provide a narrative and a record. Yet we can meanwhile speculate on the motives of abusive foster parents of wartime Britain.

Though many are nostalgic for the good old days, the lives of children were not generally as good then as they are today (even taking into account the shameful fact that Britain, today, has more children living in poverty than any other leading European nation). The idea that children needed to be thought about, rather than simply provided for and trained to obey, was not prevalent then. Many people of course loved their children in spite of the gloomy advice given out in the earlier years of the century by such "experts" as J B Watson and Frederic Truby King whose effect on a whole generation would now be regarded as frankly abusive. They advocated harsh regimes, even for infants, in order to stop anyone being spoiled. Childhood was effectively regarded as a training for an adulthood of obedient service, including of course in war. Some of these children became the foster parents of the subjects of this book. The awakening of real awareness of children's lived experience takes a long time.

Dr Kraemer is a Consultant Child and Adolescent Psychiatrist at the Tavistock Clinic, London. With a team of psychiatrists, psychotherapists and psychologists, it is one of the foremost clinics in the world for the treatment of emotionally traumatised children and adults.

CONTENTS

CONTENTS

CONTENTS

Page

CONTENTS

Acknowledgements

I have written this book because I was an evacuee who suffered physical cruelty for five years during the Second World War. I felt there must be thousands of others so I asked dozens of local newspapers if they would publish a letter inviting evacuees to write to me. I received hundreds of replies. My heartfelt thanks must go, first of all, to all of them. The evacuees who collaborated on this book are a smashing bunch of people and during the time *Prisoners of War* was being written, they gave me much encouragement. I want to thank my sister Joyce, who not only shared the trauma of our evacuation, but who has also helped me to get *Prisoners of War* publicised. I owe a tremendous debt of gratitude to Jane Reed CBE, a great friend, and a brilliant editor from whose kindness and professional opinion I have benefitted. My thanks, also, to Sally Baker, another friend and an outstanding sub-editor, who cast her professional eye over the book. I want to thank Ned Garland and Joe Widdows without whom it would never have made it to the printers and Lesley Bliss, a secretary in a million, who creates order out of chaos. And, finally, I would like to express my thanks to the many librarians I have encountered who were unfailingly helpful.

Chapter One
Like lambs to the slaughter

Some of the case histories in this book are traumatic and you will need a strong stomach to read them. Although the majority of evacuees may have been treated kindly and have lasting and loving memories of those years, this book is about the forgotten minority who lost their childhood. The evacuees who were thrown to the wolves.

It was a monstrous thing to do. Even the despised Nazis thought no children under ten should be evacuated without their parents. The British Government of 1939 is the only one in the history of the world which carried out such a policy on such a scale. Why did it do it? And why did so many parents acquiesce?

The obvious answer to the first question is that there was a war on. Well, yes. But if neither the Germans nor the French sent off their little ones like parcels, complete with a luggage label, to live with complete strangers, why did we? Even in Scotland they evacuated families, not children on their own. The fact that it worked so well says much for the kindness of most ordinary people and the resilience of children.

But for many evacuees the rather rosy myth that we were all sent away from the danger of bombs in the inner cities to the countryside where we were well treated, were fed fresh food and enjoyed fresh air for the first time, is a distortion of what actually happened. While fathers, brothers, uncles and cousins were sacrificing their lives on our behalf, to save us from being crushed by the Germans, many of their children were being treated as badly as if the enemy were already our masters. While my father, who was in the RAF, and many others like him, were engaged in the Battle of Britain in August 1940, and my mother, who was a nurse, was tending those wounded in the Blitz, which began a month later in September, 1940, many of their fellow citizens were betraying them by being cruel to their children.

It is not the purpose of this book to find fault with all those people who did generously open their homes to look after evacuees; the purpose is to give voice to all those thousands of evacuees who were abused physically, mentally and sexually. Such stories have rarely been heard, their experiences have been brushed under the carpet of history.

Truth, it is said, is the first casualty of war and it is amazing how often one version of history becomes accepted as the only one, any other slipping away into landfills. Uncomfortable though it may be to highlight what really went on behind the net curtains of so many homes in the British Isles during the Second World War, justice demands that the truth, as experienced by many evacuees, should be told. Soon it will be too late to record these first-hand testimonies.

Not only did the Government encourage parents to send their children away through the use of propaganda that amounted to emotional blackmail, the households where evacuees were to be received were given no choice in the matter; for them taking in an evacuee, if they had room to spare, was obligatory. This inevitably led to resentment among some people. Class bigotry was far worse 60 years ago and this policy was deeply unpopular with the host families who for the most part had no idea, and no wish to know, how the other half lived.

The Government could have built camps where children would at least have been together, a policy advocated by many concerned experts whose views were mostly ignored. Partly the building of camps was considered too expensive and would require manpower, builders, carpenters and so on needed elsewhere, but also some military advisers warned that the Germans would find camps for children excellent targets. Where the Government fell down, in the view of people who suffered as a result of the evacuation policy, is in not making arrangements to ensure evacuees were cared for properly. Child guidance specialists warned at the time sending children away to live with strangers was fraught with danger.

Susan Isaacs, a respected child development officer, wrote at the time, “In a misguided attempt to lessen the evils inherent in exile, many have tried to make out that evacuation is actually a good thing, something sensible, which it takes a war to bring into effect. But to me evacuation is a story of tragedies; either the children are emotionally disturbed, perhaps more than they can recover from, or else the children are happy and it is the parents who suffer, the implication being that they are not needed even by their own children. For me, the only success the scheme can claim is that it could fail.”

A government committee, latterly under the chairmanship of Sir John Anderson, had been meeting for years to discuss what to do about evacuation in the event of another war with Germany. A year before the first evacuation took place in September 1939, Miss Mary Sutherland, representing the Standing Joint Committee of Industrial Women’s Organisations, told the evacuation committee that what it was planning would not be acceptable.

"The majority of mothers would much prefer some system of family evacuation rather than any scheme for evacuating children as a special group. I think the reaction of mothers, especially ordinary working class mothers, is based on a deep-rooted instinct that it is a good thing in times of stress and strain for families to be united rather than separated. There is also the feeling that where children are separated from their parents in such circumstances great damage might be caused to the sensitive minds of the children." They say that in war soldiers are lions led by donkeys. In the evacuation children were like lambs led by wolves.

The Government was repeatedly warned that evacuating children on their own was not necessarily a good idea. In May 1938 Sir John received a letter which pointed out: "It is much easier to move children than to move children plus adults. Should the policy aim at the widest dispersal of children over small and relatively scattered localities less liable to continuous air raids, that policy may mean greater safety but greater loneliness."

A report by the Liverpool School of Social Science said that in the evacuation areas the family, the basic unit of society, would be broken up and in the reception areas the family would be gravely disturbed, which would lead to serious economic and psychological difficulties. The report went on, "For most working-class mothers the main, perhaps the sole, purpose in life is the bringing up of their children. With the evacuation of the children this purpose disappears. Each social group in society has its own standard of living and behaviour but under this scheme the different groups will be forced to live together. In the absence of imminent danger from air raids neither group will take kindly to this new way of living nor make any effort to accommodate itself to the other."

They suggested many problems could be solved if trained social workers were appointed in each reception area to visit the homes where children were evacuated, to give informal advice and to straighten out any difficulties. As most of us now know, this suggestion was not acted upon.

John Bowlby, the eminent child psychiatrist, wrote, "When small children are separated from home and given for long periods to the care of strangers in strange surroundings, their whole character development may be seriously endangered." His opinion was not heeded.

In *Psychological Trauma: A Developmental Approach*, Dora Black et al conclude, "The importance of the social context is of particular relevance when considering evacuation in time of disasters or conflict, which may serve more to satisfy the emotional needs of the helpers than the recipient. It is suggested that people in threatening situations are more likely to feel secure when they can stay with their relatives in familiar places and that removal to places of safety often causes extreme insecurity and anxiety about the fate of relatives."

Even the Ministry of Health early on assumed that "separation might involve greater risks than did air-raids" and a meeting of psychiatric clinicians at the Tavistock Centre, London, predicted, "There is in this situation a very real danger that the seeds of neurosis will be sown in an increasing number of children, and apart from the immediate distress and disability arising from this (evacuation) there is the wider question of what these children will go through as adolescents and adults."

What happened to the evacuees when they became adolescents and adults is that they were the people who became the first generation of teenagers; the people who embraced rock'n'roll in the Fifties; the people who were the Swingers in the Sixties. Some of this new demand for freedom and disregard of authority by the younger generation must have had its roots in their abandonment as children, having been left to sink or swim at such a tender age. They grew up to have little respect for authority because the authorities had let them down.

The majority of evacuees, in spite of their abuse, and in some cases as a consequence of it, have grown up to be well-adjusted, caring, successful members of the community. You simply can't let the past drag you down and most managed to shake off their bad experiences. In his study, *Long-term Effects of Early Childhood Separation and Group Care*, psychiatrist Henry S. Maas, of the University of California, puts that down to the indomitability of the human soul.

Psychiatrist Dr Sesbastian Kraemer, who has written the Preface to this book, in *Changing Attitudes to Children* argues, “Sometimes it becomes clear that quite badly abused children had a few months or years of devoted care in infancy which we can suppose provided a kind of ‘immunity’ to later harm.”

The cycle of abuse I refer to in this book, in Dr Kraemer’s opinion, “is almost certainly demonstrated by the abusive foster parents themselves, many of whose parents would have been terribly strict and negligent a generation earlier”.

Why are the people who were evacuated as children during the Second World War speaking out now 60 years later about the cruelty they suffered? The truth is, no one ever bothered to ask them before. The persistent myth that evacuees had, on the whole, a jolly time of it, is so potent no one has ever challenged it. The odd report has appeared from time to time in books that have, in the main, subscribed to the rosy-glow version of history but no one has ever devoted an entire book to a collection of the horror stories of those war years from the evacuees’ point of view.

I have a few hundred true accounts of serious maltreatment; I am sure there are probably thousands. If only one in 20 evacuees was abused, and all the surveys completed recently by the NSPCC, and other charities concerned with abused children, put the figure of child abuse in the general population at a much higher level than that, a conservative estimate would put the number of evacuees who were abused at 75,000. This would not surprise me. Almost everyone I talk to who endured those years of separation has a tale to tell if not about themselves, then about a relative or friend.

Another reason people are talking about it now is that they have reached an age when they have time to think about themselves. All their lives they have been busy bringing up families and their own experiences as children were repressed: they were too busy getting on with life, doing things, to think about what happened to them. Also, because child abuse is talked about so much more openly today, it has helped them to realise that they are not alone and that what they went through is something that should be brought into the public domain.

Everyone else seems to be getting things off their chest; adults who were abused in children's homes are, rightly, having their abuse investigated by the police. For most evacuees that is not an option, although there are one or two whose stories are told here who have justified grounds for a criminal prosecution but no independent evidence: it would be simply their word against their abuser's. What is extraordinary is that hardly anyone tried to find out what happened to the evacuees during or after the war. It is partly to redress this imbalance, to give evacuees who were abused a platform and to validate their experiences that this book has been written. The fact that the majority may have come through the experience relatively unscathed does not alter the seriousness of those whose lives were blighted.

As John Bowlby says, "Why some individuals should recover, largely or completely, from experiences of separation and loss while others seem not to is a central question, but one not easily answered. In living creatures variation of response is the rule and its explanation is often hard to fathom. Of all those who contract poliomyelitis less than one per cent develop paralysis, and only a fraction of one per cent remain crippled. Why one person should respond one way and the rest in another remains obscure. To argue that, because 99 per cent recover, polio is a harmless infection would obviously be absurd. Similarly, in the field under consideration, to argue that because most individuals recover from the effects of a separation or loss these experiences are of no account would be equally absurd."

What makes the abuse of English evacuees so special is that the evacuation was ordered by a government and therefore what happened to those children was sanctioned by a government. It was run by the Civil Service, by a network of officials whose energy was concentrated on getting the logistics right, not on the social and psychological welfare of the individual child.

It is true that 10,000 Jewish children were evacuated to Britain from Germany and Austria through the Kindertransport Movement but that was organised by the Jews themselves, albeit because of the actions of a government. I have not attempted to include what happened to the Jewish evacuees because their plight has been so comprehensively covered elsewhere. I did receive one letter from a Jewish lady who was English, not part of the Kindertransport scheme. She had five billets in all, some cruel, some just unkind, one wonderful. Another Jewish experience was given to me by a librarian who told me her late mother was evacuated with a woman who used to brush her hair back from her forehead and demand, "Where are your horns? I thought all Jews had horns."

It is surprising that there is so little published material about the psychological effects of evacuation. It was such an enormous social upheaval and its consequences, you would have thought, an interesting enough subject for investigation. It has not escaped the evacuees in this book that they have been ignored whereas in today's compensation culture people are given silly sums of money merely for have their feelings hurt.

At the very least I would like to see the Government offering to pay for good quality therapy for the many victims of abuse who are still suffering. The fact that evacuees are now pensioners makes no difference; in fact, it should make their case for counselling all the more urgent. Better they live out the last years of their lives with some inner peace than carry the psychological torment to their graves.

Terry Waite, the former aide to the Archbishop of Canterbury, who was taken hostage in Beirut and kept for years in solitary confinement, wrote recently how very fortunate he, the television reporter John McCarthy and the American journalist Terry Anderson, who were also hostages, were to receive help from a skilled team of post-traumatic stress counsellors from the RAF. "Put at its simplest," he says, "PTS counselling enables one to verbalise, and thus objectify, an experience in the company of a trained listener. This helps one to take hold of the experience, no matter how unpleasant, and manage it, rather than suppressing it and being managed by it in a negative way. I don't know where I would have been today without skilled help and I feel sympathy for those who never had the opportunity we had."

His ordeal was terrible but he was a grown man with all the wisdom, strength and resilience a lifetime can give. How much worse were the ordeals endured by small children with no such inner strengths to fall back on.

Governments, ours and others, are apologising today for all manner of atrocities, mistakes and policies of previous administrations going back hundreds of years: the Slave Trade, the Aborigines, Northern Ireland, Colonialism, Vietnam; there are even people saying sorry for the Crusades. Surely the fate of so many British children forcibly separated from their families only 60 years ago is worth at least a review.

One of the most convincing theories to explain why Stanley Baldwin's government, which was made up entirely of men, seemed to think packing children off was a sensible solution is that they all went to boarding schools. Belonging to the Eton/Oxbridge Establishment of upper-class English life, they were used to being torn from the bosom of their families at an early age and thought nothing of it. In fact they probably considered it character building. There is, however, no comparison between a boarding school, with all its faults, and a foster home.

Many evacuees hardly saw their parents again for five years; many more never received a letter, the foster parents confiscating them and often, cruelly, claiming there never was a letter in the first place. They were temporarily orphans, robbed of parental guidance and security.

Today's parents can hardly credit it that mothers and fathers would agree to be parted from their small children. Why, they wonder, did parents in those days acquiesce in such a heartless policy? A former evacuee put her finger on one obvious answer: before the war people were afraid of anyone in authority; they were afraid of the doctor, the teacher, the policeman. People were so much more cowed then, it is hard to believe how subservient and accepting of the status quo they were compared to these days of citizens' rights.

On top of that there was an incredible amount of propaganda being churned out. Parents were made to feel they were not being good parents if they did not send their children away to safety. Posters began to appear exhorting mothers to "Let them Go. Give them a chance of greater safety and health."

There was a rallying cry from one government minister on the radio immediately before the first evacuation which hammered the message home: "Big and crowded cities offer a tremendous temptation to a ruthless enemy to try to deliver a knock-out blow during the first few weeks of a war," he said. (He was quite wrong, as governments so often are. The first bombs, the Blitz, did not begin until September 1940, a year after the Government's evacuation programme began.)

"A great deal has been done to find homes all over the country where people are ready to take children and act as foster parents to them. I am not going to paint too rosy a picture of the conditions they would meet with. Perhaps for the first night or two they will just have to put up with very rough and ready arrangements. But you all know the spirit of helpfulness which everyone shows when a great emergency comes along and all of you can judge how hard everyone would work to get children fixed up with foster parents at the first possible minute. Those of you whose children have been away with the Children's Holiday Fund, or in some other way, know how kind and helpful country people can be.

"We would do our best to keep them busy and happy and I am sure the country people would do all they could for them. If you have more than one child all the children in the family would be kept together."

That last promise was one of the first to be broken. Siblings were parted as soon as they reached their destination. There is a memo from a Dr Innes of Birmingham who asked, "Who is to see that a child boarded out is properly fed?" It was an anxiety that was ignored. Too much reliance placed on this famous "helpfulness" of country people.

The argument that children would be better off away from bombs was one with which many psychiatrists and child psychologists disagreed. Psycho-analyst Anna Freud wrote, "War acquires comparatively little significance for children so long as it only threatens their lives, disturbs their material comfort or cuts their food rations. It becomes enormously significant the moment it breaks up family life and uproots the first emotional attachments of the child within the family group."

An unpalatable fact is that some mothers were only too willing to offload their children onto someone else. This may sound harsh but, as you will read, a few evacuees have come to this conclusion. A vicar from Haslemere, Surrey, pointed out in a letter to a national newspaper what many host householders complained of: that evacuees' parents were happy to leave the responsibility of their children in someone else's hands. He wrote: "Time and again we hear of children in urgent need of boots or clothing, so urgent that their hosts feel bound to supply them out of labourer's wages, and the parents, who are already relieved of the entire cost of the children's food will do nothing to help, refusing even to answer letters. The mother may be free to earn good money and it does seem that the authorities should find some way of compelling them at least to impose no further burden on our villagers."

You can't blame foster parents for being more than a little vexed if they thought they were being taken for a ride although it may be that their standards of dress for children were higher than the evacuee's own mother and that they felt it was not possible or desirable for two standards of dress to exist side by side under the same roof. As soon as the evacuation began appeals for help for clothing followed and these were responded to promptly and generously by American and Canadian organisations.

A donation came from the Maharajah of Gondal who presented a "lakh of rupees" (£7,500) to help clothe evacuees. The National Union of Teachers voted to send £1,000 from their coffers and many other voluntary gifts poured in, but there was not nearly enough to solve the problems of children sent away from home in flimsy summer clothing and worn-out shoes, coping with the cold, mud and wet of an English winter.

By November 1939 the Government decided to cough up some money but the hand-outs were cloaked in secrecy; the Government insisted there should be no publicity for fear of attracting people who could afford to clothe their children but would happily let the state do so if they could get away with it. This was, in effect, the beginning of a new social service. The Government wanted to keep children in the country but did not want to take responsibility for their wardrobe away from parents. The children were hardly to blame but they, nevertheless, would bear the brunt of the foster parents' resentment.

Since I began looking for people who were abused while they were evacuated I have received many heartbreaking letters and I am sure I have only uncovered the tip of an iceberg. Some of their letters begin, "This is the first time I have told anyone about this." Or "Thank goodness someone is telling it like it really was at last."

For some, the experience made them determined to be a good parent. That is certainly how it affected me. I was evacuated when I was only two years old until the end of the war in 1945. I was beaten constantly and locked in a cupboard under the stairs. I was shut in there in the dark for hours. It was, at times, an extremely unhappy childhood so I tried hard to be a good mother. I tried to give my children all the things I never had when I was small. I never wanted them to experience that forlornness I felt, that terrible feeling on the one hand of being rejected, on the other of waiting to be rescued.

The people I have interviewed for this book say the same. They were strict, but they wanted their children to know they were loved and they never, ever beat them. All these evacuees disprove the theory that there is a cycle of abuse. Although most abusers were abused themselves as children, being abused as a child does not necessarily turn you into an adult abuser. Far from it. Most people I have met who were abused as children are gentle: they may lack self-confidence or assertiveness but they do everything in their power to make life happy for their children and as unlike their own childhood as it possibly can be.

Some former evacuees reveal their experience has left them with nervous disorders such as agoraphobia or depression. Many have written their own accounts of what happened, spurred on by sons, daughters or doctors, as a way of getting their painful memories, their feelings of anger and rejection, out of their system. Sheila Jump of Aigburth, Liverpool, told me she could feel the hate travelling from her body down her arm into her hand and fingers, her pen jabbing and sometimes tearing through the paper she was writing on.

Many children were treated, literally, like prisoners. Barry Goodwin of Morden, Surrey, was evacuated at the age of six to a village called Hoddesdon, near Aylesbury with a family who had four sons and a daughter. He says, “I was never allowed to get up until after 2.30pm on Saturdays and on Sunday I was put to bed at 4pm, knowing on both days that all the other children were outside playing. I was not allowed to go to evacuee parties which were held regularly in the village and when the children of the house went on trips or to Sunday school I was put to bed. Sometimes I was sent to my room on a Friday after school and not allowed out again until Monday morning.”

When Barry married and had children of his own he could never bring himself to make them go to bed. “That sometimes caused a few problems between my wife and I,” he says. As an adult Barry has a lukewarm bath or shower because he was put through what seems to have been a favourite choice of torture among some of the people caring for evacuees: a scalding hot bath. Doreen Ingrams, who suffered from polio and whose story is told in a later chapter, is another who endured this barbaric treatment.

Barry also had to witness what many other evacuees saw during the war: gifts from their parents being taken from them. He says, "I remember vividly my mother once bringing me a pair of new black shoes which I thought were great but they were given to the son of my age and I was threatened not to complain.” John Gough and his brother Tony, whose story is in the Dear Mum chapter, were victims of this heartless treatment when a toy their father had made for them was given to the sons of the family, something that still rankles with them today.

Shirley Vint, who was evacuated in 1940 when she was five from Sherrington Road School, Charlton, south east London, was another evacuee who was forced to go to her bedroom at 6.30pm every evening and stay there on Sundays. She says, "I used to gaze out of my bedroom window all day and watch the steam trains, longing for my mother to come for me. I used to pray she would be on one of those trains."

Petty meanness was part and parcel of the atmosphere hundreds of evacuees grew up with. Pat Sladden, of Stratford, east London, for instance, was only allowed into the kitchen and her small bedroom. She was not allowed to enter the house by the front door and her clothes were kept in the cardboard suitcase she had been given when she was evacuated. Daphne Hoare, whose brother Peter tells their story, was only six and inevitably wet the bed. She was made to stand outside the house in her wet nightie at midnight even in the middle of winter.

Sylvia Rogan of Barrow-in-Furness, Cumberland, is still afraid of spiders because she was sent to stand in the outside toilet for wetting herself – and that was after the "kind, caring" foster father had beaten her with his leather belt. "This went on almost every day that I was with them, two and a half years in all," she says. "Today Mr Cater would have been imprisoned for being a pervert, but it happened to many children, and they just got away with it because of the war. Although it was him who meted out the punishment, his wife and daughter were always there to watch."

At some billets the lack of care and the incompetence was breathtaking. Tommy Thompson, of Wallasey, Merseyside, was only six when he and a fellow evacuee called Freddie Sloan were evacuated to Llanerchyedd, Wales. They were billeted with a woman of 24 who used to go off to Rhyl with her husband every weekend leaving them on their own with no food. "We used to dig up raw potatoes and eat them," says Tommy. Just close your eyes for a moment and think about two six-year-old boys alone, in a strange place, for such a long time with no food. It beggars belief.

For some evacuees, such as Phyllis Maloney of Kesgrave, Ipswich, who was evacuated to Northampton in 1941 when she was 12, it was the fact she was billeted with a middle-class family who resented having to look after a working-class girl that caused her grief. "They had a younger daughter who had a box of toys and books in my bedroom which I was not allowed to touch," she says. "I was never taken out with them and when they had family or friends to visit I was made to go outside. They even made me go to a different church to them on Sundays because they didn't want to be seen with me."

If the physical pain can no longer be felt, when evacuees recall what happened to them the emotional pain is still there. The child psychologist Alice Miller writes, "An unacknowledged trauma is like a wound that never heals over and may start to bleed again at any time. In a supportive environment the wound can become visible and finally heal completely." I think what evacuees are doing now by telling their stories is healing their wounds.

One evacuee said, "Speaking about it was terrible. I felt six again, unsure and afraid. When you are damaged like this as a child your memory of it is not that of an adult. You remember it as a child again and it is very frightening. You don't realise how much power someone has to take your childhood, confidence and self-respect. Talking about it is cathartic. I wake up in the morning and know I am stronger and better and nothing and no one is going to haunt me or hurt me any more."

Sometimes I have cried with evacuees as they relived terrible scenes from their childhood. For some, both men and women, the experiences they suffered during their evacuation have had a wholly negative effect on their lives. Take the man who was abused as a child of only eight by the soldier son of a widow he was billeted with. He has never married, sex in his mind forever a disgusting experience. Or the nurse, also eight when she was abused, who found it impossible to consummate her marriage, the vision of her abuser always making her recoil from intimacy. Their memories of what happened are extremely vivid. One thing that is repeated over and over again in evacuees' letters is: "I remember it all as if it were yesterday."

Some of the cruelties they endured are just mean mindedness with no horrendous longterm harm done. The sending to bed without any supper for the slightest infringement was a favourite punishment. As was the ridiculing of children who wet the bed.

Many children were starved and reduced to stealing food. For two little girls, dinner was one tinned sardine and a small piece of potato. Another wo girls were reduced to stealing pears. When they were found out, their punishment was to have the pretty dresses that had been made for them taken away. One girl bought a cabbage for a penny for herself and her little brother and they ate it raw.

A few children were rescued. They were old enough to write to their parents to tell them what was going on and canny enough to get their letters through their prison walls. One of the hateful facts of life as an evacuee was that your letters were censored or confiscated. Even when the abuse lasted only a short time, the horror of it still lingers.

One man told me that when he grew up he used to think to himself, "If ever I am told I am dying of cancer, I'll go back and kill that woman."

Many cannot face going near the same area again but others have been back to assure themselves it was not all just a bad dream. On the whole they found going back to where it all happened helped, even though it was a painful journey.

Some children rescued themselves from their torturers by running away. One young boy walked 30 miles back to his home, with only five pence in his pocket. When he arrived his house was empty so he slept in a shed until a friend of his mother's realised he was there and took him in. His mother was in hospital having another baby.

It is difficult for people who did not experience the evacuation to understand what a brutal social upheaval it was. I have suggested to friends they look at their own children or grandchildren or, if they have no children, to look in the playground of a primary school, and imagine those small children being marched off to live with total strangers. There were hardly any telephones in those days so there were no calls home that evening to say “I’m all right, Mum.” Often for days, or even weeks in some cases, parents had no idea where their children were.

I have unearthed only one example of a child being visited by a social worker. A neighbour noticed her skeletal appearance and must have reported the situation to someone in authority. A social worker knocked on the door one Saturday morning when the evacuee was scrubbing the kitchen floor, one of her many household tasks and arranged for her to return home.

In those days, children were seen and not heard. Evacuees who tried to tell their teachers what was going on were not believed. Indeed, some of them were given the cane for being such ungrateful liars. Evacuees were frequently told they were scum from London/Liverpool/Newcastle or whichever big city they happened to have been evacuated from. It was repeatedly dinned into them that they were worthless.

Sometimes they were even told their parents didn’t want them or, in a few terrible cases, that their parents were dead. As a lesson in how not to bring up children these householders knew no equal. Many of the people whose stories are recounted in this book wonder how they grew up as sane as they have

Although parents usually instructed older brothers and sisters to look after their younger siblings, when they reached the end of their journey, in a strange country village hall where they took part in what has been described as a cross between a cattle market and a bargain store sale, the majority of people who have written to me were unceremoniously parted from other members of their family. This lack of understanding for or sympathy with the plight of the evacuees illustrates a callous disregard for the feelings of homesick children.

Most evacuees now, with half a century of experience behind them, say evacuation made them grow up quickly. It taught them to be independent. Many comment, wryly, on those people today who blame unhappy childhoods for their crimes or who demand counselling for seemingly trivial reasons. And these people are adults; how would they have coped with far worse and at a tender age? Evacuees had to.

All things considered, I think most of us would rather have taken our chances with Hitler's onslaught and the bomb shelters than the hell holes we were imprisoned in.

Chapter Two
Bud of the Nation

Evacuation was a scheme drawn up by minds that were military, male and middle-class. A totally unconnected event - unconnected to the evacuation that is - helps to illustrate just how different society was then. It was announced in *The Times* in August 1939, that a Mrs M. E. Farrer, employed as a scientific officer by the War Office, "has been granted permission to retain her post in the research department, Woolwich...after her marriage". Before the Second World War female civil servants were forced to give up their jobs when they married. If women suffered inequality on such a massive scale, you could say evacuees were off the Richter scale of equality.

Evacuation was voluntary, although there were plans afoot to make it compulsory later in the war if the powers that be thought it was necessary. Cabinet minutes of the time register the fact that ministers were not happy about the way their blandishments were being ignored by the majority of parents, who refused to put their names down on lists of who wanted and who did not want to have their children evacuated. The simple truth is that most parents in the working-class inner cities, unlike the middle-class legislators, were reluctant to contemplate sending their little ones away to live with strangers. The feeling among most people in the inner cities then was, "If one of us is going to die, it would be better if we all died together."

CHAPTER TWO

The first time the Germans dropped a bomb on Britain was in January, 1915 during the First World War when Zeppelin raids hit East Anglia. In the winter of 1917-18, night after night, more than 100,000 people in London, as many as 300,000 on one occasion in February, took shelter from aerial bombardment in the Underground. This was in response to half a dozen slow-moving aircraft carrying primitive high-explosive bombs. It was estimated that double the weight of bombs dropped on the whole country in the First World War could be dropped in 24 hours at the start of the Second World War.

Backroom planners during the Thirties decreed that panic in the face of future high-tech air raids had to be avoided at all costs. The drastic scaling up in January 1937 of the Air Staff's estimate of German striking power provided a fresh stimulus to the study of evacuation. The first comprehensive report concluded that some three and a half-million people living in inner London, or approximately 75 per cent of the population would be evacuated.

At first it was thought it would be necessary to employ the police to throw a cordon around London to stop people leaving in a panic but that was abandoned because the police would have enough to do with other air raid defence precautions. And forcibly trying to prevent so many people determined to escape from the capital would not be good for morale.

In a place the size of England under the conditions of modern war, there really was no place of absolute safety. However, 11 million were considered to be in the most vulnerable, evacuable areas, 13 million in neutral areas and 16 million in reception areas. The first areas it was decided should be evacuated were: Acton, Edmonton, Hornsey, Tottenham, Willesden, East Ham, West Ham, Barking, Ilford, Leyton and Walthamstow in London; Rochester, Chatham, Gillingham, Southampton, Portsmouth, Gosport, Liverpool, Bootle,

Birmingham, Crosby, Birkenhead, Wallasey, Manchester, Salford, Stretford, Newcastle on Tyne, Gateshead, Birmingham, Smethwick, Hull, Bradford, Leeds and Sheffield in the provinces and, in Scotland, Edinburgh, Glasgow, Dundee, Clydebank and Rosyth. The first priorities were schoolchildren, women with babies or women with children of pre-school age, expectant mothers and adult blind and disabled people.

The idea of a planned and orderly transfer of people from vulnerable to safer areas in the country grew out of contemporary theories about the character of a future war. It was regarded simply and solely as a military expedient, a counter-move to the enemy's objective of attacking and demoralising the civilian population.

The Committee of Imperial Defence, set up in February 1931 to start working out the details of any evacuation and how to prevent a disorderly flight, asked the India Office for help with information on the management of masses of people. Unless the Government took firm control, chaos and confusion were bound to ensue.

In November 1932 Prime Minister Stanley Baldwin informed the House of Commons that precautions were being taken, yet plans were still in a rudimentary state by early 1938. Part of their complacency can be attributed to the self-congratulatory evidence of the London County Council who, in 1937, had brought nearly 40,000 school children to the embankment from 877 schools to watch the coronation of King George V "without a hitch". It followed, they believed, that transporting upwards of three million adults and children out of London would also be plain sailing.

According to a report prepared by the intelligence branch of the Home Office in June, 1938, the Germans had no plans to evacuate their citizens. A series of articles in the official organ of the Reich Air Protection League during 1935-36 discussed the difficulties of evacuation. Written by a Colonel Teschner of the German Air

Ministry, the articles said whether evacuation was practicable depended on three considerations: a) the number of people to be moved b) the time when the movement could take place and c) the means of transport.

The report continued: "It is impossible with any degree of accuracy to forecast the numbers involved. Those liable to military service will have left their homes already, the ARP (air raid precaution) services will absorb many others, officials will remain at their posts and the general business activity must be maintained. Thus all able-bodied men and women will be needed in the towns, whilst the old and infirm to whom evacuation would seem to apply, cannot travel alone and they would be therefore better off if they remained in their homes. Prisons, however, should be evacuated in view of the risks which the population would incur were the inmates to escape.

"Children under ten years of age must obviously remain with their parents and those over 15 will be required for ARP duties. Thus, only those between the ages of 10-15 can be considered as being available for evacuation." The writer concludes that the question is not how many but how few should be evacuated.

As an evacuee who was evacuated at the age of two, it strikes me as profoundly ironic that the Germans thought children under ten should not be separated from their family. Compare that to our government's cavalier approach to children being packed off with their teachers. Perhaps, as already mentioned, it has something to do with the boarding school ethos of the Establishment then.

Another curious comparison between the British and German thinking on evacuation at that stage is that here 5,600 convicts and Borstal inmates were suddenly given their freedom. Our powers that be seemingly were not worried about the risks to the British public of setting prisoners free.

The first evacuation began on Friday, September 1, 1939. Nearly one and a half million adults and children were transported between 50 and 100 miles in a matter of four days at a cost of approximately £2 million. By January, 1940, four months later, 43 per cent of unaccompanied children and 86 per cent of mothers with children had returned home. The period from September 1939 to May 1940 became known as the "phoney war" an expression imported from America meaning that the combatants were merely playing at war. They were not, of course, "playing" on the Continent.

Serious evacuation, when everyone realised the Germans, who had lost the Battle of Britain, changed their tactics and decided to try and bomb us all to smithereens, began in September 1940 with the Blitz.

The pictures of small children, gas masks dangling from drooping shoulders, forlorn parcels of humanity dispatched to the countryside, are now part of our national heritage. Schools reopened during the summer holidays on Monday, August 28, 1939 so children and parents could have evacuation practice. Notices were pinned up around the schools telling children to report by 7am on Friday morning. Blackboards were scrawled with various witticisms such as "By kind permission of Adolph" with a caricature of the famous forelock and the miniature moustache underneath.

Children were made to stand in single file in the school yard and their names were ticked off by their teacher, a familiar enough start to the day. The wish list of what each child should take with him or her from the Ministry of Health Government Evacuation Scheme had been circulating for some time. The luggage should be "no more than a child could carry" according to the thoughtful instructions though it was still a burden for some of the tiny tots: gas mask, a rucksack or cardboard suitcase containing a change of underclothing, night clothes, house shoes or plimsolls, spare pair of stockings or socks, toothbrush, brush and comb, towel and handkerchiefs, a warm coat or mackintosh and a packet of food for the day. They were told not to take drinks, an orange would suffice. The children should be sent away wearing their thickest and warmest footwear, was the official diktat. Teachers searched bags for missing items and made a note

Some families found it difficult to meet this list of requirements. It was estimated that before the war there were about four million families in Britain living from hand to mouth or from pay day to pay day. For all these families, the purchase of boots and clothing often meant a capital outlay beyond their means.

Before the evacuation, appeals were made for boots and mackintoshes which children in more favourable circumstances had grown out of in order that a central store might be organised. Many evacuees were dressed in flimsy summer clothing, not garments to cope with the cold.

On that first day the children walked to the bus, Tube or train station in crocodiles, two by two, to the accompaniment of loudspeakers, microphones or whistles, giving them instructions or a signal when to cross the road. One of the boys in this book was at a school where they sent their evacuees off accompanied by a brass band as if it were a jolly occasion, a day's excursion and they would be home again by bedtime.

Children at the front of the crocodile carried a placard mounted on a stick bearing the name of the school, the entraining station and the time of the train to facilitate identification by police and transport authorities, although in the event parties were sometimes packed onto the first train available. Each child was supposed to be given two postcards so they could let their parents know where they were when they arrived but that did not always happen either.

It became obvious from the start that this military-style manoeuvre was not going to be the plain sailing the mandarins of Whitehall assumed it would be. Schools were separated over dozens of villages, some 70 miles away from their teachers. While King's School, Canterbury (a private school) was moving to Scotland, Canterbury City Council took over the school buildings for the reception of state-educated children from London. While children were to be evacuated from East London to an area of Essex bordering on the Thames estuary, the Essex authority was arranging to evacuate its children away from that area.

An MP argued at the time that compulsory billeting was far worse than war. One county council protested that householders in their area would not take "the dregs of London", while members of the Government's advisory panel of industrialists suggested that evacuees might be accommodated on Ascot racecourse and in golf club houses. That idea never made it past the starting gates.

The trains were over-crowded, sometimes without lavatories and with inadequate water supplies so children arrived tired, having been up and out of bed probably by 6am to get to school for seven; they were dirty and fed up so possibly unco-operative. Nor did it get any better as the war progressed when those organising evacuations had more experience.

According to a report by the district inspector at Cambridge in December 1941, 112 children arrived nearly an hour late. "The children were taken by bus to a pre-arranged school where they were given a mug of cold milk and biscuits only," he reports.

"I spoke to Mrs S suggesting this type of meal was inadequate, especially in cold weather. She explained they had arranged hot meals before but children ate very little or did not appear to enjoy what they ate and that the children preferred cold milk to hot.

"The disposal of the children was not carried out in a very satisfactory manner. There was a dreadful muddle and the final bus did not leave the school until about 4.20pm. A doctor from the London evacuation authority sent a list of approximately 36 children who were said to be under treatment and unfit for billeting. The Newmarket doctors did not examine them but instructed the nurses to place them in a separate room until they could be sent off to White Lodge. Of those examined, a further six were found to be ill.

"No one told the council helpers so they thought they had been lost. White Lodge had been told to expect six children and were horrified. There is a suggestion of scabies. The medical officer decided brothers and sisters of sick children should accompany them. They did not arrive in villages until it was getting dark so considerable difficulty was thus caused in billeting them out. Mrs Lamb, chief billeting officer, was nominally in charge of the reception but apparently Mrs Tharp, the WVS representative, butted in a good deal and there was some confusion during the sorting out period."

Although you can sympathise with the difficulties these officials were experiencing, my heart goes out to those tired and frightened children who were being pushed from pillar to post the entire day, not understanding what was happening to them. And it was not untypical.

In one reception area a group of Ealing children arriving at Brixworth Station, Northants, were unexpectedly joined by a Croydon party and were left to sleep on the roadside. Eventually they were put up on mattresses in the council offices but there was no food for them, just packets of crisps and a cheese sandwich.

There was, too, a clash of cultures between inner city children and their urban counterparts. And it is crucial to understand the depth of animosity between the two social groups to comprehend how easy it was for some evacuees to be taken advantage of, since the one regarded the other as a lower form of life.

It has to be said that some of this animosity was fuelled by the behaviour of some parents of evacuee children. Devizes Rural District Council reported in January 1942 that some of the children sent to them were "generally badly behaved and badly clothed and a large proportion of them had been evacuated before, several on more than one occasion".

Parents, the Council pointed out, "have taken their children back to London after they have been cleaned, clothed and trained in better ways". When a boy of 11 whose school report showed that he was unruly and untrustworthy, lazy and troublesome, was charged with larceny, the London magistrate who heard his case gave an order that he should be evacuated. In view of that kind of "punishment" it is hardly surprising that resentment was rising in some reception areas.

Evacuees have generally been portrayed as children coming from poor, if not slum, homes and sent to rather better off places where they enjoyed fresh air and fresh food. The truth is that although they did come from inner cities, they were not all necessarily that poor and certainly could not all be described as slum children. Most evacuees came from homes where they were well cared for, even if it was on a tight budget, and not all the houses they were sent to were superior to those they had left behind. Far from it.

Many foster homes only had outside toilets and no running water and, unlike the city districts the evacuees were brought up in, there were few medical centres or other welfare facilities. This countryside paradise versus bombed out squalor is just another of the myths that has been built up around what happened to evacuees during the Second World War which needs to be exposed for the nonsense it is.

Some host families complained of evacuees' parents arriving in cars to take them out on Sundays, families clearly better off than they were. On the other hand, a columnist in a national newspaper who put forward a Draconian suggestion, saw the evacuees in a different light: "I have seen these pathetic, dirty children myself. What is really shameful is that our system has allowed such creatures to grow up. There is a serious deficiency somewhere in training and outlook. Our educational methods seem to have failed miserably and such children, through evacuation, have been brought mercifully to the light of day.

"But before all that can be remedied, can we not have legislation immediately to stop this senseless return by the parents to the filthy conditions they came from? The war has brought about the one condition of country life that might save these children and the Government, through inaction, is letting slip a great opportunity to improve the coming race. They have already taken on the responsibility of separating the children from the parents...I cannot see why they cannot go further and complete the good work."

There was a deep-rooted lack of sympathy and understanding between town and country which the evacuation scheme exposed when this enforced mixing of sections of the population who normally had little or no contact with each other happened.

People in the countryside were expected to welcome these alien cuckoos into their nests. Unfortunately, as we shall see, many of them did not welcome evacuees at all, they hated and resented them, they felt put upon and felt free to exact their revenge by treating evacuees abominably although, at the same time, MPs like the minster of health, Walter Elliot, were making stirring speeches in the House of Commons referring to them as "the bud of the nation".

Early complaints from host householders included that the evacuees were verminous, bed wetters, liars, rude and quarrelsome, petty thieves with no respect for property and of unclean habits. The country people felt they were being swamped by a "barbarian invasion:" Some of the country women believed that a decent wife would never leave her husband, therefore the types who came with their children to the country from the towns were hysterical. One editor, ranting in a West Country newspaper, suggested concentration camps should be built for evacuees.

John A. F. Watson, chairman of Southwark Juvenile Court, wrote an article in the *Daily Mail* of September 1942, in which he said: "Children are more unpopular in this country than they have ever been. Thousands of country people who have made the acquaintance of city children for the first time are appalled at what they find. Many children are allowed to run wild. They steal, damage property and disturb the peace. Some earn big money and make unwise use of it. They spend it in fun fairs and on gambling machines. The righteous are shocked. They point to the increase of juvenile delinquency. They prophesy the mental and moral decline of Britain."

In Evacuation Survey: A report to the Fabian Society edited by Richard Padley and Margaret Cole, the authors rightly point out that though the State controlled evacuation, once the purely transport stage had been passed, it was a highly individual business. It was bound to be, since it consisted of the placing of individuals by individuals in individual families over widely separated and widely differing localities. The billeting question was the heart and soul of the evacuation scheme and yet it was left largely to well-meaning or, in some cases, malevolent, volunteers and there was no organised system of billeting inspection.

Children were scattered at random, miles away from their brothers and sisters, school friends and teachers. Some spent their first night away from home sleeping on bags full of straw in a village hall. For many children that first experience was totally chaotic. For instance, some children from West Ham schools arrived where they did entirely by accident. They should have gone to Somerset with other West Ham schools but, being provided by the railway company with a non-corridor train, the needs of nature proved too strong and they had to be deposited at Wantage. They arrived hungry and miserable in the dark and had to be put into any available house in the black-out.

Although being evacuated was voluntary, putting up evacuees was obligatory. Not that billeting officers used their powers very often because the people they were dealing with were often neighbours: coercion was the preferred means of finding a billet. (Slough magistrates imposed a fine of 1s with 8d costs on a family for failing to obey a billeting notice, but that was a rare court case.)

Local authorities had conducted a survey early in 1939 of more than five million houses to find accommodation. This survey showed there were places for just over six million people. It was impossible to use one and a quarter million of those for various reasons, such as that the billets were required by the Services or the houses were too near aerodromes and military establishments. The final figure of available billets boiled down to four million eight hundred thousand.

The Government's aim was to billet one person per habitable room, a totally unrealistic aim as it turned out. In Scotland, where the housing shortage was more serious, one person per room over the age of 14 was established and two in the case of children under 14. The survey had to take into account the fact that a proportion of the accommodation available would not be suitable for the billeting of unaccompanied schoolchildren.

There would, for instance, be the cases of old or infirm householders and of people living alone whose employment required them to be absent all day. These and many other factors, such as the inadequacy of a water supply, had to be noted by the investigators and reported to the health departments.

That this did not always happen is borne out by some of the evacuees' accounts in this book. It is no surprise to us that nowhere in the instructions issued to billeting officers is there any mention of the moral welfare of the young children being sent to their fate. It seems to have been taken for granted that children would be treated kindly, or at least the powers that be just did not give any thought to the possibility that anything awful might happen to them. Even allowing for the fact that child sex abuse was not a subject for discussion in those days, it seems inconceivable that no one made provision for the possibility that some evacuee children might be treated cruelly by their hosts.

The Ministry of Health issued an edict which said, "It is obviously desirable that so far as possible, children should be accommodated in homes where their presence would be willingly accepted." A self-deluding bit of Whitehall-speak when people would obviously take children in simply for the money. Payment for one child was 10s 6d per week, sixpence more than the old age pension. There was no mention of weekly or monthly checks which ought to have been made to ensure evacuees were being cared for properly but, as you will see, the State considered its task was simply to ship children from A to B and to foot the bill.

Parents today would under no circumstance be willing to trust their children to complete strangers. The revisionist view of history we have been provided with for the past 60 years makes it sound as if people in safe country areas opened their homes with gladness when the nation was in peril. Not so.

Some well-to-do people in country towns filled their houses with relatives or servants in order to claim they had no available accommodation. One wealthy woman is reported to have avoided evacuees by saying she was reserving her house for air raid casualties. Since she lived as far away from a munitions factory or a shipyard as it is possible to get, she probably went on living undisturbed.

The job of a billeting officer was not an easy one. Even if they had been anxious to keep a watchful eye on the welfare of the children they had found a home for, they were handicapped by being local residents themselves and they did not want to appear inquisitive or critical of their neighbours. Even so, they quickly became deeply unpopular.

Nor was their job made any easier by those people who simply refused to cooperate. Some of these citizens, who no doubt have talked endlessly since of doing their bit for the war effort even produced medical certificates to back up their claims for exemption from taking in evacuees. One billeting officer in a university town reported he could plaster the town hall with medical certificates. In another place 37 prominent citizens, including the vicar, ministers of two churches, the town clerk, the deputy clerk, the chief billeting officer, the chairman of the billeting committee, the coroner and a bank manager all shirked their responsibilities. An MP who lived in a large house refused to accommodate secondary schoolgirls on the grounds he had confidential papers lying around.

When the Ministry of Health sent its own investigators to a town which claimed it was full, they found, in July 1941, 7,900 spare rooms. Of 28 councillors, 17 lived in houses with seven or more habitable but unoccupied rooms.

The Cambridge Evacuation Survey, edited by psychoanalyst Susan Isaacs in 1940, struck a note of incredulity about the appalling lack of planning that went into the evacuation scheme. "When the whole plan rested upon the ability of the original man and woman to cooperate in a public undertaking of such gravity and urgency, it is hard to believe that we could be so foolish, so self-contradictory," she wrote. "If evacuation had been forced upon us by war in September 1938, we might have been excused for thinking only of immediate military necessity and questions of transport. But when we had a whole year in which to plan, it is bitter to think that we, in our proud democracy, showed so little provision, so little knowledge of the parents and children upon whom we were to act so disturbingly and in whose hands the success or failure of the scheme rested."

The committee of child psychologists and social workers recommended the appointment of trained professional social workers to help with the organisation of billeting with one full-time and responsible person for every 500 children. This did not happen.

There were bitter complaints about the allowance of 10s 6d per week per child with five shillings extra for a sick child. By April 1940, reception areas were not far removed from open revolt. The allowance for 14 to 16 year olds was increased to 12s 6d and for young people over sixteen to 15s. An agricultural labourer earning 30s a week with a boy aged seven billeted on him found an additional 10s 6d a week quite welcome. On the other hand, a middle-class household, expected to give the same standard of food and care to an evacuee as their own child was receiving, soon learned that the allowance for, say, two secondary boys aged 16 was not nearly enough.

Evacuation was a carefully planned strategy yet with astonishingly little research into the needs of the individuals it was meant to save. It was designed supposedly to avoid the general population taking matters into their own hands and stampeding out of the cities, and yet it was by no means universally accepted that sending small children away from their families was the right or sensible way to tackle the problem.

An observer from the Association of Architects Surveyors and Technical Assistants Evacuation Committee, sent to study evacuation in practice in the Home Counties three months after it began, wrote: "Officialdom was either so incompetent that it thought it could treat individuals as so many ciphers, or it simply shut its eyes to what might happen afterwards in its effort to get them out of the towns at all costs. It was just a panic evacuation.

"It is obvious that in wartime expenditure must be allotted to different activities according to their national importance. For instance, money is being found for hutments for evacuated civil servants who have shown their discontent with the present position. We do not grudge this expenditure, on the contrary, but we do look with apprehension at the refusal to release money for the children. It appears that evacuation is at the bottom of the scale.

"One per cent of what is being spent on the war in a single year would transform the situation, while three times this amount would pay for a complete building programme, including camp schools, new buildings for education and feeding and nursery schools and day nurseries.

"The children are the future of the nation and therefore those for whom we are fighting. Our treatment of them is the sort which might be expected in a pauperised Balkan state, but is scarcely in accordance with the resources of the richest country in Europe."

Chapter Three
Nightmare on Elm Street

I was two years old when I was evacuated and can remember the day my mother left me with my "Aunty" Jenny - she was not a relation - as if it were yesterday. I have a photograph in my head of my mother, wearing a dark brown fur coat, walking away down the back lane on the opposite side to where we were. I was being held in the right arm of this strange woman; my sister, Joyce, was standing on her left side, and I was screaming. My mother never looked back - she was probably crying, too.

One of the awful aspects of my story is that I cried as much when I had to return home five years later, in spite of the violence and unhappiness I endured. My sister put it all behind her but I kept going back after the war to see my Aunty Jenny and was genuinely fond of her. I now think that is dreadful. How could I? I have tried to understand why and have read something about the Stockholm Syndrome which may explain in psychological terms what happened to me.

In his book *Understanding Child Abuse* psychologist Dr David Jones looks at research into the experience and reactions of prisoner of war camp inmates which has some relevance for abused evacuees. I decided to test his conclusions against my own experience and reactions, and evacuees reading this might like to do the same. Dr Jones suggests the following common characteristics: amnesia about events before incarceration (since I was only two that hardly applies to me); denial of experiences in the camp, or alternatively recapitulation at length of all that happened (well, yes to the latter, since that is what this chapter is about, and I am writing a book about other people's similar experiences); low self-esteem, guilt, self-blame (internalised attitudes of the captors) (yes, I do sometimes feel I have low self-esteem although I try to fight it and I feel guilty about loving the witch, but I don't think I feel any self-blame); need to fail (yes, but I recognise that so I force myself to take up challenges); inability to cope with anger/depression (sometimes); fear of therapist (perceived as a potential persecutor) (that doesn't apply to me. I had a wonderful therapist who helped me tremendously although it took three years and was at times extremely traumatic); children of inmates, born later, share these self-perceptions (don't think so); latency period of up to 30 years before reactions manifest (I think that's probably right. I can't remember thinking much about my evacuation when I was younger).

Dr Jones also claims that the following characteristics of hostage survivors are common: inability to hate their captors; support of captors' beliefs and objectives lasting several months afterwards; hatred of their rescuers; recurrent fears/anxieties in stressful or unexpected situations; residual guilt and sense of vulnerability; need for reassurance; need for repeated recapitulation of experience; anger with captors emerges one year later (re-birth feeling); generalised fear of strangers persists. Some of these, like a sense of vulnerability and a need for reassurance and for repeated recapitulation of the experience, I share.

What is not mentioned here are the positive things you acquire from adversity. For instance, I think I am extremely resilient, self-reliant and patient, I might mind how long it takes to do a job, but I will go at it until it is done, all qualities which I think have their roots in my having to cope for such a long period in a hostile environment.

I concur with what Dr Jones goes on to say: "Many of the characteristics, known as the Stockholm Syndrome in hostage cases, seem to us to be personality defences against a totally inconsistent environment, alternating between threat of death and occasional kindess, with massive fear and rage which have to be totally controlled, even suppressed. Many seem to be shared by children from persistently abusing families, in particular the internalisation of the parents' attitude towards them, leading to self-blame, guilt, low self-esteem and a need to fail. Inability to express appropriate anger or depression is common, with periods of passivity followed by sudden outbursts."

As Aunty Jenny was for all intents and purposes my mother for five years I suppose I reacted to her as an abused child would to an abusing parent. In the case of evacuees, our psychological responses are more complicated by the fact that everyone around us seemed to be condoning what was going on; it's not as if we were isolated as in a hostage situation. The schools, our teachers, priests, neighbours, everyone was in on the conspiracy. Our incarceration was commanded by our own Government, not some enemy.

It is a strange period of our lives which I wish psychologists had studied more so those of us who experienced the evacuation could make more sense of it. On the one hand I must have felt abandoned by my mother, yet on the other I saw both my parents as glamorous heroes. My father was in the RAF and came into my life about twice while I was evacuated, each time bringing wonderful gifts, and my mother appeared now and again also bearing presents. By the time I went home after the war I was seven years old and they were virtual strangers. No wonder I was mixed up.

My mother was a nurse at the Royal Victoria Infirmary, Newcastle, so I suppose it was inevitable that when the Government urged parents to get their children out of the big and vulnerable cities, they thought it was best for us to leave. With Vickers Armstrong, building ships for the Navy, and many plum industrial sites for German bombers to annihilate, Newcastle was not a good place to be.

One of my mother's sisters, Aunty Winnie, lived in South Moor, County Durham, a mining village close to where my grandparents lived. But she was already full up with the four daughters of another sister, Aunty Nan, who was a district nurse and lived at Tynemouth, on the Northumberland coast, a few miles outside Newcastle. Aunty Nan's husband was killed during the first few months of the war and Aunty Winnie's husband had been a miner but was ill for most of the time I remember him with the terrible miners' chest disease, pneumoconiosis.

Winnie must have known Mrs Jenny Morris and her husband Tom who lived in Elm Street, South Moor, and recommended her to my mother. So we were taken to their little terrace house where we stayed for the duration of the war. It was not all a horror story, we had some great times. I remember weddings where we danced the Gay Gordons, the foxtrot, the quickstep and lots of old-fashioned waltzes. We used to play a game of arrows in two gangs. One gang would chalk an arrow on a tree or mark one out on the side of a slag heap and the other gang had to follow the arrows until they found gang A. This game could take all day and we would roam for miles and miles. We used to take jam sandwiches and a bottle of water. There were no cars to worry about then and, looking back, we had an extraordinary amount of freedom to go wherever we wanted. Whether that is because the person looking after us didn't much care what happened to us or whether it was the way all children were brought up then I don't know.

Near our evacuation home in South Moor there were some quaintly named places. School was a two or three-mile walk to a place called Hustle Down and the next village was Quaking Houses. There was a bluebell wood and a park with an enormous oak tree under which I can remember eating the staple fare, jam sandwiches. I also remember once sitting on the front step savouring a jam sandwich when a red chow came up and snatched the sandwich and wolfed it down before I had time to realise what was happening. I have been frightened of chows ever since.

Uncle Tom, a miner, was quiet, I can hardly remember him ever speaking except on Sundays to say "I'm going to see a man about a dog". Being a miner he was given free coal and a lorry deposited a pile of it in the back lane every week, and one of my jobs when I was old enough to wield a shovel was to throw it into the coal shed. I would be able to remember Uncle Tom fondly except for one incident - and the service he used to require every Sunday which, thankfully, was my older sister's responsibility.

But Aunty Jenny was, at times, a monster. I have no idea why I never told my mother about the beatings when she came to see us or after the war. I don't recall us ever talking about it: whether I thought my parents wouldn't believe me or whether I instinctively knew they had so many troubles of their own, trying to find us somewhere to live, adjusting to each other after such a long separation and so on, that it was better not to burden them with my woes. Probably a bit of both; I think everyone in those days wanted us all to forget what went on during the war and to get on with life. Perhaps that is why no one bothered to inquire too closely about what had happened to evacuees for the past six years and what has made people not want to look back subsequently.

Aunty Jenny kept a brown leather belt hanging on a nail in the living room at Elm Street, solely for the purpose of giving us a beating. As far as I know it was never used for anything else. She used to beat me for anything and nothing. There was no predicting what might merit a thrashing with that belt. She was a tiny, wiry little woman with rather large glasses, which magnified her eyes, and frizzy black hair. She always wore one of those wrapover pinnies most women had in those days.

What saved me, I think, from feeling terminally miserable and alone was the dog. The witch had a black and white collie bitch called Lady and when she beat me I used to run upstairs where the dog was usually lying on my bed. Some dogs can be amazingly sensitive - she must have known I was going to need to cuddle her. I used to sob into Lady's coat with my arms around her neck and I was convinced she wasn't really a dog. I suppose I must have read the story of the Princess and the Frog because I just knew Lady was really a prince and would rescue me from this nightmare. I remember whispering and cuddling the dog for hours.

Often, when I was crying like this, waiting for Lady to transmogrify into my rescuer, I would sense a presence and turn around to see Aunty Jenny peeping through the gap in the door frame. She used to creep up the stairs and listen to what I was saying to the dog. That was as scary as the beatings were painful. What was she doing? Spying? Coming to gloat over her handiwork? I used to pretend I hadn't seen her.

I have read that for centuries it was considered necessary, literally, to beat good into children so I suppose that is what she was trying to do. Other times, as a punishment, Aunty Jenny locked me in a cupboard under the stairs. It was pitch black in there and she made me stay locked up for hours. I wouldn't be able to sit in my own understairs cupboard at home today with the door closed, the very idea of it makes me tearful. I was frightened and crying and she wouldn't let me out until she saw fit and eventually I used to occupy myself. In those days people made pictures out of silver paper and there were bits of silver paper in there which I used to play with, once my eyes became accustomed to the darkness.

She also used to threaten me constantly with "The bogeyman will come and get you". I cannot remember now what reason Aunty Jenny used to give - if she ever did - for the beatings. There is only one incident which I shall never forget and which gives some idea of her complete unreasonableness. One of my cousins, the family who were evacuated with Aunty Winnie, invited me to her birthday party. As parties were a rare occurrence in those days, I was terribly excited. I rushed home after school, and told Aunty Jenny I was going to Margaret's birthday party. I can remember thinking I would have to put a move on because it was nearly teatime already. Aunty Jenny not only refused to allow me to go to the party, she gave me the belt for asking. I can still feel the injustice of it today and am as mystified by her attitude now as I was then. For some reason, and I never discovered why, I believe she and Aunty Winnie were not on speaking terms so I assume that had something to do with it. To a five or six-year-old child, it made no sense at all.

I can remember one Sunday her reading out a story to us from the newspaper about two brothers who had been treated cruelly. The tale was lurid and frightening and I was sure at the time, as I am now, she was telling it with the purpose of getting the message across "If you think you're badly done to, that's nothing to what you could get." She relished reading out every detail of happened to those two boys. In my memory the story seemed to go on forever and I think one of them died at the end of it.

I said Uncle Tom was harmless and quite gentle, but now that I am older I wonder what he was really like. I once had measles or mumps and had to sleep in the living room on the sofa. Most of the living was done in the scullery. This room was used only for lunch on Sundays and for administering the beatings, and it was where the dreaded understairs cupboard was. I can remember being woken up in the middle of the night by uncle Tom getting ready for work. If I had to undress then re-dress in front of a child, even if I assumed that child to be asleep, I am sure I would turn my back and do the usual contortions you do on a beach not to reveal anything, but he stood naked in front of me and I saw his private parts. They looked disgusting and I was very frightened, screwing my eyes up tight, but once you have seen something, you cannot wipe the vision from your mind. He was looking at me and now that I am an adult I find it rather a creepy thing to do. The other revolting thing about Uncle Tom was that every Sunday he wanted his back scratched. He took his shirt off and his skin was pale and pimply. This was a job my older sister had to do and it made my flesh crawl. She says it didn't bother her so I'm glad the job fell to her. I think I would rather have had the belt yet again than have to do that.

Another sadistic trick Aunty Jenny used to play was to frighten us with her false teeth. Once we locked ourselves into the pantry while she was outside with her teeth in her hand shouting at us. My sister remembers her putting the false teeth in the cupboard under the stairs and forcing her to go in beside them. Poor Joyce didn't know whether the teeth were going to bite her. I think Aunty Jenny must have been a bit mad, unless she genuinely thought it was a fun game to play with children. I should have thought, though, that our obvious terror would have made her stop if she had been normal.

She had a daughter, Nellie who later, she insisted, we had to call Ellen. She must have lived somewhere else because although I can remember seeing her a lot, she was not around all the time. I was a bridesmaid at her wedding, wearing a dress that a friend of Aunty Jenny's had made. We were always dressed very well, in the same outfits. Someone took us ice skating and we had matching black satin dresses with white pom poms on them and I can remember another outfit of red velvet. She used to make a tremendous fuss about our hair. It had to look like Shirley Temple's so we went to bed with it twisted into rags. They were uncomfortable to sleep in and ripped your hair out when they were removed. Next morning the rags would be pulled out – painfully - and hey presto, ringlets. She also used to crimp our hair with tongs. I have incredibly fine straight hair which she was determined to make look completely different. I can even remember being sent to a hairdresser's once and having great black plugs like something from *Star Wars* fitted to my head to perm my hair. It is a wonder I have any hair left.

On Saturdays we had the choice of tap dancing classes or the cinema. My sister chose the tap dancing classes and I chose the cinema. I can remember seeing *The Man in the Iron Mask* and lots of films with Gene Autrey and his horse Trigger. On Sundays, after the back-scratching chore we were allowed to go and buy an ice cream, when it became available again.

For someone who was so handy with the belt, Aunty Jenny could be extraordinarily tolerant of some things. For instance, my sister hated Sunday lunch so, with no criticism whatsoever, Jenny used to put all the meat, potatoes, vegetables and gravy into a frying pan and give it to her as a fry-up. Joyce had to wait for us to finish ours first but still, she got what she wanted. Once, when we were out playing in the bluebell wood, Joyce lost one of her sandals in a stream and I thought, all the way home, we would get the belt but neither of us did. Aunty Jenny was completely unpredictable.

The war never intruded on our lives, we heard no bombs. The nearest to a major worry was when we heard of a pit disaster. I remember there were two in quick succession and everyone was talking about there being a third to come because bad things always happened in threes, and they were right.

I was also aware of the lack of everything. Sweet rationing began in 1941 and we were all allowed two ounces per week. Everyone was issued with a ration book. Parents of children who were evacuated could hold their ration books in order to send them presents of sweets although I can't ever remember receiving any. I think Aunty Jenny had our ration books because I can remember going to a shop at the bottom of the road occasionally, but I think most of our sweet ration was commandeered by her because she used to have a linen cupboard in her bedroom stacked full of sugar and tea. Perhaps she was storing it up against a possible German invasion.

Our mother used to come occasionally, always on a Sunday. She used to wear make-up and had her hair bleached in the front and rolled around her head in the style fashionable at the time and she always brought a lovely present. I have no idea why we didn't spill the beans to her. I think children just have an instinct about these things. Anyway, Jenny probably never left us alone with her. She was fiendishly cunning.

We saw our father a couple of times when he was home on leave and we went to see him in Newcastle. He was handsome in his RAF uniform and he once brought us lovely embroidered raffia baskets and nuts, an unheard of luxury, from Italy or Greece. He used to pretend he was having a great time in the war but he never spoke about it much. Even years later it was like trying to get blood out of a stone. All I know is that he had a narrow escape. He showed us a bullet wound in his leg years later but where he got it or how I could never get out of him.

I have no idea how old I was when I had my tonsils out but I can remember waiting in the room before the operation and being afraid. I can also remember coming round and seeing stars on the ceiling. The nurses were kind but the reason I am telling this story here is that I was put on a bus and came home from hospital on my own, wrapped in a tartan blanket. I don't know how far it was but it seems an extraordinary thing to do. Talk about learning independence at an early age.

As I said earlier, one of the saddest aspects of my evacuation is that I cried as much when I had to go home as I had when I was first evacuated. In spite of the beatings and being locked in a cupboard, apparently I still loved the witch who had been my tormentor. Although I feel absolutely no affection for her now - I am hurt and perplexed by her treatment of us - I know I cried and it must have upset my poor mother. My sister never looked back and I think hers is a far healthier reaction. For years I kept returning to South Moor to see Aunty Jenny -- maybe it was my way of facing the demons.

It is only since having psychotherapy and reading books about child abuse that I am beginning to understand why I felt such affection for the person who was so cruel to me. It baffled me for years and I felt, somehow, as if I had let myself down by not hating her which I ought to have done. I was helped tremendously by a psychotherapist, who showed me how to look back at the child then, to be a mother to myself in a way. It made me realise that I was much too young to be blamed for anything, that what happened to me made me immensely vulnerable and I should understand and forgive that little person. The counselling sessions certainly helped me to put that part of my life into perspective.

I can remember the VE party in Elm Street and I can also remember sitting on my dad's shoulders in Grey Street, Newcastle, watching the bands and people marching past in a victory parade so we must have returned home by May 1945.

After we left, Aunty Jenny fostered a teenage girl but sent her back because she would not come home at the times she was told to. Presumably she was someone old enough to stand up to her, otherwise Jenny would have beaten the foster daughter into obedience. She also adopted a baby called Carole who came while I was still evacuated because I can remember wheeling the pram down the street and telling the baby to copy me. I'd walk along with my eyes closed and Carole did the same. I thought it was such a clever wheeze to get her to go to sleep. The last time I saw her, Carole was quite big so I don't know how many years after the war that must have been. Nellie/Ellen married a miner who decided they should all emigrate to New South Wales, Australia, which is where they must all be now. Aunty Jenny is most probably dead and I don't suppose, even if I had the chance, it would do much good to ask, "Why did you do it? Why were you so cruel?"

Chapter Four
Opportunistic Pederasts

Because evacuees were regarded as slaves, they could be subjected to sexual slavery. We now know, after numerous commissions of inquiry into the running of children's homes, that there has been widespread abuse of children in Britain – what the child psychologist Alice Miller refers to as "the cancer in our society". Adults have come forward to bear witness to the crimes committed against them when they were too young and vulnerable to protect themselves.

The sexual abuse of evacuees goes back even further than those first reports which began to emerge during the Seventies. They, too, were too young and vulnerable to protect themselves. They were unceremoniously billeted, on their own, into houses with men and women who had never been vetted. Some were pederasts who took advantage of this golden opportunity: a child delivered to them on a plate and given to them, what's more, with the blessing of their Government. The experience of these evacuees proves that there are many sexually deviant men – and their accomplice wives whose silence is almost as abhorrent – whose proclivities may be latent but who are ever ready to take advantage of a victim.

Many years ago a pregnant woman whose car broke down on the M4 motorway was brutally raped and murdered as she tried to telephone for assistance. I was asked to write an article for *The Times* about the type of killer who could carry out such an evil crime. A criminal psychologist I interviewed warned people not to think of this person as a slavering maniac with staring eyes: he would be a completely normal-looking person even though an opportunistic rapist and murderer. It is hard to imagine there are people walking around the streets looking perfectly ordinary who harbour such evil thoughts, but obviously there are. That is how I imagine these people who took in evacuees to be like: seemingly normal to their neighbours but hideously depraved behind their net curtains.

Psychiatrist Ann Fillmore claims that "a revealing, stark and even frightening dimension to the experience of the abused child is gained from comparison of his situation with that of hostage victims and concentration camp inmates. The abused child, like a camp inmate, is told to love and obey his warders or be injured, but at the same time given the message that he is abhorred and unworthy of love and protection. He is asked to perform acts of loyalty but at the same time psychologically and physically degraded. Most important, he is constantly threatened with life-destroying violence and often receives violence for no consistent reason or for a reason which is patently untrue. To complete the comparison, neither the abused child nor the camp inmate has a time-limited sentence - there seems to be no end to their situation...That a few days under the threat of death (as a hostage) can change the entire psyche of an adult should be a clear indication of what intermittent violence, emotional battery and intermittent kindness can do to an unknowing and inadequately verbal child."

What happened to Helen, a gentle, compassionate nurse from Merseyside, when she was evacuated has had tragic consequences for the rest of her life. She could not have the children she always wanted because she was unable to consummate her marriage. She could never bring herself to tell the sister who was evacuated with her, but to a different foster home, what happened to her. Her sister died two years ago and it was when she was grieving for her sister that the sorrow that has been with Helen for more than half a century broke through her defences.

Helen is still, at the age of 66, so ashamed of what happened when she was just an eight-year-old girl she asked me not to reveal her name. She cannot, she says, face the public humiliation. My assurance that people would be sympathetic could not persuade her to come out in the open. Even talking about it to me was painful.

This is one of the consequences of what happened to evacuees that makes me so angry. Women like Helen are left, even after all these years, harbouring a guilt that is not theirs, that should be laid at the door of the perpetrators. If she had had counselling she may have been able to save her marriage or at least rid herself of some of the shame she feels. It is such a waste of a wonderful person that she should have been made to suffer all these years because of the lusts of a grisly father and his vile son.

The son is still alive - Helen managed to track him down. And although she would dearly love to see him prosecuted, there is no evidence, it would be her word against his. The perpetrators of abuse have it so easy, their victims are their prisoners to do with what they want. We speculated about this man, now in his seventies, who abused her when he was 15. Did he grow up to abuse his own children? We wonder.

Helen's mother died when she was just three. She and her older sister were evacuated to Wales and, like so many siblings, were split up. Her sister went to a lovely family who wanted to adopt her. "When my sister died two years ago I went to the library to try to track down the family I was evacuated with. They had an unusual surname and eventually I did track down the son. I telephoned him and he denied everything, he even said he couldn't remember having an evacuee in the house. He said to me 'You are a very sick woman'. I rang our local rape crisis centre and told them I had not been raped but I had been sexually abused and could not stop crying, thinking about this episode when I was a child. They were sympathetic, they assured me he was in denial. The fact that I wasn't actually raped did not make any difference to the effect the abuse had on me. It totally destroyed my self-worth and my ability to commit myself in a physical way to my husband."

Helen remembers setting off for evacuation with her sister, labelled and mystified, and at first her billet seemed fine. "I had my own little bedroom which I thought was beautiful but then the father started coming in at night. The son, who was about 15, came in as well and did the same things. The son also made me go with him 'to play' in the family car. Then the father, on a few occasions, started taking me into his bedroom. He'd say, 'I have been a naughty boy and I need caning'. He used to lie across the bed, his fat bottom in loose underpants and make me smack him with a big cane.

"I think the wife must have found out because I was told she had a nervous breakdown and I was put with the people next door. I can remember the wife being very angry with me. She'd given me a tea set and I remember her taking it back from me."

So an eight-year-old girl was punished, made to feel guilty, for the gross desires of a fat, middle-aged husband and father. It was a trauma that, sadly, marked Helen mentally for life. With help she may have been able to overcome it and even now could probably be helped through counselling to recapture some peace of mind.

Helen says, "I want people to understand how something like that ruins your life. I was an eight year old girl on my own. It was frightening and degrading. It became a standing joke in my family for years that I had caused this woman to have a nervous breakdown. 'But Helen is so easy to look after' they'd say, not understanding how a timid little girl like me could have driven a woman to having a nervous breakdown and of course I never said anything about what really happened. I never even told my sister. If she'd known she would have found them and slaughtered them. You don't tell anybody about a thing like that because you take some of the blame. You know somehow it is wrong, you feel it is wrong, but you don't know what to do about it.

"In the new foster home the people were old and they weren't cruel but they weren't kind either. I was given my own shelf in the pantry where my rations were put and that's all I had. I somehow managed to let my father know that I was unhappy and I went back to stay with him. After the war I trained as a nurse and became a staff nurse on the medical and surgical wards of a big hospital in Liverpool. I'm still a practice nurse now.

"I'd met my husband as a child and we married when I was 21 but the marriage was never fully consummated. There was a hang up about sex on my part. I just couldn't get over that sense of revulsion when I saw my husband in his underpants. My poor husband, I could never explain it to him. We divorced after 12 years of marriage and afterwards he wanted to remarry a Catholic girl. He asked me if we could get a divorce on the grounds the marriage had not been consummated but I said no. I was too ashamed to say yes so they had to get married in a registry office instead of church which is what they wanted. I still couldn't bring myself to tell him, even though I am really sorry for him and would like to have helped. I just couldn't bear the shame of admitting in public what our marriage had been like. He now has two lovely children. I love children and wanted five of my own...

"I did meet someone later and told him what had happened to me but that relationship didn't work out. When I was on the wards I know I had an aura about me that said, 'Keep away'. There was a barrier between me and the male patients which in a way I think helped me to look after them. I am a very maternal person and now

I pour out all my love into looking after lost and hurt animals."

I once interviewed pederasts at a clinic in Birmingham where psychologists were trying to rehabilitate men, to try and make them understand that what they do to children is evil. It sounds incredible, but these men really do kid themselves that what they are doing does not harm children. Even supposedly intelligent people seem able to fool themselves that raping children is of little consequence.

Virginia Woolf was subject to schizophrenic episodes from the age of 12 and took her own life in 1941 at the age of 59. From the time she was four until she reached puberty she was sexually molested by her much older half-brother, virtually on a daily basis, without being able to tell anyone about it. Yet her - male - biographer wrote that he did not know whether this trauma had any permanent effect on Virginia or not.

Shirley Wilson, of Altbridge Park, Liverpool, could enlighten him. "I was evacuated to north Wales when I was five," she says. "And for almost two years I was physically abused by the lady who billeted me. On one occasion I was locked in an outside toilet all night for wetting the bed and lashed across the legs and back with a cane when I didn't please her. My brother was three years old and he was billeted with good people.

"We were both transferred to Denbigh, north Wales, where my older two sisters and older brother were evacuated. For me it was a case of from bad to worse. The lady of the house was crippled with arthritis and slept downstairs. My young brother and I slept in the same bed as her husband upstairs. There, for the next two years, I was sexually abused almost every night of the week. Put through all kinds of abuse at the hands of this man.

"My older sisters and brother were all physically abused. I told my sister what was happening but when she told older people we were not believed. My little brother was run over by a motor bike and had facial injuries and they lied to my parents, telling them it was just a push bike.

"After telling my sister and us getting nowhere trying to tell grown ups about the abuse I suffered at the time, I did not tell anyone of this chapter of my life until I was turned 40 years old, but for years and years I kept getting flash-backs. We were never given counselling, it wasn't heard of. We were just left to get on with life.

"Recently I retraced my childhood by going back to look at the cottage where all my pain and suffering occurred. It was 58 years after my terrible experiences. I am now at 64, crippled with osteoarthritis, I have had both hips replaced, but I can die happy knowing what happened to me was not my fault."

Chapter Five
Thrown to the wolves

As I said in the first chapter, some parents regarded the evacuation as a welcome excuse to rid themselves of the burdensome responsibility of their children. I have interviewed only a few evacuees who actually asked their parents the question, "Why did you leave me there?" Perhaps we were afraid of the answer. Or maybe, after the war was over, there were so many other problems to face – bombed-out homes, relatives killed, jobs to find, the atrocities committed by the Nazis, that we accepted what we had suffered was simply our share of the horrors of war. But it hardly seems fair that ours is the only suffering that has hardly been acknowledged or given any sympathy since.

There were lamentably few follow-up visits by anyone in authority to ensure everything was all right and where such rare visits were made, the emphasis tended to be on making sure it was the billeting household which was satisfied. No one seems to have worried about the welfare of the children, beyond a superficial check at the beginning, when they arrived off a train, to see if they had shoes on their feet or a winter coat.

It was not as if the thought that something terrible might happen to evacuees had never occurred to anyone. An unsigned letter appeared in *The Times* in 1940 suggesting that parish councils should have some sort of compulsory right of inquiry. "One has only to read the sad records of the NSPCC to realise that some people cannot be trusted with their own children," the letter said. "Far less with those of strangers in the country. There must be many who would need supervision to ensure that the allowances were being spent on the refugee children and that these children are adequately maintained. Only the local councils would have the necessary knowledge of individuals to ensure this being properly done; but there seems much doubt and some timidity in the whole matter."

In the spring of that year the NSPCC brought out a special edition of its newsletter in which an editorial admitted that although they had been hopeful they would not have any serious cases to deal with concerning evacuees, this was not to be. "Cases of actual ill-treatment of evacuees brought to our notice," it went on, "have been of a particularly abhorrent nature.

"Probably the worst of these concerned four little London boys whose ages ranged from eight to five who were sent to Hove, East Sussex, in September. They were placed in the care of a young man of 25 and his wife. The accommodation was poor and consisted of two basement rooms and a scullery, in which were already living five people, three adults and two children.

"At first the little evacuees slept five in a bed and afterwards four in a bed. They were, when sent to this 'home' quite clean, but when their mother saw them at Christmas their condition was terrible. All were suffering from scabies and impetigo and the body of one was covered with bruises.

"The Society was informed and the story these boys told of their sufferings was a very painful one. It cannot all be related in the columns of this paper, for the details are too revolting, but in giving evidence at the Police Court, the eldest of these boys said, 'We were not happy because Mr Short was cruel to us.

'He made us lie on the bed with our legs up and our hands above our shoulders so that we should ache. He made us stand near the fire and burn our stomachs. We only had a shirt on and he made us lift it up. Mr and Mrs Short hit Johnny. He said if we told tales he would burn us again. He burned Johnny and Edward twice and me and Jimmy once. He whipped us with an umbrella-stick. He hit Jimmy with a shoe and punched us in the stomach.

'He made us box. When he boxed with us he wore ordinary gloves. I hit him in the mouth once and broke one of his teeth which went into his gum. He punched me in the jaw and in the stomach and I went into the fireplace. He picked me up and punched me again and made my mouth swell.'"

The man denied the allegations but admitted that he had hit the five-year-old boy with a slipper. Called for the defence, the chief evacuation officer stated, with reference to the skin trouble from which the boys were found to be suffering, that quite a large number of evacuees brought such diseases with them. He thought it possible, indeed probable, that the boys caught the diseases from other evacuated children.

The case against the man's wife, who was charged with neglecting the boys, was dismissed, but the man was sentenced to six months' imprisonment for ill-treating the children.

The mayor of Hove, in passing the sentence, said to the man, "There are no words that will allow the magistrates to express their disgust and abhorrence at your conduct towards these defenceless children. It does not seem possible that in these days a man can be found who would treat defenceless evacuated children in the manner we consider you have done."

Regarding the neglect allegations, the mayor added, "To a large extent the circumstances seem to have arisen because the billeting authorities allowed the children to be billeted in a small basement flat where there were already five other persons."

Widespread publicity was given to this case in the press and among the editorial references was this comment, which appeared in the *Daily Herald*: "Nothing more revolting has come to light for a long time than the case of Mr James Short, sentenced at Hove yesterday for cruelty to small evacuee children. He has been sentenced to six months hard labour. But surely the question is whether an unbalanced sadist of this kind is fit to move freely in society at all...Yesterday's case is a nasty warning of what may still happen when children get into wrong hands." Sadly, though there was this and other evidence that children were sometimes badly treated, it did not seem to occur to the authorities to check on all evacuee children.

In her book *Thou Shalt Not Be Aware*, Alice Miller writes, "One of the greatest discoveries of this century is that the period of early childhood is of crucial importance for a person's emotional development. Children who are respected learn respect. Children who are cared for learn to care for those weaker than themselves." If a little child who is abused, she goes on, and is not permitted to talk about it, this very taboo against expressing himself robs him of his self-confidence. "Rage is a proper reaction to cruelty but how do small children show rage? A child experiences feelings much more intensely than an adult: feelings of helplessness, fear, powerlessness, feelings that inhibit a person's vitality."

And Miller poses this question, which, she says, abused children ask and which evacuees must have asked themselves many thousands of times as they cried themselves to sleep at night: "Why don't my parents come and rescue me from this?"

One evacuee who saw neither her mother nor her father during the war and who, with her sister, suffered the most appalling sexual abuse is Mrs Rita King from Liverpool. She was evacuated at the age of six until she was ten years old to Builth Wells, mid-Wales, and the isolation from her parents added to her sense of rejection, a sense of loss that remains with her today.

Now a widow of 64, Rita won an award for best adult student at college where she recently studied catering, but she feels she has been deprived of a life. She is convinced she was never able to reach her full potential because of what happened to her when she was evacuated.

"It's like living behind a closed door," Rita says. "I am trying to make something of my life at last but I resent all those years I have missed. I put my needs on the back burner because I was told I would never have anything, never be anything. It's difficult to explain but now that I am older, I feel anger and despair. I felt I was utterly soiled and worthless. We evacuees were there for the picking, we were thrown to the wolves."

Rita never told her mother what happened to her while she was evacuated and she and her sister Barbara, who suffered the same fate, only started talking about it to each other two or three years ago.

She sobbed as she told me her story. She shed tears for the way the sexual abuse she was subjected to has warped her life, and I cried in sympathy for the plight of a little girl disgustingly mauled first by a father and then by his son. She tried telling her late husband once but he told her, "It was a long time ago, forget it." As if she ever could. She has now told one of her three sons who asked her, "Can't you do anything about it?" But what? "The father is probably dead now and the son must be in his seventies. I hope they both lie in hell.

"I was six when I was evacuated. I come from a large family and most of us were evacuated. I was sent to join my sister, Barbara, who was seven. We were evacuated to a small market town and were in a block of four houses that shared an outside toilet and had one tap between them. It wasn't the foster parents who abused us, they could not have been nicer. It was their neighbours, a father and his son. I don't know what the wife was doing while it was happening but she must have known something was going on. We were frequently sent to stay with the neighbours for a weekend or longer so the foster parents could have a break. What those men did has scarred me for life. It still distresses me to talk about it. Even now, and I am 64 years of age, the smell of Lifebuoy soap, which they used to use, makes me feel sick."

Rita's words come haltingly at first then she takes a deep breath and they speed up. It is only because I am a woman and also suffered abuse when I was evacuated that she feels she can talk to me about what happened. She doesn't want her full name to appear in print - we have used her mother's maiden name - because she still can't face up to it: the experience is still too painful and she feels ashamed. It isn't easy for a woman to talk publicly of sordid sexual gratification but we both want the world to know - and care - how brutally some of us were used. And Rita bravely put into words the experiences which are always there in her memories. She doesn't have to drag them up from long ago. They are lurking like dark shadows, just beneath the surface, affecting everything she does, everything she thinks.

"I think about it with such utter revulsion," she says. "You are the first person I have been able to talk to about it in detail. The father or son often used to say, 'I'll take her to the toilet' and you'd feel sick, knowing what was going to happen there. At other times they'd say, 'Let's go to bed and play our little games' or the father would say, even in our foster parents' home, 'I'll put the girls to bed'and the son would say, 'I'll help you dad'. And no one suspected anything. It was so revolting... All the time he used to grin at me...I was only six years old when it started...The son was a teenager and used to read the *Beano* and *Dandy* comics. He'd say, 'Come upstairs and we'll read the comics' and I'd have no choice. They abused both of us, first one sister and then the other.

"I can remember once being told to sit on this man's knee at my foster parents' house and having to do as I was told. He would do things to me even then. It was so gross. I still can't bear my face to be touched. Even going to the dentist is difficult for me because of him touching my face. We used to crawl on our hands and knees to get past their window without them seeing us so they couldn't drag us inside but I felt they were always waiting for the next time to get you alone, looking at you, gloating."

Rita can't believe she is telling me all this and we stop to talk about something else, what happened to me or I tell her about another evacuee story I have been told. Yet she wants the world to know how betrayed evacuated children feel and how easily and ruthlessly paedophiles operate.

"These two men used to taunt us, telling us we were 'Bootle Bucks' which implied we were from Bootle, which we weren't, and low, common, not worth anything. They frequently told us no one would believe us and we felt they were right because being evacuees we were of no importance, we had no status. You were so helpless as an evacuee. You had no one to turn to. They used to say to us, 'If you don't do what I say, I'll send you back to the bombs.' I can remember a WVS person coming to the house but she never asked us how we were, as an evacuee you were spoken about but never to. She'd say to the foster parents, 'Are they behaving?' and 'Are they alright?' You were a little baggage in the corner, that's how we were made to feel, like a piece of baggage.

"Because I didn't see my mother and father during the whole of the war that added to my feeling of rejection. I felt I wasn't important enough to my mother and father for them to come and rescue me from this. My father was never a real father, he was just a figurehead which they were in those days and my mother probably didn't come to see us because she couldn't afford the fare, although she never showed us any love anyway. She never gave us cuddles or kisses and we never had intimate talks or that sort of thing.

"And the teachers at school were so vicious you didn't feel you could go to them for comfort. You were not allowed to blink at school or you got the cane. One teacher caned me every day because I refused to answer to the name of Margaret which she had down in her book. Eventually my foster mother sent away for my birth certificate to prove to her my name was Rita and only then did she stop caning me but there was no apology. Children were treated like dirt in those days. I'm glad they stick up for themselves today.

"You just knew all the time no one would believe you so you were isolated with this terrible pain. It's hard to explain to people who have not endured abuse. You know they must be thinking, 'surely there's something she could have done' but when you are so young you feel completely helpless. You just had to put up with it. We were given the impression all the time we should be grateful."

When the war ended, Rita's foster parents wanted to adopt her but she couldn't get away from there fast enough, although they never knew the reason why. Anyway, her mother would not consent to an adoption. When she left school she went to work in a chemist's shop in Penny Lane, made famous by the Beatles, but her troubles were not over.

"There was a man there who tried to touch me and I became hysterical, absolutely hysterical. I always wore a cardigan to hide my bust which was large and I began to think that there must be something about me, that I must be giving out the wrong signals to men. Now I understand that many men are so sexually motivated they only see women in crude terms but in those days I thought it was my fault.

"My husband was in the Navy and was a pen pal. I thought marriage to him would be wonderful and all my anxieties about what had happened to me and men's attitude to me would be at an end but I'm afraid marriage exacerbated my problems. When he started to touch me I became frigid; bed became a battle ground. I would give in to sex for peace in the family but there was never any enjoyment on my part. I did it out of duty and that was frustrating for him. He could not understand what was the matter with me. As far as he was concerned, what happened to me was a long time ago. He loved me and I can't say I didn't love him but I felt he degraded me. I felt I had sex with him as a prostitute in my marriage, in return for kindnesses to my children, holidays and so on. I thought I should not have to do this with my body, other people should not have to touch it. It sounds a dreadful thing to say, but when my husband died fourteen years ago, what came to my mind was, I don't have to have sex any more. I don't have to be touched anymore."

Mrs Anne Bowes of Oxford, also had to put up with perverts at one of her foster homes but thankfully for her, although the memories are revolting, they did not stop her from going on to live a happy, fulfilled life. She is secretary to a don at Oxford - one of the lucky evacuees who says if it hadn't been for the evacuation he would not be where he is today - and she has a husband she loves and two wonderful grown-up children she is proud of.

An articulate and sensible woman, Anne says, "Evacuation for me was hateful and I would never, ever, have sent my own children away under similar circumstances. I don't blame my mother, parents were encouraged by the Government to send their children out of the cities, and she couldn't possibly have realised how unhappy we would be or for how long we would be away.

"When the war ended I was eleven. I always felt I deserved more love than I got but I don't think I was permanently affected by our experiences during the war, but I am not so sure about one of my sisters.

CHAPTER FIVE

"They were eleven and seven and I was five when we were sent away. Our dear mother had been deserted by our father who was a musician and evacuation of her children gave her the opportunity of having us properly looked after - so she thought - while she worked fulltime to provide us with a decent home. My mother had offered her services to run a children's home so that she could look after us at the same time but she was turned down.

"She never knew about all the abuse we were subjected to; it would have broken her heart. Our older sister was parted from us on the first day of evacuation and eventually she returned to London at about the age of 13 because she was living in filthy conditions.

"First of all let me say that, although evacuation of children had been planned long before it was actually carried out, it does seem that eventually it was done in haste and things were wrongly handled. For instance, my second sister and I, who remained together for the entire war period, lived in six billets in total and every time we were moved it was by the same billeting officer, a Mr Johnson, who drove us in his car. Each time he sat me in the front passenger seat and my sister sat behind and each time he would put his hand down the waist of my knickers and fondle my bottom. I endured this, hating every moment, but not knowing what I could do about it. I am so glad that today children would speak up if anyone did anything like that to them.

"We were sent first to Bedfordshire, this billet lasting only 24 hours because we were too young for the two elderly ladies who had taken us. Then we went to a kind family and for the first year we were content but, because our foster mother became ill, we were moved to a new home in Buckinghamshire. At this home we were inadequately fed and clothed. Despite a harsh winter we walked the mile or so to school wearing summer clothes and sandals. My sister developed chilblains on her feet which broke and she still has the scars.

"Our breakfast consisted of a few crumbs of cereals and the evening meal consisted of yesterday's pudding for starters while the family tucked into a hearty meat meal. We became so hungry we ate berries, nuts and leaves from the hedgerows. Our mother used to visit us regularly on Sunday, sometimes bringing our elder sister and she noticed how thin we had become but we tried to reassure her that we were well.

"However, we discovered we could reach the family's store of pears which were on the rafters of a garden shed where we played each day after school and it became our custom to take and eat one or two. This must have gone on for some time because by the time the theft was discovered, there were very few pears left. Our mother was sent for and she was outraged with our foster parents. She accused them of starving us and had us moved immediately. The woman had made us rather pretty dresses which were taken back again as soon as she found out about stealing the pears.

"We were sent back to Bedfordshire where, after two short-stay billets, we spent the last three or four years of the war with an extended and very religious family. The matriarch was in the Salvation Army and she thought she was wonderful. She used to say to us, 'When I die, Saint Peter will say, 'Come in Mrs Gasgoine, I have a front seat for you'. We discovered what hypocrisy was staying with this family.

"My sister lived most of the time with one married daughter and her husband who was engaged on war work and their small daughter and I lived most of the time with another married daughter who, at first, was alone because her husband was fighting abroad. He came back home because he was discharged from the army after having contracted VD. I know this because, although I was young, I was intelligent. I didn't know what VD was but I had seen posters on the buses with the shadow of the letters VD across a baby's face and the words Venereal Disease. When the daughter with whom I lived received a letter from her husband telling her about the VD she called to someone who was in the house, 'What's VD?' and I piped up with 'venereal disease'. The daughter was furious with me and told me I shouldn't listen to other people's conversations.

"When her husband returned I was required to sleep downstairs on the sofa instead of sharing their double bed which is where I slept before. I had a bad dream one night and the husband came down, ostensibly to comfort me, but allowing his pyjamas to expose his horrible penis. There were many similar occasions when he exposed himself to me.

"Another time he took my sister and me to the cinema. My sister left her seat as soon as the lights dimmed and didn't return. She was waiting for us outside the cinema two hours later. No questions were asked of her and she gave no explanation and I thought it was very odd. She had decided, on that occasion, that she was not going to be forced to touch him and had left. She didn't tell me about this until we were back in London.

"The family thought nothing of landing one or other of us a hefty whack around the head and my sister suffered severe headaches. In those days a good hiding was not considered to be physical abuse and we certainly had our fair share. There was an occasion when my sister broke her leg and she was sent, alone, to the hospital in the next town to have it treated.

"She still remembers the shock the nurses had on seeing a seven-year-old with a broken leg being sent for treatment all by herself. It happened on a Monday which was wash day and nothing was allowed to interfere with their routine; it was too inconvenient to take her to hospital.

"Sometimes I had to sleep in the matriarch's home where her youngest daughter, aged 18, lived, and on those occasions I had to share this daughter's bed. What happened to me then was repulsive. I would be awakened from sleep with her abusing me. I was horrified and disgusted by this, as well as scared.

"She used to ask me whether I liked it and I was so used to being obedient that I couldn't even say how much I loathed it, but just put up with her foul behaviour. I could not understand this 'rude' behaviour as I thought of it, or how she could behave perfectly normally at other times, as though nothing untoward had occurred. You had an intuitive feeling you could not tell your parents or anyone else about it.

"There were lodgers, war workers, as well as evacuees and foster children with this family and one of the lodgers, a particularly unattractive man, I recall, called Harold Love, would sometimes take the children for a walk and he would suggest, on summer afternoons, that we remove our top clothing. At the age of seven or eight, it never occurred to me that I should not do so. In any case, I had been taught to be obedient and to do as instructed by grown-ups.

"I don't think he ever touched us but on one occasion, as a group of us strolled, half naked, across the Downs with this man, a member of the family saw us. My sister and I were in severe trouble, but I don't know whether anyone chastised the lodger or the other children. My sister and I were the culprits. It was considered to be our crime.

"Our mother knew nothing about this ghastly family. The extraordinary thing is that after the war they used to ask me back for holidays and I went, yet I hated them with a passion.

"We went to a school where there were two classes to a room, one facing one way and the second the other. On one occasion a friend and I were sitting in an empty classroom and we started to draw pictures. In my maths book I drew two little match stick people with a head, two arms and two legs and an extra bit for one of them.

'They are having a fuck,' I announced. God knows how I knew anything about such things, I was only about seven.

"The student teacher reported it and my mother was sent for and a Salvation Army officer was sent for. 'How did you learn things like that?' they asked. I can remember thinking, 'What a hypocrite'. I had heard it or seen it somewhere certainly. There was hatred and disbelief in my heart during that confrontation.

"Another terrible scene that is in my memory is to do with a pair of shoes. We heard Freeman Hardy and Willis were going to have shoes in on Wednesday and we all queued. The ones I was bought were black with red insets. They were to be for Christmas but this was only Easter and by the time Christmas came my feet were too big. I still tried to cram them into the shoes and the back seams burst so I was given a good hiding. It didn't make any sense.

"In fact, I was always very confused about the reactions of this family. What I would have expected them to find degrading, immoral and sinful seemed to be quite acceptable, yet the relatively minor occurrence I have just described seemed to them to be the most wicked sin possible.

"We witnessed, or were involved in, so many sexually-related activities with this family that it surprises me my sister and I grew up to be normal and to enter into loving and successful marriages."

Chapter Six
From heaven to hell

Once the hierarchy in the Catholic Church woke up to the fact that many of its flock were being educated in non-Catholic schools and living far away from a Catholic church, all hell broke loose. The situation of Roman Catholic children evacuated from London was so regrettable, from the point of view of the practice of their religion, and was causing the Church so much anxiety, that Cardinal Hinsley, the Archbishop of Westminster, set up a Commission under the chairmanship of Dr John Vance to sort out the unholy rows which were beginning to surface all over the country.

Letters began winging their way between Church and State, imploring "something is done". In all, the Commission listed 31 schools - later reduced to 18 - where, especially in winter, children were in places where it would be impossible for them to attend mass on Sundays. By October 1939, a map was produced marking out, in the reception areas, where there were Catholic churches and schools. The beleaguered Minister of Health, Walter Elliot,wrote a sardonic note on the bottom of the map to his civil servants: "When you wish me to arrange for further distributions so that Methodists, Plymouth Brethren, Quakers and Freethinkers can each enjoy their particular brand of spiritual comfort you will no doubt let me know."

Dr Vance proclaimed, "It has been our guiding principle for centuries, and for generations in England, that we have built our own schools at enormous expense to safeguard our conviction and principle. We Catholics have always held that our children should be taught by Catholic teachers and gather in Catholic schools. This is no sudden wish or principle we now mention. In the name, therefore, of the Cardinal Archbishop of Westminster, in my own name and that of our Schools Commission, I ask on religious grounds that transfers may be effected forthwith. I should like to say that we are extremely grateful to the householders and billeting authorities who have done everything they possibly could for our children. Moreover we are all distressed to think that our application for transfers should be any reflection upon their goodness and kindness." Sadly, for the children who had to bear the brunt of it, the transfers caused considerable bitterness among receiving local authorities and families.

Since a large part of the cost of Catholic schools was met from Catholic funds, the ecclesiastical authorities felt it was only right that the Government should have some regard to their wishes. When the next wave of evacuations was being planned, in March 1940, the Church was consulted by the London County Council. Priests were asked to indicate which of the various receiving areas would be most acceptable from the Catholic point of view. They were asked to assume responsibility for seeing that their people reached the right assembly point to enable them to get on to the proper main line train and charged with arranging for their schools to travel on trains scheduled to arrive at those destinations.

Why no one thought, during all the years of planning the evacuation, of the difficulties that would arise if you put Catholic children into Protestant schools remains one of the many mysteries connected with the organisation of the evacuation.

Dr Vance was not above using a little blackmail to get what the Church wanted. Although the initial plan was to evacuate schools together, when the children arrived at their destinations they were often scattered over a wide rural area and it became a physical impossibility to make sure they went to a school with their old teachers and friends. Trying to reshuffle schools was one of the major headaches facing the reception authorities during the first wave of evacuations. Such movements invariably excited great local opposition, especially on the part of householders on whom children were billeted and also on the part of the children's parents.

The reshuffles were often followed by the return of a number of children to their evacuated areas. It was a vicious circle the government was desperate to break and Dr Vance offered a helping hand: if he were notified of suggested moves in advance, he could write to teachers asking them to use their influence to dissuade parents from bringing their children back to London.

In Liverpool, where 38 per cent of the schoolchildren were Catholic, the Catholic School Managers' Association held a meeting attended by practically all the parish priests. They roundly condemned the Government for not consulting them before the first attempted evacuation began and threatened not to support any more evacuation plans unless they were consulted properly.

Archbishop Downay wrote to Walter Elliot and Lord De La Marr, president of the Board of Education, "As the clergy had experience of many spiritual and moral evils resulting from the evacuation of September last, they felt that they could not be expected, in view of this experience, to support willingly any further scheme of evacuation which did not take into consideration the religious interests of the evacuated schoolchildren." The diocese also wrote a letter to the local paper accusing the authorities of behaviour that was "morally and spiritually dangerous".

The main difficulty for Liverpool children was the relatively few places with facilities for Catholic worship: the Liverpool reception area was principally Wales. Children like Tom Glavin, whose story is told in this chapter, had to be rebilleted 'as a matter of urgency' according to local priests. Catholic priests were beside themselves with worry and fear as well they might be: the war went on for six years and six years in the life, education and indoctrination of a child, is a long time. The fundamental teaching of the Jesuits - "give me a child until he is seven and he is mine for life" - was, and still is, a central belief of the Catholic Church.

Typical of many anxious clerics was Father J. Dukes of St Francis Xavier's, Liverpool. Just after Christmas 1939 he wrote to parents, "The children s religious and educational interests are in jeopardy and will be in very grave danger shortly. The authorities in Montgomeryshire are offering you a challenge which I am sure you will not delay to take up. They will not stir a finger to help your children to learn and practise their Catholic faith, save in the present most unsatisfactory way.

"Ours must be a strong line of action. We must convince them that Catholic parents regard their children s souls as of infinitely more importance than their bodies. Hence, I beg you to write at once to your children in these five villages, recalling them to Liverpool. If you cannot afford the fare, I will do all I can to help you. Many of them will weep at being separated from homes and kindly folk they have learned to love, but you will have the satisfaction of knowing that once again you have put your children's eternal interests before their temporal welfare."

Fr Dukes followed up his letter to parents by writing to a Rural District Council criticising it for refusing to appoint a Catholic priest as a helper with the evacuated children. He pointed out that two priests were helping in other areas and receiving the government grant of one guinea a week. Fr Dukes's letter went on, "Conditions are serious from both the educational and religious point of view. In most of the places named there has been, and there probably would be more, difficulty with the local teachers; at two places these difficulties had been very grave on several occasions and at two other places the children have been taught in circumstances that would not be tolerated in any Liverpool school."

At the council meeting a billeting officer shouted that the priest was arrogant, the letter was branded "ungenerous and objectionable" and the council adopted a resolution declaring that it was wrong in so many of its statements that it did not deserve any further consideration. It is probably fair to say that priests were anxious on their own account, but they were also wound up by pleas from Catholic teachers who found their conditions deplorable. They wrote telling him that with the arrival of winter it would be impossible for many of the children to go to school for days on end, impossible for the visiting priest to reach the place they were evacuated to and therefore often impossible for some, and sometimes impossible for all, to go to mass on account of floods and snowdrifts.

One letter, guaranteed to put the fear of God into a parish priest, read: "Get us all out of this village at once. It is totally unfit for human habitation. The whole village is flooded, a swirling river is rushing through it in a torrent and we cannot get out of our houses at all. The institute will be under water so it will be impossible for any of us to be there when the floods subside. We had no mass today (Sunday) as the waters are in all the houses. It is inhuman to expect any of us to remain here under these appalling conditions. Mr – has to go in his sea boots to post this.

"All the shop and lower rooms are flooded; we have all been bailing out water. They tell me the floods are of constant occurrence and the winters here are a perfect nightmare. In any case I will not allow any of our children to remain in that dreadful institute, in complete darkness, the so-called electricity has failed, and the room is full of their sodden clothes drying all day long, the stench is quite unbearable."

CHAPTER SIX

The Government was getting flak from both sides. The Rev Wilfred Monk of the Congregational Church, Castle Camps, Cambridgeshire, wrote a disgruntled letter to Florence Horbrugh, private secretary to the Minister of Health, on behalf of his parishioners who had received letters from Catholic school teachers asking them not to take their charges to churches of other denominations. "Perhaps you could help the many mothers in this parish who are striving to do their bit so willingly under difficult circumstances," Mr Monk wrote. "Our great object is to help the children to forget the war, nothing is said at any of the services to change their religion, that is avoided.

"Many families who attend my church naturally bring the evacuee children with them as they cannot leave them in their homes at night nor leave the children on the street. Surely the mothers are not expected to give up their religious practice to remain at home with the evacuee children.

"We love our country and our freedom and also respect others' freedom. I don't think it is fair that my parishioners should receive such letters, when they have cleaned the children from the pests they brought with them and are giving them the very best a country home can give of food and love."

You can hear the resentment resounding in this missive. The trouble is, it was the evacuees against whom anger at the unreasonableness of others could be vented; they were a physical presence, the Welsh churchgoers could prod, pinch, beat and generally show their irritation.

The chairman of one receiving council wrote to the minister without mincing his words. "If these children are moved and householders are asked at a later date to take other evacuees, considerable difficulties will be experienced and opposition will be met in most cases."

And Trevor Hunt of Sheringham Urban District Council, commenting on the transfer of Catholic children from St John the Evangelist School, Islington, London, to his area, said, "The children seem a nice lot and the two I have myself are very well behaved. I hope they will all settle down well but the teachers are rather tiresome and hard to please."

The Commission originally represented that they were speaking for the Catholic community as a whole, but gradually it became clear that in a number of cases they were at variance with the views of the school authorities in the localities and particularly of some of the parents. This led to cancellations of moves at a late stage with all the extra disruptions that entailed. A good deal of controversy was sectarian and sometimes there was counter-canvassing of parents not to allow their children to be re-billeted. While the Government had to play piggy-in-the-middle it was the evacuees who had to pay for the chaos.

Local authorities were irritated at having their careful plans disrupted. Householders were resentful at having their benevolence rejected. Local newspapers reflected their mood with increasingly hostile articles about the fecklessness of big city mothers, the ungratefulness of evacuee children and the general thanklessness of everybody putting themselves to so much trouble for nothing. Moving evacuees from pillar to post caused untold aggravation. It also caused misery for many helpless evacuees, such as Tom, who was moved from heaven to hell.

Tom Glavin was 11 and lived in Stanhope Street, in the Toxteth area of Liverpool, when the children at his school, St Vincent's, were evacuated to Wales. He, a brother David, nine, and three sisters, Annie, 13, Nellie, seven, and Sarah, five, were marched from school to Lime Street Station, accompanied by a brass band from their church. "The brass band often accompanied us on outings," says

Tom. "We used to be sent away for a day out at Southport every year and the band always came with us. They would play in the hall where we were given our food so it didn't feel unusual for them to be playing us off to the station. I can't remember the journey except that we were excited at seeing fields with cows and sheep in them. We'd never seen anything like that before.

"Our family was very poor. My dad worked for Walker's the brewery company, delivering beer. Almost every pub in Liverpool was a Walker's. I'm not telling stories when I say I really didn't have shoes to wear."

At first Tom and his brother were billeted at a farm called Glan-Alan in Wales with a Mr and Mrs Pearce and their two sons, Tom and Richard, and they were set to work on the farm. "We loved it," says Tom. "We had to do milking, collecting eggs and weeding. We were on our knees until it was dark weeding in between the mangles, sometimes it was bitterly cold but we didn't mind. We weren't unhappy, we enjoyed it and I don't think it did us any harm. They also had two wonderful shire horses, Star and Megan.

"The sons used to throw us on to their backs and we'd be 20 feet off the ground. I fell in love with those two horses and have loved horses all my life. I have a wall full of horse pictures and could tell you what horse won the Derby any year you name. Once I went to the races at Haydock with £5, my wife had £1.50 and I won a jackpot of £1,200 with six winners. Without the experience on the Pearce's farm I'd probably never have developed such a love of horses.

"For kids, working on a farm was more fun than going to school. The Pearces were a nice family and treated us well. They bought us clothes and took us to a Methodist church on Sundays where they had their own pew. I can remember being stared at by other people in the congregation and feeling self-conscious because we looked like posh kids. I suppose evacuees were a bit of a curiosity then as well.

It was a tiny little chapel and I remember there was wonderful singing. Well, being Welsh, there would be."

But their idyllic billet did not last. The full weight of the Catholic Church bore down on the small Welsh village in the shape of a Father O'Malley. "Because we were Catholics the Church was very concerned we were not getting a Catholic education. They were afraid we'd all grow up Methodists or anyway not Catholics, so they moved us all to another village where they set up a special school in a memorial hall. The Church was worried we'd lose track of our religion and they couldn't let that happen." Nellie was sent to a farm which translated means Little Palace. Tom and his brother were sent to a farm which could have been translated as Little Hell.

"It was run by a Miss Jones, I can't remember her first name, we were never allowed to use it, who was a sadist. She must have been about 30. Her brother was about ten years older but he was terrified of her. From the word Go she took a dislike to me. My brother was younger than me so I looked after him, and she left him alone.

"Whatever you did was wrong. One of my jobs was churning the butter and she'd stand over me with her legs apart and her hands on her hips waiting to find fault. Then it would come, she'd always ask 'What did you do that for?' and I'd answer, 'I don't know Miss' – that's the way we addressed her – 'I didn't know I was doing anything wrong.' And she would hit me with a walking stick."

Tom remembers that there was only some respite for him when their tormentor was taken out by her suitor. "Miss Jones used to knock about with the milkman, who was married, and as soon as she was through the door, her brother was transformed. He used to cut us great big slices of bread plastered with best butter – butter which we used to make on the farm but which we normally never saw – to make up for the way she treated us. He'd make us big cups of tea and say, 'Right lads, get that down you'. He was a really nice man but terrified of her. I suppose today you'd call him a wimp.

"Once, she caught me eating a potato and she really lost her temper. One of my jobs was boiling up potatoes for the pigs in a cast-iron boiler. I had to light a fire, cook the potatoes, then feed them to the pigs. They were good potatoes, there was nothing wrong with them at all, so I ate one. Miss Jones came in and caught me with my mouth full of potato, munching away. She went back to get her walking stick, raised it high above her head and whacked and whacked, over my back, my arms and my face. I can't remember now how many times she struck me.

"One night I was going to bed with my brother and she called me back. She told my brother to go on up then she got the walking stick – she used to keep it at the bottom of the stairs – and beat me so hard with it, a huge lump, like a big sausage, swelled up on my cheek. She beat me all the time with this walking stick, for trivial things. She'd often get me out of bed on some pretext to give me a beating. Nothing we ever did for her was right. She seemed to have this hatred for me. I often wondered if she got something out of it, some satisfaction.

"Next day I told our teacher, a Miss Power. She said, 'Come here,' and she gave me the cane on my hand for lying. The thing is, Miss Jones was a totally different person when anyone came to the house. When she took my brother and me to introduce us to the school she was as nice as ninepence so, of course, the teacher thought she was wonderful.

"My brother was dancing around on his feet saying, 'Miss, he is telling the truth, our Tom's telling the truth' but she took no notice of him.

"In many ways it was quite normal in those days for children to be belted. My parents were strict and they used to knock ten bells out of us but it was always done for our own good. That was different. I knew what this woman did was not right, it was way over the top. I wrote to my parents, 'Dear Dad and Mum, this woman hits me with a walking stick and I want to come home. I told the teacher and the teacher gave me the cane.'

"Dad sent a letter back to Miss Jones, and give her permission to chastise me in her own way. I was gutted. There I was, locked in a prison with this terrible person controlling me. Apparently my mother lay awake for three nights tormented about my letter and eventually couldn't stand it any longer. Although she often hit me when I was naughty, she did not think anyone else had the right to. She wondered if there was a little bit of truth in what I had said and she couldn't get the worry out of her mind so she came from Liverpool during the day, with the latest baby Margaret, and went straight to the school.

"When I saw my mother it was like a great weight was lifted off my shoulders. I knew she would not leave me in that place. When David and I saw her I rushed to her telling her all about it and David backed me up. She knew we were telling her the truth. Besides, the weal was still on my cheek so she could see the evidence. My mother addressed the teacher, 'What's this about this woman?' she said to Miss Power.

"My mother was small, 4 foot 11 inches, if that, and she gave the teacher a bit of her mind for not believing me. The teacher replied that she believed grown-ups and thought I had been lying. My mother demanded why she hadn't looked into it and, since she got no satisfactory answer to that, we trudged off to walk the one and a half miles across the fields to the farm. We had to climb over stiles and through someone else's farmyard where my little sister Nellie was billeted, but it was quicker than going by road which would have been about four or five miles.

"When we got to the farm my mother tore into Miss Jones. To tell the truth, at the time I was crying and laughing at the same time. I was relieved my mother was taking charge, glad someone was sticking up for me against this evil woman, but the sight of my tiny Mam laying into this terrifying female who had turned white with fear was also funny. My Mam ran at her as if she was going to hit her but she managed to hold herself back and she called Miss Jones a few names then demanded she pack our clothes. She was taking us back home.

"But that nasty woman tried to do us down right to the end. The Canadians sent parcels to the evacuees, lumber jackets, boots, woollen hats with ear muffs, all the sorts of things you need in a cold climate, and some of the stuff came to the school in Wales where we were. David and I were given a colourful lumber jacket each, which of course we were thrilled to have. We'd only had them a couple of days when our mother came to get us and Miss Jones tried to keep them.

"She told our mother they were not really our jackets, they belonged to the school. But my mother was not having any. 'If they belong to the school, I'll take them back myself,' she told the wicked lady. And we were off. Needless to say we never went near the school again and we kept the jackets.

"For years I used to think to myself 'If ever I'm told I'm dying of cancer, I'll go back and kill her'."

Chapter Seven
The Herod impulse

The 20th century was called - optimistically - "the century of the child". Reformers began to see that abuse of children was damaging not only to the children themselves at the time the abuse was happening but that it affected those children when they became adults, when their contribution to the social fabric of society was weakened because of their physical and mental health, and when their treatment of their own children caused even more problems to themselves and to society.

One of the first breakthroughs for children came about in 1874 when the lamentable details of the Mary Ellen case, the first of a series of children whose tragic life led to a public outcry, became known. The scandal occurred in New York where Mary Ellen was living with her adoptive parents. Neighbours were concerned that she was being ill-treated and neglected and contacted an organisation providing voluntary help to immigrants. A visit was made to the flat and she was found in a terrible state, beaten and cut with scissors. The parents refused to change their treatment of her and insisted they could do as they wished.

There were laws against the ill-treatment of animals but no similar laws to protect children, so it was decided to bring the matter before a court on the grounds that Mary Ellen was a member of the animal kingdom. The case was found proved and she was granted protection. This case resulted in the formation of the New York

Society for the Prevention of Cruelty to Children which was the inspiration for the founding in Britain of the NSPCC. Nevertheless, it was still possible in 1892 for a defence barrister in England to argue, albeit unsuccessfully, that a Mrs Montague should not be convicted of the killing of her child who had suffocated when locked in a cupboard as a punishment, because parents had absolute rights over their children.

The overriding aim of reformers during the first half of the last century was to map out a territory called "childhood" and put in place frontier posts which would prevent too early escape from what was seen as a "garden of delight". Within this garden children would be cared for and acquire the "habit of happiness".

Social change takes a long time to happen. There were more dramatic improvements at the end of the 19th century, through legislation such as the Factory and Education Acts, which protected children from punishing working conditions like sending them down mines at the age of 12 or up chimneys when they were just eight, and criminal legislation which halted the use of barbarous penalties for children which included transportation, imprisonment and death.

But by halfway through the 20th century, when we were evacuated, most children were still regarded as an underclass who should be seen and not heard, whose views were rarely canvassed by the adult world. It was not until 1989 that the United Nations Convention on the Rights of the Child came into being. This stipulated a child's right to contribute in any decision that may affect his or her life and even to have the right to bring legal proceedings against his or her own parents. If evacuees had had such rights we might have been able to use them to protect ourselves. Instead, we just had to accept what was done to us and suffer the lifelong consequences.

Three deep needs have to be met to counteract any negative

psychological effects of evacuation: the foster home must offer warmth of atmosphere, love and friendliness; secondly, play and creative opportunities must be afforded through "an active social life among their companions"; and finally, foster parents must help their temporary charges to keep alive the images of their parents and their loyalties to their own homes. These laudable sentiments were expressed at the time by Susan Isaacs, a specialist in child development, in her book *The Uprooted Child* and will be read with some cynicism by former evacuees. That these ideal conditions did not happen for many thousands of us is what this book is all about.

More in line with our experience is the view of child guidance officer Theodora Alcocks who studied 1,140 evacuee children aged from two to 16 between 1939-45. She observed that evacuation exacerbated the social disunity that normally exists in the perceived dichotomy of child and adult life:

"The fear possessed by adults of their being ultimately supplanted by the next generation, which manifests itself in hostile impulses directed towards the young and which the child guidance officer had winessed several times as anger and hatred visited upon evacuees by their foster parents.

"The Herod Impulse, normally concealed and confined by the 'natural identification' of parents with their children, is likely to be activated where identification breaks down or never existed, a phenomenon of particular importance in the care of all family-less children." Alcocks says she observed the apparent condoning by the authorities of such behaviour, for example, in dismissing a case of gross negligence in which, among other things, a billet mother refused to change a boy evacuee's soiled bed linen as a punishment for an undoubtedly fear-induced, emotionally-based problem. Rationalised cruelty was not, she claims, rare.

Alcocks's evidence is doubly interesting because few of the

evacuees I have spoken to were ever visited by a billeting officer but it was obviously known in some quarters that not all foster parents were the upholders of sweetness and light that they have been been portrayed. I can only repeat once again that the views of children were rarely sought in those days. The views of evacuees have rarely been canvassed since either.

It is curious how many of the evacuees who have written to me recall being the last child or children chosen in that cattle market that happened in the country village hall at the end of their long train journey. Rita Parker of Dagenham, Essex, (I have changed Rita's surname at her request) was eight and her brother, Laurie, five, and she remembers being the two leftovers when they were dumped for inspection at Paignton, Devon. "I don't know whether it is because people wanted just boys or just girls and no one wanted one of each but as I had been instructed not to let go of his hand, I didn't. I literally held Laurie's hand at every opportunity for the next three years," says Rita.

"Evacuation has a lot to answer for. My experience has left me so insecure I cannot accept anyone or anything at face value, I am always looking for a reason behind everything. I don't trust anyone. I was married at 17 to a man of 30, possibly looking for a father figure - my father died just after the war, in 1946, when I was 14. I desperately wanted a family, to belong. I used to press people to see how far I could go before they would leave me, I always expected people to leave me, I never expected them to want me for myself.

"I have been married three times and the breakdown in relationships has been as much my fault as theirs. I am too clinging. I have two daughters and one son all in their forties and I am always trying to do this family bonding thing. I get upset if I don't see them, I want to keep them nearby. One of my daughters now lives in the Shetlands and I phone her every day. If I won the lottery I would buy her a house close beside me, I hate her living so far away even though I have been to stay with her and they live a wonderful life up there. They don't have to lock their doors, they can leave their car unlocked when they shop at the supermarket, my grandchildren could sleep in tents in the garden without a worry. It's wonderful but it's too far.

"My brother, Laurie, committed suicide when he was 34 and I don't think the treatment he had as a child helped. I asked his daughter if she minded me talking to you about our evacuation and what happened to him and she said 'no'. He had moods and depression and he had attempted to commit suicide before but I thought he was better because we had all planned to have a caravan holiday together, staying on the same site. He spent a couple of years in the Merchant Navy, a couple of years in Australia. He married a friend of mine and had two children; he wanted a family, but he didn't know how to hold a family together. But he was a good dad, it's very sad.

"He and I were first billeted with an old couple who had two grandchildren, I think their mother was in service somewhere, because she only came to see them occasionally. We had only been there for a week when the woman we were told to call Nanny Bud, bathed us in the same water as Doreen and John, who were about the same age as us, with the result that we caught impetigo and had to attend a clinic. She knew they had impetigo yet she still made us use the same water. I had it worse on my left hand and my brother on his feet. His was so bad he was off school for a long time.

"Doreen once told me a lady had given her six shillings and we had a lovely day spending it. When we returned - I can remember we had stewed plums and custard for tea - and Nanny Bud said there was six shillings missing from her purse and accused me of taking it. She screamed at me and sent me to my room and made me stay there for a week. But she knew it wasn't me. She later tried to apologise without actually saying she was sorry. To this day I never touch plums, if I ever see them stewed this incident immediately comes into my mind. I didn't tell anyone about it at the time because there was no one to tell. Evacuees always got the blame for everything.

"When we sat the eleven plus we were told we couldn't have pens, we were given two pencils and a slate on our knee. Then the teacher came round in the examination room and I was rapped on the knuckles for not having a pen. Evacuees were the black sheep and could not do anything right.

"I am 6ft 2in tall now and was very tall for my age then, I probably looked older than I was. My father was 6ft 7in and I took after him. I had lovely long chestnut coloured hair, nearly down to my waist, and the grandfather - who we were told to call Granfie - used to stand behind me to brush it with a piece of velvet material tied over the brush.

"There was no electricity, only oil lamps and candles in the bedroom and Laurie used to sleep in a baby's cot which he hated. Every Sunday we had to sit in Granfie's bedroom cutting up some big leaves, which he said was tobacco, with scissors. When the others were called down for tea he always kept me back and would call me to his bed and ask me to hold him for a penny.

"I never did but I was frightened. He used to wear a nightshirt with a massive hole in it so everything was on display. This went on every Sunday for a long while. Then one Sunday he kept me back and asked me again. I still refused, despite his pleading and I backed away from the bed as I was so scared of him. He was a stockily built man, very broad, and he suddenly jumped from the bed and lunged at me, landing us both on the floor. He fell on top of me. The wife heard the noise and ran up the stairs and he told her I had been teasing him. I was dragged downstairs, put on a chair and a basin was put on my head and my hair was cut really short. She told my mother I was running alive with fleas so my hair had to go.

"I used to be sent to the shop next door which sold sweets and tobacco at eight o'cock every night. It was always shut and looking back, I realise it must have been a pre-arranged thing. Now I know why I was sent there, supposedly to pick up the tobacco, but that was just a pretext and the grandfather of my billet was sending me so his neighbour could do what he wanted. Otherwise, why didn't he go and get the tobacco himself? Or send me during the day when the shop was open and the two old maids who I suppose were the shopkeeper's sisters were there?

"I'd ring the bell (I was about ten by then) and there was a long, dark passage to go through to the living quarters and it was always the old man who owned the shop who opened the door. Then I was pinned up against the wall. He had more hands than an octopus and they were all over me. This went on for months.

"Then I got an interview with the evacuee people, I can't remember how that came about or why, and we were going to be sent home. The old man next door threw bars of chocolate and sweets up into my bedroom window and begged me not to name him. He must have thrown about a pound's worth of chocolate. Obviously he knew what he was doing was wrong and that he could get into trouble. I didn't tell the evacuation people because you didn't know who you could trust, so you didn't trust anyone.

"We went home and were there for about a year when the raids began to get really bad and our house was bombed out. My brother was sent to a farm in Gloucestershire where he was beaten and treated badly by the people on the farm. He was about ten then. When he came home he had to be operated on; he had three broken ribs and complications. As he is unable to tell you anything I am speaking for him.

"Next I went to Derby with a friend and we were billeted with a miner and his wife. I had an accident on a bicyle and fainted and when I came round my friend, Kathleen, was locked in the bedroom because she had objected and hit the man for things he was doing to me while I was in a faint. The woman used me as a skivvy but Kathy, who was the only girl in a family of four brothers and was never expected to do any housework at home, refused to scrub the floors etc so they wanted to move her and keep me. I was as helpful as a child could be, I was so desperate to be liked but I wanted to stay with Kathleen and we were placed in a hostel but shortly after that they put us in separate billets.

"I went to stay with a Mrs Murphy and her husband who was a doctor in a mental hospital who always walked around in a white towelling robe. Once I had a sore eye and the woman put something she called 'hoarser' iodine on my eyes and it blinded me for six weeks. One day when I was sitting by the fire, the man came down in his white terry towelling dressing gown, the wife was out, and he asked me how my eyes were. I looked up at him, they were getting better, and he grabbed my hand, bent down, pushed his tongue down my throat and pulled my hand through his towelling robe to touch him. I beat him on the head with my fists and ran out of the door and into the street. I tried to find the evacuee people but their office was closed.

"I was so frightened of him all the time I lived there, he used to catch me on the stairs. In the end I wouldn't come out of the bedroom if he was in the house, not even for meals so I became thinner than I already was. I was always hungry when I was evacuated and if ever there was jam or cake on the table I knew we must be having a visitor.

"When I started my periods Mrs Murphy hit me and told me I had been messing about with boys. She could not have been more wrong because I was an incredibly shy child and terrified of boys. Because I was so tall I stood out in class and this made me extremely nervous. This woman would not give me anything to wear when I had my periods and each month Kathleen's lady used to give me clean rags to use.

"It all came to a head one day, I don't know how or why, possibly because I wouldn't come out of my bedroom, and the man admitted what had happened. The next day I was put on a train to Paddington and I sat on a suitcase all day waiting for my aunt and uncle to collect me. I found out later they had gone to another station, there had been a mix up. I waited until six o'clock and a lady from the kiosk said they wouldn't be coming now and gave me the money and showed me which train to get home to Dagenham.

"My dad lost a forefinger so he was not accepted for the Forces, they said he would not be able to shoot a gun. Before the war he would not allow mum to work, he was very much the man of the house and the provider, but women had to work in the munitions factories and she was pleased to work and earn a wage. I begged her to bring me home but she refused and gave me £2 instead, which was a lot of money in those days. But I didn't want money, I wanted to be home. I think she liked working and didn't want us back with her. I used to hear that song, *Goodnight Children Ev'rywhere* and used to cry myself to sleep.

"She married a policeman, a widower, a year after my father died and went to live in his house because it had more bedrooms but his son and daughter walked out on the day of the wedding, then Laurie left home and I got married at 17, probably to get away. I was looking for affection. My mother never showed me any affection, she never kissed or cuddled me after I came back from being evacuated, yet I was a very helpful child, I never minded how much housework I did. She said she didn't understand me, I suppose I must have picked up new accents from Devon and Derbyshire.

CHAPTER SEVEN

"Just before the evacuation I had been in hospital with diphtheria and dad had bought me a mechanical Charlie Chaplin toy but because it was such an infectious disease, I was forced to leave it behind in the ward. So, when I went away, I insisted on not taking my doll, Belinda, with me because I was convinced it would be taken away from me, which it probably would have been. My mother once sent us a parcel of clothes, she had been a dressmaker, but we never received them.

"It is odd but I can't remember what I had for dinner yesterday yet these things stay in my mind and sometimes I get extremely upset about them. When I came home the first time I was with my mum and dad at a neighbour's and they sent their daughter and me out to buy fish and chips. She was about 15 at the time.

"As we came out of the shop, a man came over to us and asked us if we knew Purcell's, the sweet shop. He said, 'My daughter came home from being evacuated today unexpectedly and the lady took her case for her but the shop is locked, do you know another way in?' We immediately said, yes, there's a door in the back alley. So this other girl said to me, 'you take the fish home and I'll show him the way'.

"When I got home I explained what had happened and my dad shot out of the house. I remember he had no shoes on and his long legs just moved very fast; he ran for all he was worth. When Vera came back her clothes were torn and she was crying and I can only assume what happened, or nearly happened.

"What struck me, though, was being amazed at how my dad had run so fast to protect her. Where were they when I was in trouble? No one was there for me and I feel bitter about that. I am sure my father never knew what was happening to me but my mother did. She virtually told me I imagined it and that the doctor was only trying to be a dad.

"If I did anything wrong, my mother would lock me in the front room, wind up the gramophone and play a song, *You Will Never Miss Your Mother Until She's Gone* and if Laurie did something wrong, he would be locked in the room and the gramophone would play, *A Boy's Best Friend is his Mother*. I can still remember once, when I managed to put a gardening fork through my foot, she took me to hospital in the buggy and told me, 'If you don't stop crying they will cut your foot off'.

"Recently I was asked to pick up my nephew from his primary school. I'd never picked him up before and was waiting by the school gates, searching the faces in the playground. They all look alike in their little uniforms but I couldn't see him and waited and waited. Eventually I decided to go into the school and found him there sitting at a desk with his lunch box and tears in his eyes. I hadn't been told that you had to go into the classroom to collect them.

"When I looked at him I thought of Laurie and me. Laurie had been the same age as my nephew and I wasn't much older. We must have looked as forlorn as that when they sent us away."

Chapter Eight
Only a thought away

No one suspects the difficulties many older people have faced - and overcome. They look normal, they are normal, but inside many thousands of evacuees there is a sadness that only they know about. I often say to my children that it is how you cope with the difficulties, how you manage the hurdles, that marks you out. Anyone can get by and make something of themselves if they were born with a silver spoon in their mouth. If they had a happy family and childhood, if everything went well for them at school, of course they will do well. Why shouldn't they? It is those who have been cruelly treated who have had to rise above their backgrounds, who have had to find some inner strength to deal with the blows life hits them with.

For them, because the start of their lives was so difficult, life is never easy. And often it is when a crisis occurs they find old wounds opening up. Sometimes they don't even know that it is those early childhood scars that are causing the problems but they often are. The psychoanalyst Dr Alice Miller, in her book *Thou Shalt Not Be Aware*, writes: "An unacknowledged trauma is like a wound that never heals over and may start to bleed again at any time".

Anne Perrett - another victim who is using her mother's maiden name to disguise her identity - and her twin brother Tom of Gravesend, Kent, wrote down her story at the behest of her GP because she is still so troubled by what happened sixty years ago. In spite of being the totally innocent victim in this horror story, she is still embarrassed and ashamed. The fact that she could talk to me at all is testament to the emotional distance she has travelled in the last few years. Her ordeal has always preyed on her mind and eventually she sought medical help. Like so many people, she found the act of writing her story on paper cathartic.

Anne and Tom were first evacuated at the age of six to Windsor, wearing, of course, their labels. "My brother and I were the last children to be billeted because no one wanted twins," Anne says. "Eventually we went to a young family and while there we suffered from malnutrition. After three weeks our father came to visit us and we did nothing but cry. A week later Dad came back to Windsor and took us home to Gravesend. On our return to infant school Tom and I had to have free school meals with second helpings to build us up.

"We were next evacuated to a village, Whitminster, in Gloucestershire, with our older sister Jean, to live with our paternal grandparents. We were alright because Jean was 12 and was capable of looking after us. We returned to Gravesend in 1941. When we were seven we were evacuated yet again to Whitminster to live with our grandparents' next door neighbours but with no big sister this time to look after us. The neighbours had three sons. The eldest son was called Derek and he was a few years older than us. Derek had some friends and the nightmare began.

"In the field adjoining the foster parents' back garden Derek and his friends would gang up on Tom and me. First of all, they made me lie down in the field on my back with my arms and legs spread out. They then took it in turns to put pieces of twig into my private parts, forcing my twin brother to stand and watch.

"Another thing they did to us was I was made to stand up and my twin brother was made to bend over forward behind me and hold my hands with his hands. One of the boys then jumped onto my brother's back and we had to trot round the field 'horse and cart' style giving them a ride. Then we reversed roles, Tom the horse standing up and me the cart, bending forward. This went on until all the boys had had their horse and cart ride. We were often chased across the fields and pushed into cow pats – it was horrible.

"Every Sunday lunchtime the foster father would stand at the meal table and swing his leather buckle belt in front of us and ask which end we wanted first for a good thrashing – although he never actually hit us. all these things happened on a regular basis for a 'bit of fun'. Looking back, I wonder who the enemy really was, the people we were fostered with who were supposed to be looking after us, or Hitler. We returned to Gravesend in 1942.

"Next we were evacuated to Darlington, Co Durham to live with our sister-in-law's mother and brothers. Nothing much to report there, it was as happy as it could be I suppose. The end of the war came while we were evacuated in Darlington.

"There were street parties to celebrate though Tom and I were not allowed to attend because we 'did not belong up North'. Gravesend, too, had celebration street parties but we were not allowed to attend those either because we had been evacuated away, to safety. Some safety.

"Tom and I gradually settled back into Gravesend. Tom completed an apprenticeship then joined the Royal Marine Commandos for his national service. He married, had a daughter and now has two grandchildren. I never married, I could never see myself in a happy marriage. There were quite a few men friends, but I always wanted to run away as soon as they started getting too serious. I don't know why.

"I am retired now and keep busy with a one-to-one youth dependency scheme which involves being a friend to a young child who has suffered abuse, cruelty etc.

"Tom and I never had anyone to talk to during our stay in

Whitminster, we seemed to have been struck dumb - still are to a certain extent over the abuse and cruelty. We never talk about it even though it is nothing to be ashamed of. I did try talking to an uncle about the leather belt and cow pat incidents but his reply was, 'Oh, that was just a bit of fun'. I rest my case. We evacuees were 'just a bit of fun' to a lot of people who were supposed to be looking after us.

"I heard recently that Derek, the ringleader, committed suicide. I wonder why? Did he know I was trying to find him? Or perhaps it is something else, to do with his behaviour later in life. Maybe I will never know. All I know is that he violated my body while my brother was made to watch. And we were only seven. He ruined me. He prevented me from having a happy life with a man. He made me distrust men. I used to think, whenever I went out with a boy, 'Please don't touch me, please don't touch me'.

"I have waited 59 years to have my say about being an evacuee. The secret is out and I am beginning to feel better although a little tearful and angry. Fifty-nine years ago it happened but it is never more than a thought away."

Chapter Nine
The education lottery

For some evacuees education was virtually non-existent. The ones who were set to work on farms often missed school for weeks on end or were just never sent to school at all. Others had their education so disrupted it affected the rest of their lives. One headmistress reported there were children who returned from the country who were so ashamed of their lack of reading ability they had to be persuaded to come back to school at all and when they did, to help them, she taught them privately in her room. "We have to try and restore their self respect, overcome their sense of shame. They are the casualties of evacuation,' she said.

Young teachers were drafted into the services or were required to do ancillary work so the teachers who were left to teach were, in the main, older some brought back from retirement, or teachers who had children of their own who accompanied the evacuees and who were therefore excused from other war work.

Teachers' representatives made it clear at meetings about the evacuation before it began that they would not wish to have any responsibility for the actual general care of the children. They would look after their education and form a link between the children and the home but they would not be responsible for their physical wellbeing. "The woman in the home will have to be relied on, someone has to see that the child washes its face every day," a union official pointed out to the Board of Education committee.

CHAPTER NINE

It was passed off as inevitable that the education of evacuees was bound to suffer, given the fact there was a war on, yet some parts of the country managed the disruption much better than others. In London, for instance, all the schools children had been evacuated from were closed or taken over by civil defence bodies so when evacuees began to trickle back to the capital that first Christmas in 1939 they could only roam the streets.

It was an absurd situation because many of the schools and health clinics were empty but the cinemas and fun fairs, which were just as vulnerable to air attack, were crowded with children. Some schools reopened for part-time sessions, but children who were playing in the streets all day were not disposed to go to school part-time. One of their favourite amusements was to go around banging electric light bulbs with sticks to hear them pop. They were probably disappointed there had been no bombs so wanted to create their own excitement.

A school manager wrote to *The Times* about the "ridiculous" situation. "More children are congregated at a matinée at the local cinema than would at any time be assembled in the schools. If the refusal of local authorities to reopen schools is justified, other authorities ought to issue instructions making the assembly of large numbers of children in any one spot illegal." Mr F. R. Dale, president of the Incorporated Association of Headmasters, in another letter to *The Times*, commented, "Evacuated schools, as a whole, are not getting their work done. They are diminished and scattered, their school hours varying from almost full-time to almost nothing. Many of them, as regards examinations, are out of the hunt."

After eight months of war, the position of elementary schools in the evacuated areas of England and Wales was that roughly one half of the children were receiving full-time instruction, 30 per cent were on half-time, and 10 per cent were receiving less or home tuition, while another ten per cent, about 115,000 children, were not receiving any instruction whatever.

Children were often huddled like sheep in makeshift shelters, and air raid protection measures in some schools reduced education to a farce. A schools inspector, Mrs W. Loch, commented after one of her visits, "Is there any sense in this shelter business when half the bombs drop before a warning is given? Shelter rooms would be death traps. Better by far to disperse the children throughout the whole school building and let them get down on the floor or under the desk and take a chance."

In some schools teachers were instructed to cover the windows with muslin stuck on with rubber paint. Other methods of shielding children from flying glass, such as wire netting and cellulose paint, had been turned down, but one inspector pointed out that the effect of the muslin would be to render the glass opaque, reducing the lighting to the room. He added that the children's eyesight might be at risk as they were writing in shadow.

Bookcases and door panels had to be boarded up, wood and glass partitions folded back and instructions given that they were not to be used. Bricked up lobbies, cloakrooms, and shower compartments were ordered and even windows in some teaching spaces were bricked up so the rooms were practically unventilated. One head teacher was so afraid of bombs she refused to allow any paintings on the wall and not even a vase of flowers adorned her school.

It is hard to say which age groups suffered most. Each seemed to have its own share of problems. A school inspector wrote this distressing report about infants after a visit to Penge: "I had occasion to visit a social settlement where two workers from the Shaftesbury Homes were doing their best to keep occupied a group of about 40 children of school age who were out of school. I was greatly shocked by the obvious deterioration of the children during their enforced absence from school, particularly of the younger ones in whom school habits had not yet become firmly established.

"They were largely unwashed and uncared for, with tousled hair and some of the children had matted eyes; their voices were raucous and uncontrolled, and their manners were self-assertive and boisterous. It is very many years since I saw the human child in the raw as I saw him that day and the realisation of the change that has come over the slum child by the steady influences of the schools was more profoundly impressed on me than I could have believed possible.

"The deprivation of the regular routine of school attendance and of its effects on personal care and social habits will be a most serious loss to the children, especially the infants, and I feel that it is of the greatest importance that we should do all that is possible to get the infants under some sort of school influence, even though it may not be possible to give them the normal amount of formal instruction. It is quite evident that in the lower grades of society the parents slip back far too readily into slack habits and cannot be relied on to fill the gap left by the absence of schooling."

Arnold Platts, a school inspector from Devon, reported on some of the difficulties experienced by teachers at the time of the initial evacuation which inevitably had a knock-on effect on evacuees. He wrote, "The children, teachers and helpers were strained and tired and a good deal has already happened that was not according to plan. Teachers whose previous experience was with children of a certain age, infant, junior, senior, etc, were with children of other ages. Specialist teachers became maids of all work. There were jealousies about pay and criticisms of local shortcomings such as inadequate playgrounds, no staff rooms, no water and how local teachers came early and went late." This latter was, he said, anathema to London teachers. Then there were the untraceable officials who seemed to ruin all chance of any hope of a satisfactory educational arrangement.

Some children who had been in the 400 or so residential nurseries in the country, on reaching the age of five, had to leave. About 600 billets or places in hostels were required every month for this group during 1942-44. Good homes were almost impossible to find in many areas, partly because these children needed intelligent and sympathetic handling. Many had spent several years in an institutional environment; they were young for their age; they were unfamiliar with streets, shops and money and with the routine of a home.

Usually they had not been brought up to do things for themselves and they were accustomed to a life where toys were shared. This occasionally resulted in some being accused of petty theft when they entered a world with different standards. From this point they descended to hostels for difficult or problem children. By 1943 many were, in fact, transferred from one institution, the nursery, to another, the hostel, without any attempt at billeting. Others remained in the nurseries until they were six or seven years old, without any school education because of the shortage of billets and hostel places.

Sir Percy Harris, MP, told the House of Commons that he had visited schools to find out for himself about the "evacuation muddle. One headmistress told me 'Some of my pupils were evacuated to different districts six or seven times; few of these received any schooling.' She said that at the beginning of the war the Ministry of Health instructed her to call a meeting of parents to warn them that the school was to be evacuated. The parents were promised that the children would be kept together. Ten teachers and 400 pupils were sent off to East England. Once there, the children were spread over an area of 40 miles and the teachers lost track of many.

"Eighteen other schools shared the same district and there were only two village schools for the lot. The headmistress went on, 'We teachers were unwelcome. We arrived and were left standing in the market place until someone would take us in. The billets eventually found for us were all miles from the schools, all separated from each other and from the children we knew. It was impossible to round up the pupils.

"In September 1940 this particular school was brought back to London, then in the spring of 1941 it was re-evacuated to a mining village in the West of England. The same troubles happened again. The headmistress said her staff had little time for teaching, they were too busy finding out where the children were and, having found them, acting as nursemaids to them. 'If only the elementary schools had been evacuated to hostels, specially built so that each school became a self-contained boarding school, the children would still be in the country today and their education would not have suffered' she said."

Because of the pressure on places, in some schools no children under seven years old were admitted and in other areas, owing to the large number of seniors and juniors who had claims on the same building, even the seven-years-olds were excluded.

A system called the Home Group was started to provide some education for these excluded young children. Head teachers were often left to make their own arrangements which meant drawing up a list of children with reference to the roads in which they lived and then asking parents to offer rooms for teaching.

Religious organisations and scout companies offered to lend their halls; factories with unused offices gave them over to become classrooms; some children were even sent to "classrooms" in pubs. The average number of children in each home group was six or seven but some were as small as three and others as large as 12. In most cases children received some tuition, varying from one to two hours daily.

Sometimes teachers stayed in one home the whole morning and

different groups of children visited her. Other teachers visited three or four homes in a day. These details were almost entirely dependent on the wishes and domestic arrangements of the host parents in whose home the "school" was to be run. Some preferred to give up their rooms for one whole day per week, others preferred to have a group for a short time each day and one or two mothers had groups for the entire day every day. Difficulties sometimes arose when Mrs A turned up her nose when it was suggested that the somewhat grubby children of Mrs B should come to her house.

The work was almost always confined to reading, writing and numbers, the occasional stories and handwork of a "tidy" kind. It was difficult to do more than this as the periods were usually short and there was a general desire to be as little nuisance as possible to the household . This cut out all noisy activity and messy handwork. The teachers said they preferred not to use paste because it might spoil polished tables; they were afraid to paint because of the danger of splashing curtains and carpets, and paper cutting was impossible because the bits stuck to carpets etc.

Boys as well as girls knitted in those days and they all did raffia work and rug making. One father bought some cheap chairs and cut them down to the right height and cut off the legs of a table to match. Mostly the under-sevens sat on the floor holding drawing boards on their knees to support papers and books. Another father wrote all the multiplication tables on large sheets and pinned them up. Rows of pegs had to be put into the parents' hall so children could leave damp clothes. At one home, each child was asked to take a bag of coal, which was rationed, on one day of the week.

The Home Group scheme meant children only had to travel for a few minutes from home and being in small groups helped them to concentrate. They learned early to do homework and to employ themselves profitably in the absence of a teacher. One schools inspector commented that "by concentrating on the three Rs, they were sewing the seeds of self-education". I can't recall learning to read and my arithmetic never got off the ground. Possisbly the difficulties we faced as evacuees taught us how to make the most of self-education later.

Peggy Taylor, whose story is in the chapter on camps, remembers going to one of the home schools when hers closed down, although her memories of them were different from the reports I found in the Public Record Office. "There was a girl called Doris Clark who was rather posh, she came from a better street, and the teachers used to come there and give us lessons for a few hours, but no one was really interested," is how Peggy recalls her home group sessions.

Just as they are today, schools inspectors during the war were refreshingly frank about what they encountered. Here is one whose comments would no doubt raise a few eyebrows nowadays. "One is particularly struck by the clean, tidy appearance of these children who come to school for work, their happy, friendly relationship with the teachers; the quiet, businesslike way they come along into school with their books and wait for their bit of attention.

"Though aged only between seven and 11, they are purposeful, self-respecting little citizens and the contrast with the 10 to 20 per cent of grubby little barefooted rapscallions of the same neighbourhood who are joyously refraining from education is astonishing. One might hope that the prodigal 20 per cent would eventually return through sheer boredom, on the Montessori theory, but at present they are having far too jolly a time. Weather seems to make no difference to them as they climb about sundry piles of debris in the slum-clearance patches, or play with absorbed interest with refuse in the gutters."

Another inner city inspector wrote that in one neighbourhood there were no halls or rooms and he had the impression little attempt had been made to find any. "Teachers spent three quarters of their time sitting round the headmaster's fire doing little or nothing."

An astonishing side effect of the need to give young children left behind in the cities at least a modicum of education came to light which proved that in many ways they fared better, in spite of the bombs, than children who had been evacuated.

A report by Wimbledon local education authority stated that there were not more than four teachers in one building and not more than 10 children per teacher at any one time. "Within range of each building is a public air raid shelter, part of which will be labelled 'for children only' and will have an air raid warden of its own to exclude the general public in school hours."

The report goes on, "Probably the teachers have learnt more than the children and now have a much better idea of what the backward child is and what he needs. It is certain, too, that the progress made by the backward children thus attended will cause a demand among teachers and others for much smaller classes now that they have seen what can be done with small groups."

And a report from Hendon, north London, claimed, "An infants' head teacher compared the reading ability of 33 of the oldest children after three months of home tuition with that of the previous three months, using standardised tests. It was found that the rate of progress was twice and sometimes three times as much as normally achieved during this stage at normal school. Physical health was good, even though there was no physical education. This was because children spent time on roller skates, with ropes and balls, on swings or on see-saws in the parks."

An article in the *Liverpool Daily Post* on May 15, 1940, reiterated this amazing by-product of the awkward arrangements for children's education in inner cities: "Children are definitely ahead of their standard in the three Rs than pre-war days. They have been subjected to more concentrated individual tuition and supervision during the restricted hours of teaching and parents have come, for the first time, to be interested in education and to realise its importance in character building as well as its mere vocational value."

This was reiterated in a report from Sheffield where they said the success of the Home Group teaching scheme had exceeded all expectations, particularly in the building up of parent-teacher contacts, with mothers keen to assist teachers in every possible way.

"The barrier which has sometimes existed between home and school is now completely broken down as a result of the emergency," the report reads. "Teachers have been working with enthusiasm and ingenuity. For instance, an upturned billiard table has been used as an improvised blackboard."

It was noted that infants missed the corporate life of school, assemblies and so on, but that the scheme had done a great deal to keep up the morale of children and prevent the physical, mental and moral deterioration that was evident where children had to run the streets for long periods without any supervision.

"The children, particularly the boys, had improved in manners, social habits and consideration for the property of other people. For example, they are more careful now to wipe their feet on the mat when going into houses," was the observation of one schools inspector.

In the Norris Green area of Liverpool, regarded as a "neutral" zone which did not need to be evacuated, the closure of schools had resulted in children soon "getting out of control and the results of ten years of social work were rapidly being undone".

However, once the Home Group scheme was launched, 93 per cent of them were getting some education and "of equal importance has been the resumption of social training. When they were out of school the children were not infrequently unkempt and difficult to manage. Now they are clean and neatly dressed, more amenable and better mannered. That they have to visit someone else's house is an important factor in this training."

In July 1944, local education authorities were advised to keep education going and not to take legal proceedings against parents who kept their children at home for fear of the school being hit. In Kent and East Sussex bombs were liable to be shot down over small villages where there was no public siren so a modified arrangement was necessary: each school would appoint a local spotter who would warn them as soon as a flying bomb was heard and the children would immediately be taken to the shelter. Of course, in many local schools air raid shelters did not even exist.

Just as it is today, 60 years ago the money for educational needs was a political football with three teams kicking it from one to the other: the Ministry of Education, the Ministry of Health and the Treasury.

In April 1939, five months before the first evacuation, Thomas Walling, director of education in Newcastle, wrote to the Minister of Education: "In reviewing the details of the children's kit, the schools' evacuation sub-committee realised, as all our head teachers have already realised, that many children would have the greatest difficulty in providing themselves with the articles of clothing and footwear which would be required if they were to be evacuated. This lack would materially affect the success or otherwise of the evacuation scheme.

"The committee were especially perturbed when they remembered that the education committees of England and Wales had in conference repeatedly requested that they should be given statutory powers to provide necessitous children with footwear and clothing in addition to free meals but that their repeated representations had met with no success. The sub-committee were astonished that the

Scottish education authorities had now for several years been empowered to provide footwear and clothing as well as free meals for necessitous children and that these authorities were in receipt of financial assistance from the national exchequer in respect of this expenditure.

"The scheme for the evacuation of school children makes this question all the more insistent. Is it not absurd that an English education authority like Newcastle should have no statutory power to provide necessitous children to be evacuated with the necessary clothing and footwear when the Edinburgh education authority will be able to do so for Edinburgh children?"

This is typical of the toing and froing between local education authorities and the ministry in London about payments and it was exercising the minds of a considerable number of civil servants. With the detached approach of their breed, one wrote a departmental paper explaining the dilemma: "Of the essential items, the warm coat or mackintosh and boots appear indispensable. It is arguable that children lacking a serviceable pair of boots or shoes and a reasonably waterproof coat or mackintosh could not be evacuated into the country in wet weather without a grave risk of incurring illness, that any such illness might involve the payment of a doctor's bill and that this would probably fall on the State as the presumption is that it could not be recovered from a parent unable to provide a child with boots or a coat; that if the illness resulted in death, questions of compensation might conceivably be raised; and that a serviceable coat would be the equivalent of an additional blanket.

Any refusal to consider proposals to meet the cost of such items in circumstances so serious as to call for evacuation might very well lead to a renewal of the agitation which has been carried on by educational associations for some years to adjust English to Scottish practice. Although such an agitation might be resisted, the ventilation of the problem could hardly fail to reduce the efforts which evacuating authorities might be making to ensure that all children were adequately equipped either by their parents or through voluntary resources.

"I have no doubt the right line to take is to approach the Treasury with a view to obtaining their consent to the authorisation of a limited expenditure as a proper evacuation charge confined to boots, clothing and bags to carry gas masks and equipment to be incurred only if and when the first evacuation warning is sent out.

"I think we would be placing ourselves in an untenable position by accepting as proper evacuating charges items such as the provision of lavatory accommodation at the detraining stations, options on the purchase of a supply of consumable school materials, the supply of blankets and camp beds and the meeting of medical expenses for children whose parents could not pay while endeavouring to sustain an objection to the provision of boots and coats for children so poor as to be unable to obtain them."

There was a study of four thousand children, some of whom had been in hospital for periods during their early life, and its detrimental effect on their education in adolescence, which probably applies equally to hundreds and thousands of evacuees. The study showed that those who had been in hospital before the age of five years, either for longer than a week or on two or more occasions, were found to differ from other children in the following four ways:

more likely to have been rated by teachers as troublesome at ages thirteen and fifteen years

more likely, in the case of boys, to have been cautioned by police or sentenced between the ages of eight and 17 years

more likely to have scored low on a reading test

more likely, in the case of school-leavers, to have changed jobs four or more times between the ages of 15 and 18 years.

According to the study, the tendencies to delinquency and an unstable employment record are significantly increased for children who experienced a further period in hospital between the ages of five and 15. Dr John Bowlby in his book, *Attachment and Loss*, concluded, "these findings tend to support the belief that the effects of separations from mother during the early years are cumulative and that the safest dose is therefore a zero dose."

Recently I came across work by an American psychiatrist, Lawson G. Lowery which throws more light onto the question of why children are disruptive which also struck a cord with me. Referring to two different studies he directed when his team spent two years working in kindergartens, he writes: "We were in the rooms observing, testing, examining, during every day for two years. We made extensive and intensive studies of one hundred children and followed them for two years. The teachers invariably said the aggressive, impudent, demanding youngsters were 'spoiled', had obviously always had everything they wanted and were given their own way at home.

"What we learned in studying the family life of these children was that, without exception, these were rejected children; either obviously and patently rejected, or suffering from a less overt rejection, often masked as over-solicitude. There were among the one hundred some who really were the family pets, loved, respected, indulged. In the classroom, again without exception, these children were poised, secure, well-behaved and regarded by the teachers as their dependable leaders. May I leave you to draw your own conclusions?"

I think it is no coincidence that establishments such as the Open University, and courses for mature students have been taken up in their hundreds of thousands by older men and women who are still trying to catch up on the education they missed during the war.

Many, many of the evacuees I spoke to had their educational

opportunities seriously blighted by the evacuation. Joan Ashley of Woking, Surrey, actually lost her place at grammar school because she arrived back from the war too late: her place had been given to someone else. "We thought you weren't coming back so we filled your place," they told her.

Joan says, "My aunt, whose son was at the grammar school, wanted to fight the decision but we were not as well off as she was and my mother said No. She didn't want to fight the authorities but she was also concerned about the uniform she would have to buy and that played a big part in her decision not to try and get me in there. I was heartbroken but I was also sensible enough to realise there was not much my mum could do about it. I did lose out and have regretted all my life not having an education but it is too late now. I love talking to people who have been educated, I feel as if I am picking their brains.

"When I left school I just did dressmaking which was hard. I can remember having to get the underground from Hendon to Goodge Street and I was so small I couldn't reach the straps so when the train was full I used to get swung about.

"My husband, Geoff, and I did a school count recently and we worked out I went to 12 different schools altogether, six months here and six months there. I can hardly remember the school work I did at any of them except once when I went to a convent where the nuns were writing on the board and the children were using pen and ink which I had never used before. I had only printed - and with a pencil - so I could not read what they were doing."

Joan was 10 and her brother, Charlie, five when they were sent to be evacuated with a Mrs Hartley outside Lancaster, who had three children of her own. Her husband was away in the Forces and, according to Joan, she was incapable of looking after her own three children, never mind two more. Joan remembers her foster mother always having a cigarette dangling from the corner of her mouth, the ash showering everything.

"We never had proper meals, we were always hungry," says Joan. "I think she used to feed her own children on the quiet. Sometimes she would cut the fat off the bacon for us and give the meat part to her kids. I can remember buying a cabbage for a penny because we were so hungry and we ate it raw and unwashed. Charlie's abiding memory, he says, is stealing potatoes from under the sink and eating them, also raw and unwashed, under the blankets in bed.

"One of her sons wet the bed but she never changed the sheets or put the mattress out to air. When mum sent us coupons for sweets and a postal order for 2s 6d we always had to share them with her children but I don't remember her ever giving us anything like that.

"Once Charlie and I were nearly machine gunned down by a German. He was attacking a goods train and we happened to be walking along a dirt track by the railway line. He must have seen us through the gaps in the hedges on our right and opened fire. I was used to being bombed, coming from the Elephant and Castle in south east London. We used to go into a deep shelter in Borough High Street with so many stairs to descend and then climb back up after the air raid was over. We had a bunk which was ours and we carried with us our bundles and bedding. I am a good walker now because I've had a lot of practice climbing those stairs. There was a particular smell down in the shelter, I have never smelled it before or since, it was awful.

"Dad was in the Air Force and mum worked in a munitions factory and I was told, 'Look after Charlie' when we went to be evacuated. I tried my best but they would do things like not let me collect him from school, I can't remember why not, but I can still feel how upset I was about it.

"Charlie suffered from asthma and once they wanted to send him to the infirmary. I thought it was somewhere you went to die so I wouldn't let him go. I must have been adamant because I won in the end, and he didn't go. I said 'I'll look after him' and I used to spend nights with him staying awake to make sure he was breathing properly.

"When it was time to return home my mother could not afford the train fare to come and collect us and Mrs Hartley put us on the train with just a little bottle of orange between us, diluted with water, for a journey that lasted eight hours.

"Other passengers on the train felt sorry for us, and one woman gave us an apple. She could see we didn't look well-cared for and was upset about what had happened to us, how we had been treated. When the train arrived in London these passengers stayed with us and told our mum what we had told them. 'I have been listening to your children and what happened to them and I think it would have been better for them to have stayed with you than where they have been' she said to my mum.

"When we got home my mum put a plate of baked beans and bread and butter in front of me and I said, 'Is this all for me?' I couldn't believe it, I had not been fed so much for so long and from that day on, 'Is this all for me?' became a family joke.

"To be taken from your parents is a wrench. I was soft before then but it probably made me harder. It also made Charlie and me very close, I felt he was mine, not my brother. When he had a stroke a few years ago I was devastated. He was in a coma for days but then he said to me clearly and plainly, 'I love you'. It broke my heart at the time because the doctors had told me there was no hope. But they were wrong – he survived."

Chapter Ten
Unwanted guests

Some children who were sent from the inner cities to be evacuated were from poor homes. Their clothes were tattered and torn but they were what their parents had provided for them. Imagine their feelings then, when they arrived at a strange place and the people they were to stay with were so shocked they stripped them naked and burned all their belongings?

Psychologist Margaret Lavenfold offers an explanation of what would be going through their minds in *Child Psychotherapy, War and the Normal Child*: "Children who are billeted on householders who are either above or below the social and educational status of their parents will be conscious of the difference. If urged to adapt themselves to a higher level of cleanliness, speech, manners, social behaviour or moral ideals, they will resent these demands as criticism directed against their own parents and may oppose them as such.

"There are children who will refuse new clothes and hang on to torn and dirty things which they have brought from home. With young children this may be just an expression of love and a desire to cling to memories; with older children it is simultaneously an expression of their refusal to be unfaithful to the standard of their homes. Their reaction might, of course, also be of the opposite account: the quickness with which they drop their own standards may be an expression of the hostility against their own parents.

"When, on the other hand, children are billeted on families who are poorer than their own, they easily interpret the fact as punishment for former ungratefulness at home."

To understand why evacuees were so reviled by some of their hosts you have to appreciate the amount of hostility there was to the children who came from a different culture. Feelings were often whipped up by jingoistic local newspapers which dwelt on, and exaggerated, any case of head lice, of bad behaviour and manners. Disgust at some of the children's unkempt appearance when they first arrived in the village hall, plus irritation at having to be inconvenienced by them at all, fuelled many an outraged heart.

It is true, as I have repeatedly acknowledged, that many evacuees found happy billets, but it is equally true that many did not. We just have never heard much from the latter group before. We have been given this spin of a country pulling together, a cornucopia of wonderful characteristics that make us feel proud to be British but it might be better for our long term psyche if we acknowledge the truth for a change. Many people, given an opportunity, are extremely nasty and cruel. Don't take the word of abused evacuees. A survey completed recently into bullying in the workplace came to the conclusion that Britain is the bullying capital of Europe.

Many schools were evacuated en masse, and managed to stay together which, for those children who were ill-treated, was some consolation: they still had their familiar friends and teachers and their education was not totally disrupted. It seems strange to us today to hear that evacuees rarely told their teachers what was going on and those who did so were not believed.

Eileen Wickenden attended Portsmouth Southern Grammar School for Girls which was evacuated to Salisbury. It had been her ambition to get to the local grammar school and she was thrilled to win a place. But she soon discovered there was a none-too-subtle form of blackmail attached to grammar school places which reinforced

Eileen's feelings of powerlessness. She was billeted with a couple in their forties who had two teenage sons and who also had the wife's father, in his seventies, living with them.

"My parents wrote to me during the war and they used to send me pocket money but they never came to see me. It was impressed upon you that if you didn't stay in your billet there would not be another one available locally and you would lose your place at the grammar school. I knew, anyway, that if I tried to get away from this one I would be evacuated somewhere else which might be even worse. You knew that from each other, you learned there were a lot of us in the same boat so you just kept quiet.

"Staff used to visit to see if everything was alright but I expect they made an appointment. You didn't tell the teachers what was happening because teachers, particularly at grammar school, appeared so superior, they were not the sort of people you felt you could confide in."

Once, the school of one of Eileen's grandchildren put on a school play called *Evacuees*. "One of the school teachers stood up in front of the audience and asked, 'I expect there are some grandparents who remember what happened. Are there any of you here tonight?' My grandson said, 'Nan, put your hand up' but I was sitting there in tears, that play brought it all back...

"I went first to an emergency billet which was wonderful. It was just a little two-up-two-down terrace house but it had two peach and two nectarine trees in the garden and it was September and there was masses of fruit to eat. Also, the woman's husband was a baker and he made the most beautiful bread. But after a month I had to go to another billet.

"This time I went to a Mrs Horder who insisted I call her 'Aunty' but I could never bring myself to say it. Although I was well fed, she made it quite obvious she thought evacuees had to supplement their keep by being a servant to the household. My bedroom was a little box room over the kitchen with rolls of carpet in the corner. It was used for storage. I was allowed no hot water for washing, even in the winter. There was often a thin layer of ice on top of the water jug which I had to break through before I could get washed in the morning. The family all washed in warm water. She refused to do any washing for me so my mother had to supply my bed linen which I had to send home to be washed, together with all the rest of my laundry.

"My duties before going to school each morning included emptying all their washing water from the wash basins in their bedrooms, also their chamber pots. After laying the breakfast table, then washing the dishes after, I had to make all the beds. They all had feather beds and I had to shake their eiderdowns and dust and mop the bedrooms. The toilet was in the yard and I was not even allowed to sit on the toilet without working. In a corner was a pile of newspapers which I had to cut up with a little pair of scissors while I sat there.

"On returning from school my duties started again, helping with the tea, then washing up. Once this was finished I was allowed to do my homework, which was often difficult to complete as bedtime was 7.30pm - not a minute later. I always did finish my homework because I was a timid girl and very frightened of her. Saturdays were spent polishing the floors and furniture in the four-bedroomed house which was all lino with slip mats, which had to be taken into the garden, hung over the washing line and beaten. She considered herself a Christian; she read the Bible and listened to church services on the radio.

"Apart from going to school the only time I was allowed out was from 3-5pm on Saturday afternoon to enable me to cash my postal order from home and post my dirty clothes back home. I had a staunch friend called Pat who was my prop. We were at infants school together then went on to the grammar school together. One good thing that came out of those war years is the many people you made friends with and that friendship stayed with you for life. When it was Pat's golden wedding anniversary I insisted we had our photograph taken because we didn't have a photograph of us, even after all those years.

"Pat knew about my awful life and she used to meet me at the Post Office every Saturday afternoon and we spent two hours together. It was wonderful. Sometimes we wandered around the market and bought a cake to eat by the river. Other times we went to the pictures but often I could not see the end of the film because I had to be back to make their tea.

"One day there was a function on at my school and all the evacuees' hosts were invited. I remember walking in front with a friend called Hazel whose host mother was walking with mine and I overheard them talking. Hazel's foster mother said 'What a rush to get away. By the time I got the dinner on and the washing up done'. 'What do you mean, you washed up? That's Hazel's job. The money we get doesn't pay for their keep, they have to earn their keep, that is what they are here for'."

These evacuees went home for the school holidays and when that happened the host family was paid a retainer for the room, but Mrs Horder considered that was not enough to keep Eileen's room so her mother had to make up the difference. She was mean in other ways too. When, on the grapevine, she heard a shop had oranges for sale which you could only buy with a child's ration book, she would send Eileen to buy them, but the schoolgirl had to pay for them out of her own pocket money - and then share the fruit with the rest of the family. Eileen also had to pay for her school lunches so Mrs Horder only had to provide two main meals a week for her evacuee - and still she grumbled that she was such a burden.

"We used three different buildings for our lessons and when we were told we were going home for good we were instructed to make our way to the main building, the art room, which we used as our assembly hall. I can still remember that feeling of intense excitement at the thought of going home. A big cheer went up from the whole school when it was announced officially and we were all excited.

"When I told Mrs Horder she went bananas. 'How ungrateful can you be? I have looked after you all these years and you say you are excited to be going home'. She went crazy. We lived opposite a car park and I had to walk through that to the station on my own with all my things. The day I left I said 'Goodbye and walked across this car park with my suitcase knowing she was standing at the door but I thought to myself 'I'm not turning round, I'm not going to wave'. I never wanted to see her or the house again and I walked straight on until I was well out of sight and I thought to myself, 'I will never go back'."

Eileen married and had two daughters and four grandchildren. She always appeared to be coping well with life but it was mostly a front. She was in turmoil inside. Like other evacuees who went through hell during the Second World War, Eileen comments wryly on the people today who demand counselling for minor things.

In Portsmouth she had been reading about the wives of naval officers sent to Yugoslavia during the Kosovo war who said they needed counselling. Not for the first time in my conversations with evacuees we wished the younger generation had some idea of what we went through then maybe they would not feel so sorry for themselves.

"Being treated so badly completely destroys your confidence although people don't realise it. They used to say 'Eileen has all the confidence in the world' but little did they know how I felt inside.

Your insides can be gnawing away but you build a shell around yourself which comes over as self-confidence but you know how frightened you really are.

"I did go back to Salisbury after I retired just out of curiosity. It was strange because until then I could not even face going near the place. Now I have laid the ghost and it doesn't bother me one little bit.

"There must be many children who suffered far worse but I shall never forget those dark days. I doubt whether anyone who has not experienced evacuation can really understand how these childen could suffer mentally for the rest of their lives. I was first evacuated at the age of eight, finally returning home when I was 14 years old.

"My two sisters were eight and ten years older than me and both married during the war. Please don't think I am unkind for saying this but although I don't blame my parents for wanting me safe from the bombing, I never felt part of the family again."

Eileen's friend Pat suffered from strokes and heart attacks and she was nursed by her husband, Dennis, for 18 years before she died in 1994. Eileen's husband Charles also died of a heart attack after Eileen had neen nursing him for, coincidentally, the same length of time, 18 years. He died in 1997.

Now she and Dennis are together. "We are doing all the things we could not do when we were nursing our partners. We don't begrudge what we did for them but we are making up for those lost years and having holidays galore. I was cheated of my childhood and I am not going to be cheated of my retirement. I am living life to the full."

Chapter Eleven
Why me?

Children who were sexually abused by strangers can never understand what it is about their looks, their character or their personality which made them a target. The obvious fact that they were, unfortunately, simply in the wrong place at the wrong time is a fact their minds seem unable to comprehend, even when they reach adulthood. It is a sad legacy of child abuse that children grow up believing they must in some way have asked for it, either by signals, body language, what they said, or the way they behaved. There has to be something, their mind reasons, that made their abusers choose them.

Roy Draper has never married because of what happened to him when he was evacuated to Pear Tree Cottage in the village of Lopen, near Crewkerne, Somerset at the age of nine. In 1941 he and his sister Joyce were packed onto a train at Waterloo with thousands of other south London children. They were excited and forgot for a while they were going away from home.

They were taken on coaches from Chard station to the village hall where people walked around them choosing those they liked the look of. "They split up brothers and sisters, I don't know why," Roy says. "My sister went to stay with a school teacher and I went to a widow whose son was in the army."

Now 67, Roy, who lives at Trowbridge, Wiltshire, is retired. He was the old fashioned kind of farmer who had ancient hedges, wild flowers and skylarks on his land. His was a smallholding with 40 red and white Ayrshires but, like many small dairy farmers, in the end he could not make it pay. "Ayrshires don't give much milk," he explains. Roy has had a happy enough life, the farm keeping him busy, too busy, mostly, to dwell on what happened to him all those years ago.

"If I'd stayed a townie like I was when I was born and until I was sent away to be evacuated, I don't think I could have coped. What happened would have been preying on my mind all the time. But because I've had my own small farm and been busy, I haven't had much time to think about it except when I've been particularly lonely and wished I could have married someone."

What happened to Roy at Pear Tree Cottage where his mother and father had sent him, hoping to protect him from the ravages of German bombs, was that he was sexually abused by the widow's soldier son. When the soldier came home from leave he slept in the same bed as Roy and abused him while the boy was fast asleep.

"Except for me and the man who did it, you are the first person to know the truth, and I'm relieved to get it off my chest. Today people go to prison for doing those sort of things. And they are called the good old days. They weren't for some of us. I didn't know at the time what was happening to me, I'd wake up and he stopped. I just couldn't understand why it was so uncomfortable when I went to the toilet. It wasn't until I was older that I realised that what he had been doing was regularly sexually abusing me. I didn't tell my sister or my parents, I was too frightened. You just didn't talk about things like that. Some years ago I went back to the village – I don't really know why – to try to find the cottage to see if it was solid or whether it was all a bad dream. I don't know if it is still there but I couldn't find it."

Not all Roy's memories of his evacuation are of this nightmare. He also has, thankfully, some happy memories, particularly of the farm where he used to spend all his spare time, helping in any way he could. His favourite job was leading out the two dark brown shire horses and grooming them. "One was called Prince and I loved looking after them. It was that enjoyment that led me, after the war, to take a farming course and I worked on a farm for ten years before I got my own smallholding."

His older sister, Joyce, hated being evacuated and one day they decided to run away. Like most of the evacuees before her who had tried to escape that way, they were picked up and sent "home" again. But the authorities were obliged to tell their parents and Joyce made her views known in no uncertain manner. She hated it and wanted to go home and went with her. So, although she was never aware of it, through her determination to get back to their mother and father, Joyce saved her younger brother from the misery he was too young to understand or fight against.

"People wonder why I never married, I am not shy, although I was shy when I was younger. What happened upset me psychologically. I never had a girl friend, something in the back of my mind held me back. I used to go out with other boys in a gang but I always held back. I used to ask myself about that terrible time with the soldier, why me? It makes me bitter to think of it but presumably he has lived his life in a normal way but mine has been ruined by him."

Fred Johnson of Cleethorpes, North Lincs, was evacuated from Hull to Crowle, Lincolnshire, in 1940 at the age of seven. He has been haunted all his life by the dreadful, unanswerable question, why me?

Fred says, "My story may sound far-fetched but every word is true. I was physically, mentally and sexually abused by the teenage daughter and her friend and physically abused by her father at the farm we went to. My first few weeks were spent at the local vicarage where I was well treated. After this short spell I was moved to this farm and there were also six other children there. We were treated as cheap labour, having to work on the farm feeding pigs, threshing, gathering, sugar beet, potatoes, etc. The only good thing about this is we were well fed.

"The 15-year-old daughter had a friend who had a cottage on the farm in which we used to play. After a while we were made to strip off while the two girls used to play with our private parts. We were all terrified to tell their parents as I believe the oldest of us all was aged about nine.

"The parents were not aware what was going on. For some unknown reason the daughter seemed to dislike me more than the others and I was terrified of her. I was told that I
was not allowed to go to the toilet even when I was at school, resulting in me wetting my trousers.

"I was so terrified of her that I dare not wee at night resulting in me wetting the bed. My punishment for this was the farmer taking a two-inch belt to me. I tried to tell him what was going on but who would believe a seven-year-old boy? This went on for approximately eight months after which I was sent home. Even then I couldn't bring myself to tell my parents as I was still under the impression she would get me.

"In later life I didn't really blame the farmer as I realised he wouldn't have known what his daughter had done to me. I would like you to know that I have never told anyone else about this as I felt so ashamed, although I now know it wasn't my fault. About 15 years ago I went back to the farm but I was informed that the family had all passed away, even the daughter who I would like to have seen and asked her why she had done this to me.

"In conclusion I would like to say I am now 65 and have been happily married for 45 years, having five children of my own and 16 grandchildren. It is a relief to get this off my chest after all these

Chapter Twelve
Stinking kids from the slums

The first evacuation of children happened at the end of the summer holidays when the routine inspection of schools and of cleansing centre activities had not been undertaken for some weeks. As a result, about 10 per cent of children evacuated were infested with vermin - mostly nits and scabies - on arrival in the reception areas. Where the billeting authority and the education authority happened to be identical, immediate steps were taken to deal with the problem and no further trouble erupted.

In many reception areas, however, owing to a shortage of staff and facilities, there was little or no medical inspection of the evacuees on arrival and no medical or nursing follow-up visits with the result that slight cases very quickly became severe and uncontaminated children became infected. In those areas a great outcry ensued, fanned by prejudice and resentment.

So, instead of the sympathy they ought to have received which would, in most cases, have led to an improvement in their condition, the children were harshly criticised. They were labelled "undesirable", never mind that they had been suddenly wrenched from their homes and families and were therefore subjected to all the mental strain that brought in its wake.

Their reception was not helped, either, by some parents who sent their children off subtracting all the month's supply of soap coupons from the ration books which one billeting officer described as "a particularly mean action which has occasioned great indignation".

It has been said that the British Government of the time was influenced in its thinking on evacuation by events in the Spanish Civil War. After the destruction of Guernica in 1937, 11,000 children were evacuated from the Bilbao area to France and Belgium. If this is true then it is a pity the British Government did not also take a leaf out of the Spaniards' book and emulate some of their good medical practices. The height and weight of the each Spanish child was recorded; each child was checked for infectious diseases; they all had vaccinations and they were lodged in reception centres for a month to enable them to adjust to their new life before they were dispersed. And, according to Dorothy Legarreta in her book *The Guernica Generation: Basque Refugee Children of the Spanish Civil War*, the private families they were sent to were "screened for good moral and health backgrounds". If only.

A particular anecdote from Legarreta's book which struck a chord proves that prejudice is an international commodity. The daughter of a well-known bank official, who lived in a beautiful house and was considered the most beautiful girl in Guernica, was smuggled to France with her mother and sister where they were greeted with cries of "scum of Spain". They were eventually found a temporary adoptive home in Belgium.

London's permanent medical and nursing personnel had been posted to emergency hospitals but when the condition of the evacuees in some reception areas had been allowed to get out of hand, permission was obtained from the Ministry of Health to make urgent appeals to former staff to return and help. With the re-establishment of the general system of overseeing their general hygeine, the conditions which had been so grievously complained of soon disappeared.

That it had not occurred to anyone to worry about the physical health of the children underlines the lack of careful thought that had been given to their general welfare. Considering how long various committees had been meeting to discuss the evacuation, it seems lamentable that more thought was not given to this aspect. The Establishment's almost manic desire for secrecy stemmed from a belief that the proletariat, given the truth, would panic or would react in some other reprehensible way which would make them uncontrollable. From day one evacuees were victimised as "verminous, stinking kids from the slums". They were accused of being liars, petty thieves, rude and quarrelsome, with no respect for people or property. No doubt some of these criticisms rightly applied to a few children but all evacuees were tarred with the same brush.

Evacuees were also, apparently, ungrateful. Many householders in the receiving areas reported tantrums when they burned the "rags" their evacuee had arrived in and issued them with smart new clothes. But in *Child Psychotherapy, War and the Normal Child*, Margaret Lowenfeld explains the complicated feelings of children in such situations: "Children who are billeted on households who are either above or below the social and economic status of their parents will be conscious of the difference. If urged to adapt themselves to a higher level of cleanliness, speech, manners, social behaviour or moral ideals, they will resent these demands as criticism directed against their own parents and may oppose them as such.

"There are children who will refuse new clothes and hang on to torn and dirty things whch they have brought from home. With young children this may be just an expression of love and a desire to cling to memories; with older children it is simultaneously an expression of their refusal to be unfaithful to the standard of their homes. Their reaction may, of course, also be of the opposite kind: the quickness with which they drop their own standards may be an expression of the hostility against their own parents. When, on the other hand, children are billeted on families who are poorer than their own, they easily interpret the fact as punishment for former ungratefulness at home."

It was not until January 1941, 18 months after the first evacuation, that a report on the conditions in reception areas by a committee under the chairmanship of Geoffrey Shakespeare, MP, concluded, "The provision of adequate welfare facilities is the essence of good reception". By this time, of course, the Government was concerned about the number of children and families returning to the cities and it was emphasised to local authorities that to discourage any flight back to the towns they should provide adequate health and welfare services, including milk, school meals and dental treatment for those who had made their own evacuation arrangements as well as those families and children evacuated under the government scheme.

Since not enough consideration was given to their physical welfare, it is hardly surprising that the effect of the evacuation on children's mental state was also ignored. Imagine you are a child: you have been travelling all day, at first in excited anticipation but increasingly with anxiety. It is dark, you have been sitting cross-legged on the wooden floor of a strange hall for what seems like hours while people walk up and down pointing to your classmates. You are not allowed to go with your brother or sister nor any of your friends. You are taken to a strange house where a woman barks at you to go to bed. There is no mother, no familiar face, no one to hug or kiss you goodnight. You climb into a strange bed in a dark room where you are not allowed a light because of the black-out. You shiver and whimper and eventually go to sleep.

This scenario was played out by hundreds of thousands of children. Many of them did what is absolutely inevitable for a child to do in those circumstances: they wet the bed.

Enuresis - bed wetting - is, according to the medical dictionary, an expression of mental protest, primarily a symptom of emotional disturbance, except in a few rare cases when it may be the result of lesions or congenital abnormality of the urinary tract. It was the cause of a great deal of distress, both for the evacuees whose unhappiness manifested itself in this way, and for the foster parents who had the thankless daily task of washing sheets and mattresses. Although many evacuees were treated kindly by householders who managed to get over their natural distaste and irritation without making too much fuss, for some evacuees it gave their foster parents a ready excuse to hurl abuse and mete out humiliating punishments.

The fact that neither the Government nor the medical profession prepared the families in evacuated areas or the families who were to receive their children about the possibility of wholesale bed wetting displays a lamentable lack of foresight. They had no excuse since, as long ago as 1934, a study was made for the London County Council on the incidence of enuretics in various schools and homes and it was found that the percentage of enuretics was significant: 26 per cent for the under fives, 13.3 per cent for the five to 11-year-olds and 6.6 per cent among 11 to 15-year-olds. On top of that, a government committee, appointed to inquire into the provision for children deprived of a normal home life, found that enuresis was one of the most frequent complaints in voluntary and public assistance homes.

The most telling evidence which came out of that inquiry was provided by the matron of a local authority home who said that when children were ill they did not wet their beds and she thought this was because they were getting the extra attention they needed. If only that had been taken on board by the Government and an effort made to educate the host families to understand the problem, untold misery could have been avoided.

The same committee came to the conclusion that in many council care homes the trouble was made worse by bad treatment and a system of punishments. In a number of charitable homes, for instance, the enuretic children were distinguished from the rest in their sleeping arrangements and in one such home they had a red light by their beds.

Even basic necessities such as rubber sheets did not arrive in time. In May, 1939, five months before the evacuation was due to start, rubber overlays were ordered for sixty per cent of children under the age of five who were to be evacuated. Only a small number had actually been delivered by the time the evacuation began in September and no provision at all was made for older children. *The Lancet* wrote chirpily, "Somewhat unexpectedly, enuresis has proved to be one of the major menaces to the comfortable disposition of evacuated urban children every morning every window is filled with bedding, hung out to air in the sunshine. The scene is cheerful, but the householders are depressed."

The country was shocked, even outraged. Bed-wetting was misunderstood because it had not been discussed and its occurrence was exaggerated. According to Professor C. Burt, writing in the *British Journal of Educational Psychology* in 1940, the loss of stability and protection led evacuees to revert, temporarily, to irresponsible babyhood. He believed the emotional effect of evacuation on children had been under-estimated. He can say that again.

In the first week or two of September 1939 evacuee children had an acute sense of insecurity and foster parents ought not to have been so hard on them. Even "normal" grown ups can sometimes suffer from the same unpleasant complaint. According to a report in *The Lancet* of August, 1944, among a proportion of the soldiers evacuated from Dunkirk in 1940 enuresis was noted as a response to feelings of stress and insecurity.

By 1940 the Government was beginning to learn from the earlier mistakes and rubber sheets, or mackintosh sheets as they were called then, were supplied, free of charge; extra payments of 5s a week to householders for an enuretic child were introduced; and special hostels were established for persistent bed-wetters to be sent to. Needless to say, the householders who received an extra payment for a bed-wetting evacuee, those so-called "guardian angels", soon began to abuse the system.

Once the news that one householder was earning extra money became known in a district, others decided to jump on the bandwagon. Although a doctor's certificate had to be obtained as evidence that the child was suffering from enuresis, the sum of about £350 for the year was paid out to the villagers of one Welsh rural district by the local council, in spite of a considerable reduction in the number of children billeted there.

Rubber sheets wear out fairly quickly and became difficult to replace. By 1942 the price had rocketed from 1s 9d each wholesale to 6s 6d each. Yet if a child's bed-wetting was not handled well and as a result he or she returned home, that would be contrary to the government scheme. It is regrettable more sympathetic medical attention was not shown to this unfortunate condition in the first place, then money would have been saved and many evacuees might have been spared some of the shame and agony they were subsequently subjected to.

Scabies was another distressing malady rife among some children at the time. It is an intensely itchy disease of the skin caused by a mite which is about a sixtieth of an inch in length and lives in the outer horny layer of the human skin, sucking blood. When the mites get into the skin they deposit their eggs, forming a characteristic burrow that looks like a pencil mark. It affects adults as well as children and is spread by direct contact with infected individuals, sometimes by sharing clothing or bedding. As a result of the irritation children would scratch and this damaged the skin allowing it to be invaded by other organisms, causing a secondary infection to occur.

Scabies is cured when all the invading parasites are killed. Some unfortunate children grew up illiterate as they had scabies at five years old and were not cured by the time they were fourteen, according to Dr Kenneth Mellanby in his book *Human Guinea Pigs* in which he describes experiments - by infecting conscientious objectors with the mites - to discover how to cure scabies.

Warmth from the body makes the itching worse and people have been known to tear their pyjamas to shreds. They also used brushes to scratch skin which, although presumably horrendously painful, did have the advantage that it took away the offending creatures.

Scabies became common during the Second World War and many dermatologists at the time were worried it might never be controlled. Because it had not been around for twenty years, doctors and nurses had not been taught how to deal with it at medical school, so a film was made to be shown at health centres around the country to demonstrate what it looked like, how the condition developed and what should be done about it. At the end of 1941 it was estimated that between one and two million people must be infected with scabies throughout Britain.

According to a report in Studies in the Social Services by S. M. Ferguson and H. Fitzgerald, the Minister of Health declared at the time, "I am satisfied that scabies is so prevalent as to prejudice the efficient prosecution of the war." An order under the defence regulations enabled local authorities to get to the real root of the trouble, ie treat the whole family and not just the individual. Previously it was almost impossible for a doctor to insist on treating the family if they were not willing when only one member appeared to have scabies.

Treatment was with a disgustingly smelly concoction which was painted on to every bit of the patient's skin, except for the head.

Sometimes an equally obnoxious sulphur ointment was used.

A great number of evacuees suffered from scabies and although the received wisdom at the time, not in official circles but among householders and writers of scurrilous newspaper articles, was that they brought it with them from the inner cities, the truth is they were just as likely to catch it while they were evacuated. It is simply another of those myths that was abroad – that every pestilence in the land was attributed to the evacuees.

Ken Riley, of Sandy Lane, Salford, Lancashire, ends the tale of his evacuation with a funny story about scabies, although I don't suppose suffering from it at the time was all that amusing.

"In 1939 I was evacuated to a large farm in Littledale a few miles from Lancaster," he says. "They were Methodists and were the meanest people I have ever met. They made us wear clogs which eventually ruined our feet causing hammer toes. My elder brother, George's feet are even worse than mine. On the farm were three daughters: Nancy the eldest, Sally and Betty. There were also three sons, Harry, the eldest, he had a farm of his own nearer to Brookhouse, then there was Bill, a big raw-boned lad about 22; he was OK, but the villain was Edward, a pure, sadistic bastard. The head of the family was their father who we called Uncle Ted; he was about 60. His wife was dead and he was the gaffer.

"There were three evacuees on the farm, David Phillipson, from Withington, myself and my brother, George. We all stood together, cried together and ran off together. Sometimes even now I wake up with tears still streaming down my face and wonder why, after all these years, the pent-up unhappiness should come out again. Sometimes I feel violent anger which cannot be released against these religious hypocrites who caused it all.

"Every day for four years we walked three and a half miles to school. Our lunch was brawn sandwiches which I hated. I threw the brawn away every day. We also had two potatoes each which we roasted in their jackets at school. Everyone carved their initials on their own spuds as some were bigger than others. The best about school was we met other evacuees from our home town, Salford. One lad, Cliff Neild, used to take us to this large house up the road where his mother was a cook and she gave us plates of rice pudding and other things and seemed to sense that we needed it and felt sorry for us.

"In the summertime we had to work in the fields haymaking and we rode on the haycarts to the barn where our job was to tread the hay down. This is where Ted, the youngest son, always tried to get one of us on our own. He used to pretend to be wrestling with you while all the time he was rubbing his hardened penis against us through his pants. None of us complained to anyone, we were scared to. He never tried anything else because we all stuck together. I hate to think what he would have done if there had been an evacuee on his own.

"Sometimes, we used to climb a hill called Pott Yeats Hill and, by looking up at the clear blue sky, talking about home and day-dreaming, we could see Blackpool Tower. It seemed that on that hill all our unhappiness would disappear like magic. On Sundays we walked to the Methodist chapel in the village. Most of the family either rode down on bikes or in the car they had – we were never allowed in the car. On Sunday afternoons all the neighbouring farmers gathered at the farm to pray and sing hymns with a local parson leading them. In my opinion, they were all hypocrites. After the show there was a big spread put on with homemade cakes. The parson sat at the head of the table like a God. Every morsel you ate was begrudged and you were scared to wolf any. Religion was their forte and they made us pray every night, kneeling by the bed. They really believed they were angels of mercy.

"We all had our different chores. At ten years old I was snaring rabbits and trapping rats and I saw hundreds of rabbits in the market at Lancaster every week and I was told I would get money for them but received not a penny. What you must visualise was this farm was of a massive size and the land was worth millions. They had hundreds of sheep and cows and hundreds of hens - we often collected their eggs in buckets. I can honestly say, of all the eggs I collected, we never had any for breakfast or for our lunch during all those years when we went to school.

"We accepted all this, what else could we do? Because we were so hungry and because I resented the mean way they treated us, I used to steal money out of Ted's bedroom, which I spent on meat pies at the village shop near the school.

"In the winter it was hard. We used to go into the woods for kindling wood for the fire and with the farm being way up on the hills, it was cold. They had to dig the sheep out of the snow drifts. If it had not been for the fact my mother was in a mental hospital and my father was working in a steel works, I would have run away but I knew there was no one at home to look after us. My mother lost a child in 1939 and suffered from post-natal depression as it is now called. In those days women were classed as nutters and she was in hospital for years.

"Myself and my brother George did run away once. We were sent to the woods for kindling and we walked nearly 20 miles to Lancaster and planned to get a train home. We had an old sack over our shoulders to keep us warm but not one penny in our pockets. They came looking for us in their car, I think with the police, and that was the only time we ever had a ride in their car.

"I remember my Dad and Aunt Annie coming up to see us and having to walk the three and a half miles from Brookhouse to Littledale and the three and a half miles back to get the bus home because they were too mean to give them a lift in their car.

"I went back to that farm in 1964 – in a car – with my cousin, who was mad on fishing. By then they were all married and I only saw the eldest daughter, Nancy and Sally, her sister. They wanted us to stay for the Sunday service. What a farce. When I got home I went out and got drunk.

"Some of the farmers' sons used to go on to the Fells to act as Home Guards in case of any German paras dropping. They might only do one night a week, as they were exempt from being called up. I remember as clear as day being sat in the farmhouse in 1942 when this young man came in with an army greatcoat on asking for the youngest son, Ted. The two of them used to do Guard duty together, but Ted was ill with flu and unfit to go. Ted knew the moors inside out and they didn't want the young man to go, fearing he would get lost but he was determined to do his duty and carried on. He never came back.

"A massive search party was organised but he could not be found. I read in a newspaper that Ted found his skeleton in 1946 behind a grouse hide where the shooting party used to wait for the grouse after the beaters had disturbed them for the shooting party. I think the young man who died was only 19 years old.

"After the war was over and we went home we all had scabies, which were rife, and we gave them to my dad who was cursing and swearing as he was scratching. We were all lined up at the public baths in Salford and stripped naked and this little man came along with a bucket of white stuff and a six-inch brush and began to paint us all, paying more attention to our private parts. When he reached my dad he was fascinated by the size and spent more time painting him than any of the others. Eventually, my dad hit him, shouting, 'You're not painting the lobby now'."

Another medical horror for evacuees was head lice. The

proportion of infested children at that time ranged from 22 per cent to 50 per cent. Besides being sent away when they had not been under eye of the school medical service for some weeks, on the journey itself, the louse had many opportunities to pass from child to child and if a child's head is left uncombed for some nights, infestation can rapidly become serious.

One or two lousy individuals will quickly infest others so they spread rapidly through a community. It was particularly galling for medical officers of health in the receiving areas as well as the families who had volunteered to take children in since Walter Elliot, the Minister of Health had issued reassuring statements earlier about the condition of the children. He boasted to the House of Commons, "these are not scrofulous and verminous children...they are the bud of the nation".

The excuse of the medical officers of health at the evacuating end where it was confidantly expected Hitler would be raining bombs, was that to search for lice and nits while bombs were falling would have been impossible. Dr Kenneth Mellanby, appointed to investigate the problem of head lice found it was high, especially in poor homes. The percentage of girls aged 14-18 with lousy heads rose by eight per cent in the early years of the war.

He admitted, however, it was difficult to know the real incidence of head lice before the war because reports then simply said heads were "unclean". There was a reluctance on the part of local authorities wanting to paint themselves in a good light to call a spade a spade. Consequently their figures drew a self-satisfied, self-deluding and optimistic picture.

In those days comprehensive national statistics were not so easy to come by. No one knew, for instance, how many houses had no bath, piped water or indoor lavatories. Or how many shared a loo although there are reports of anything up to 30 people to one lavatory in some places. In York about 66 per cent of homes were without a bath and in Stepney 90 per cent. A survey in 1944 showed 14 per cent of middle-class homes and 50 per cent of the poorer classes had no indoor sanitation. Approx 54 per cent of the poorest group could only obtain hot water for washing clothes by using kettles and pans on stoves.

The deterioration in the standard and output of social facts partly explains why it was that many people were ignorant of the conditions of life for a large number of town dwellers. It was these conditions, the insanitary homes, the lack of baths and lavatories, the crowded rooms and the congested streets which, along with poverty, helped to generate the dirt, fashion the behaviour and dull the mind of a people long inured to drudgery and disease.

These mothers were children during the First World War and many went out to work as children, lost fathers or their fathers were disabled. The chief medical officer of the Board of Education, as early as 1916, in drawing attention to the premature employment of a very large number of young children, asked an important question which resonates with implications for the mothers who sent their own children away to be evacuated during the Second World War: "Physical injuries in childhood are often insidious and inconspicuous. They do not catch the eye, or arrest the observer but they may undermine the growth of the child at a critical point in its life. What will be the condition of these children in five, ten or twenty years?"

Incidentally, there was no shilly-shallying about head lice in Wigtown, Scotland, where they took mothers and children from Glasgow: their hair condition was regarded as so bad the medical officer sent messengers out to buy hair clippers. With the aid of many helpers, all the heads were shorn. The thing was done without formality and without permission.

When evacuees started returning to their homes in great numbers, a few months after the first attempt at evacuation, the schools had closed down so the school dental service was not available and eye defects were uncorrected. Many children who needed glasses went without. Speech defect classes were suspended, the special schools for handicapped children were disastrously affected; no tonsil adenoid and rheumatic conditions were seen to and there was a sharp fall in the consumption of milk at schools: a fall of over one third in England and Wales and by nearly half in Scotland.

Joan Waite, whose story is told in a later chapter, remembers returning home with nits, scabies and malnutrition. "My sister and I were taken to have hot sulphur baths," she says. "I can remember my mum crying as she took us to be attended to. We were lucky in that mum carried on the work at home as we had a bathroom then (you put a penny in the geyser for hot water) and she spent hours under the table 'shelter' combing our hair and removing the nits. We were eventually spotless and had shining hair to be proud of but the smell of sulphur comes back to me when I remember those times."

Margaret Flack of Netherton, near Liverpool, did not have a bad time as an evacuee but her sister and husband did. Her sister's story is in the Dear Mum chapter and here Margaret recounts what happened to her husband, who contracted ringworm at his first billet.

"My husband is from Liverpool and he was evacuated to Wales where he didn't do very well. The first couple who took him in chose him because he looked the biggest and strongest. They were old and had a small farm with no hot water, electricity etc. He was made to get up at dawn, milk cows and so on, and do all the chores until he went to school. When he got home he worked again until it was dark.

"They worked all the daylight hours, this was a normal way of life. They never changed their clothes unless they fell to pieces. One day in school a girl complained of an awful smell and the teacher took each child out one at a time to examine them. The smell was my husband who had ringworm which was covered in a dirty rag with goose grease on it. His leg was ulcerated and sceptic.

"The teacher was kind and arranged for him to be moved to a well-off couple which he thought at first was marvellous. He was told he had to do the washing up after the evening meal. He had to run the hot water, swish a bar of soap in the water to get up a lather and dry each piece at once so there were no smears on any of the crockery or utensils. If the woman found one smear he would have to do them all over again.

"Some nights this would happen over and over again with him standing on a stool because the sink was too high for him to reach from the floor. Usually he would be crying his eyes out. I think this was worse than the first couple because they were well-educated. The elderly couple were uneducated and I don't think they thought they were being cruel. He ran away and eventually his parents took him home."

Although many children did go to country villages and towns from inner city slums, many others were from perfectly decent homes and actually encountered much worse conditions than they knew at home. It is a pity the opinion of professionals on the ground, such as Dr Allen Daley, medical officer of health for the London County Council, was not listened to - and acted upon, then there would have been no need for evacuation at all.

He is quoted in daily newspapers as saying, "It is the unanimous opinion of doctors who have been working daily among the children that they stand up to the air raids as well as, or better than, the adults. The greatest fortitude is shown by children under 14, possibly due to their ignorance of the real dangers. Then there is the natural resilience of youth, the tough constitution of London's children, good food and good shelters." He declared it was the major medical discovery of the year. It was 1941 and we could have been saved four more years of torture.

Chapter Thirteen
A life sentence

A lot of people say evacuees should put the past behind them, that it is no use dwelling on what happened all those years ago. And, of course, most of us did just that. We got on with our lives happily and successfully but the terrible experiences we had when we were evacuated cannot be wiped out. They are part of our character and have affected the way we think about ourselves and therefore the way we have reacted to other people and circumstances.

I have found that most evacuees who suffer from major nervous disorders such as agoraphobia have had other traumas in their lives to deal with, abusive relationships with men being the most common. They all think the cause of their agoraphobia has its roots in what happened to them all those years ago. Child abuse has lifelong effects. It is impossible, and abusive, to say to them they should put all that behind them. If they are still having to cope with the result of the cruelty they suffered, the fact that they buried it for years does not make their complaints now any less urgent.

Agoraphobia is a particularly difficult condition because it can strike victims out of the blue when, for no apparent reason, they begin to tremble like a leaf at the prospect of having to make a short journey. The word "agoraphobia" is derived from two Greek words - phobos meaning "fear" and agora meaning "a place of assembly or market-place". It is estimated that eight to ten people in every thousand of the population suffer from it.

CHAPTER THIRTEEN

Common symptoms include palpitations or difficulty in breathing which make sufferers believe they are having a heart attack. Another is the feeling that your legs have turned to jelly. A choking feeling, sweating, headaches and a churning stomach are other indications that an agoraphobic attack is on its way.

All these classic symptoms have been experienced by Barbara Birchall of Brixton, south London. But before we get on to her agoraphobia, read the story of her evacuation, where, she feels, it all began.

"I was evacuated with my sister Shirley to Reading with a couple who had one child, a daughter, who was older than us by about five years. I was three years old and my sister, who had infantile paralysis, was four years old. We went in 1940 until the war was over, five years later. We suffered awful mental and physical abuse. We were locked in our bedroom for hours if we spoke out of turn and sometimes she locked us up in the dark in the coal cupboard under the stairs all night if we just asked for a piece of bread. The woman, a Mrs Eves, knew I didn't like spiders so she used to lock me in the outside toilet or the shed at the bottom of the garden where there were lots of the creepy creatures.

"We were always hungry, always fed the leftovers, especially the food their daughter left. They used to say, 'Give the scraps to the orphans'. We were so hungry that on our way home from school – I used to push Shirley because she wore leg irons and was in a wheelchair – we would stop where they scraped the leftover food for the pigs into dustbins and we helped ourselves to the slops because we knew we would get hardly any food at our foster home. We used to have to go with them in the early mornings to pick mushrooms. My sister wasn't able to pick any as she wasn't well.

"They didn't think that was a good enough excuse not to do any picking so she was made to stand and watch us while we ate our breakfast. I used to slip some food into my apron pocket and give it to her when we got upstairs.

"When the billeting officer used to come round, Mrs Eves used to lay on a big feast and cuddle us just in front of him to make them believe we were happy, but inside we were screaming for help. I had a problem with food as an adult because when I finally got on my own and there was no one to tell me not to eat I went mad. I was eighteen stone at one stage but now I am back to eleven so I am a bit more in control of that.

"We used to get smacked on the bare behind with a hair brush which was made of wood. My sister used to scream when she was hit and then I would too. But we couldn't help each other. Our mother wrote to us but we never got any of her letters. There was a cherry tree in the garden and I used to hang onto my sister's legs while she hung out of the window to pick the cherries. We hid the stones up the chimney wrapped in newspaper but one year when the chimney sweep came they were found and Mrs Eves gave us a beating for that.

"I ran out of the house to the church and shouted at the vicar, 'Help, help my sister, she's being beaten' but he didn't believe me. Anyway, Mrs Eves had followed me and she told him it was a lot of lies and that we had done something terrible. I had the feeling that no one would ever believe me.

"The woman, she's dead now, never gave us anything to drink. I can remember once we crept down the stairs to the kitchen and climbed up on a chair to the sink where there was a dripping tap with a bowel underneath it. We pulled our hair back and drank from the bowl but she caught us and we got a tremendous beating for that. We even drank water out of a flower vase because we were so thirsty.

"Today I suffer from agraphobia and bad nerves. I am now 61 and my sister is 62 and she suffers with nerves also. It was the most dreadful start to our young lives and I wouldn't wish it on anybody."

CHAPTER THIRTEEN

Barbara has received counselling to deal with her agoraphobia and it is better than it was, although she is still in many ways a prisoner of her past.

Obviously it is impossible for me to analyse everything about the evacuees in this book and since I am not a trained therapist I would not have the temerity to attempt it. But some of the strange things I have been told do make you want to dig deeper. For instance, one of the inexplicable things about Barbara's illness, one she certainly cannot explain, is that sometimes, when she is feeling really low, she will take a doll into her own understairs cupboard and she stays there cuddling it. "It brings tears to my eyes but for some reason it also comforts me," she says.

Barbara's marriage and every other relationship she has had with men was violent. Now she lives alone although her seven children and fourteen grandchildren live close enough to visit her all the time so she is not lonely.

"I brought my children up by myself, we lived in homeless hostels some of the time and it was a struggle but I love them and am proud of them. There was no way I was going to let them be put in a home where they would get beaten. None of my children has taken drugs or been in trouble. We are a loving family and they look after me. One of my daughters lives opposite and I sometimes phone her in the middle of the night because I have terrible nightmares. I wake up thinking I am having a heart attack or worrying about someone dying.

"My own mother died of a heart attack when she was only 54 so I used to think the palpitations and sweating I got were signs of a heart attack. It was almost a relief when it was diagnosed as agoraphobia. When the children had all left home I had time to think about me. I didn't know who I was, I didn't know what sort of personality I had. The men in my life had always put me down, I'd had a terrible childhood and here I was, unable to go out of my own home. It was terrible and for a long time I didn't know I had a phobia. But now I help myself a lot. I am getting more confident all the time. Sometimes I look in the mirror and tell myself I am a worthwhile person, I am not being controlled by anyone and I have to get on with things."

Agoraphobia is a debilitating condition with a close link between it and depression. According to specialists, agoraphobic patients stand a higher risk of developing depressive illnesses than do other people but it affects people in different ways. It is incredible how some people manage to live a happy life in spite of the affliction while others are imprisoned by it. Listening to some evacuees, you can't help admiring how strong they are in spite of what they have been through. Undoubtedly it made some of them tougher, although it is a high price to pay.

Irene Mapletoft of Nottingham is an evacuee who has had agoraphobia for most of her adult life although it did not debilitate her as much as it has Barbara. She at least is able to travel, so long as she is with someone. Irene has three daughters and seven grandchildren and she wrote this letter about her evacuation experience:

"My elder brother, Ronald, younger sister, Christine, and I, along with quite a few other evacuees from Portsmouth, were sent to Winterslow, a little village just outside Salisbury. I was seven at the time. We suffered the usual humiliation of being eyed over like cattle. One lady only wanted boys so my brother was picked and off he went. As I remember, no one wanted two girls so we were left until last. A very tiny woman was asked if she would take us and she reluctantly agreed.

"My memories of her were that she was always in a bad mood. That first night at her house she showed us to the bedroom, told us to get to bed and threatened that there would be trouble if either of us was a bed-wetter. There was no welcoming cup of tea or sandwich. We were really miserable and I wet the bed that night. She slapped me around the next morning. I should mention that she was tiny and I was tall for my age so we were the same height.

"We only ever had margarine sandwiches for every meal. She had a son of about three years old and he always got proper food. She verbally and physically abused us all the time. I continued to wet the bed and we were terrified of her. I presume her husband was away at war because there was no man around.

"One day her son came running into the house screaming because he had poked a berry up his nose. She beat me with a wooden and copper stick – as if it was my fault – before rushing off to the local doctor with him. He ended up having to have the object removed at the hospital in Salisbury.

"She hated us with a vengeance and we suffered at her hands. Eventually we were moved to another house in the same village. I don't know if she got rid of us or if her treatment of us came out, but we were glad. We nicknamed her The Midget – but only after we'd got away. I was emotionally scarred by the whole thing and suffered for years afterwards.

"From my teens until my fifties I suffered from agoraphobia which, looking back, I blame on my years as an evacuee. I used to get palpitations and thought it was a heart attack coming on but as it happened so often and I was still here I realised that it probably was not my heart, that it must be my nerves.

"I could only ever go out if I was with someone else, never on my own. Luckily I always had my sister or a friend so that it did not curtail my life too much. I never went back to the place where I was evacuated although my brother did, but then he had a good time and got on well with the family he was evacuated with.

"But we are survivors and I survived. I married a wonderful man, now deceased, who was my crutch and helped me in more ways than he ever knew. I know there are thousands of adults who suffered far worse at the hands of their so-called 'guardian angels' than we did. After the war we settled down again as a family but it took a long time. Now my brother lives in New Zealand and I have been to see him, although as I said, I had to have someone with me before I could travel that far.

"I am pleased evacuees are at last talking abaout the abuse and hardship they went through, it might help the sufferers by knowing that they weren't alone. The emotional scars, although faded with time, are still there. Can you imagine it today? Thousands of vulnerable children sent off into the unknown to be randomly chosen by any Tom, Dick or Harry who could be a child molester, pervert or paedophile? The social services would have a field day."

Chapter Fourteen
A vicious circle

In their report on evacuated children in nurseries during the war, psychoanalysts Anna Freud and Dorothy Burlington noted: "We deal with a minority of mothers who are not affectionate, intelligent, hard working, ready to make every possible sacrifice for their child. They are lazy and negligent, hard and embittered and unable to give affection. There are others who are over-strict in their demands and make the life and upbringing of the child extremely difficult. It is a known fact that children will cling even to mothers who are continually cross and sometimes cruel to them. Attachment of a small child to its mother seems to a large degree independent of her personal qualities and certainly of her ability."

Sylvia Jump thinks she had one of these mothers. And her grandmother was also one of them. After an article about this book appeared in the *Liverpool Post*, Sylvia wrote: "I agree wholeheartedly with your remark that physical pain does ease but other degradations are there for life. Let me say how delighted I am that someone has the courage to speak out on behalf of evacuees, some like myself who have bottled these experiences deep within themselves. Since retiring I attend college, as a mature student, and amongst other courses, did one on Women's History where, for the first time in nearly 60 years, and with the help of an understanding tutor, was able to speak of my horrendous experiences."

Sheila. from Aigburth, Liverpool, was eight, her sister Joyce, nine, and her younger sister Eileen five when they were evacuated. They went on a train with their mother to their grandmother's small village in north Wales. Mother left with no explanation whatsoever. I can't even remember her saying goodbye. I feel the long-term effects of evacuation should be highlighted, it's always been swept under the carpet; I still get upset about it. I would have said our torture lasted 99 years but apparently it was only nine months, which I still find hard to believe.

"I remember feeling so lost, mother not there, not even saying 'I am going home'. Grandmother could not look after us, she was too old, so we were sent to a house in the village where they had two daughters, older than us. The first thing I can remember is we were isolated in a little room at the side of the house with a lot of old furniture stored in it – and we weren't allowed to eat with them.

"The foster mother, Mrs Williams, I couldn't tell you her first name, was very, very clean. It makes me wonder if she was trying to wash something away. Her husband was blind and he used to abuse us. I think he had been in the Navy because he used to show us his scars from an explosion. He wore dark glasses most of the time but sometimes he took them off and you could see the damage to his eyes. He would come into the bedroom, and we were too frightened to do anything about it.

"I always felt so dirty. I used to think it was my fault. It happened right after you were sent to bed out of the way. He used to say, 'I will see them into bed'. I have no idea if his wife suspected anything, but when I think about it now, it is so unusual for a man to want to put children to bed, you would think she must have. When I see the NSPCC adverts on television about child cruelty, they make me creep, they remind me so much of him. He used to say, 'Come and do my nails, I can't see to do them'. While we filed his nails he used to abuse us. I remember being like a zombie, I would not feel happy and I would not feel sad. I learned how to clamp down my feelings and I am still inclined to do that. We were too terrified to tell anybody. Even now I feel physically sick thinking about it.

"I didn't see him abusing my older sister but she said everything except rape took place. When I told her I was contributing to this book she said, 'I don't know how you could'. She is very bitter, she blames our mother for leaving us there. She reckons mother could at least have come to see us but I make excuses that travel was so difficult then. We didn't tell anybody because there was no one to tell, no one would have believed us. No one listened to children in those days.

"I used often to think how I would love to have met that foster mother now I am an adult and tell her I feel she ruined our lives but now I don't know if I could be so cruel. Because I didn't show any emotion, I didn't retaliate and she disliked me intensely. Her husband obviously didn't work and they were hard up so she was trying to make money by taking in evacuees but she didn't spend it on us - we were starved. We were so ravenous we would pick things up off the road to eat, anything, even a crust. It didn't matter if it was dirty, we were so hungry. It's amazing we are alive today, the germs we must have eaten then. I suppose it must have built up my immune system. If we found a sweet that was a field day. My younger sister had a little friend at school who gave her a corner off her sandwich and she would share that with me so we had a few crumbs each.

"Eileen was put to bed on the floor in their bedroom at 6.30pm and the wife would go up and see if she was asleep. She was thrashed, I think with her hand, every night because she wasn't asleep. The woman didn't thrash us much, well, she hit me occasionally and she hit Eileen most nights, but hers was more mental cruelty. She'd say things like 'You will never see your mother again'. I was nervous, the most nervous out of the three of us, and I started wetting the bed. I can understand her now, it must have been awful to cope with. She used to call me a 'dirty little devil' and add 'you are going into a home'.

"One morning she announced I was not going to school and I immediately had a feeling of fear in my stomach. I was taken into Prestatyn to what looked like a big red house which I realise now was probably an office. I was terrified of her and her husband, they were whispering about me but I didn t know why I had been brought there or what I was supposed to have done that was naughty. I probably thought it was the home they were talking about and it was because I'd wet the bed.

"A man came out of an office with a bunch of keys. He unlocked a door and went into a room where there was a long table. We had to follow him and he sat on the edge of the table, one leg on floor, and he threatened me, 'You will never see your mother again, you will be sent to a home where you will be whipped black and blue until you are a good girl'. I still could not for the life of me work out what I had done wrong. I could pick that man out of a crowd today.

"Evacuation spoils relationships between sisters because you become jealous of each other. Sitting in this little room with its drop-leaf table we'd see her put the plates in front of us with such tiny amounts on them, each of you would look at her sisters' plates and think 'their potatoes are bigger than mine'.

"She had our hair hacked off to an inch on top of our head and she told me she was writing to our mother for new shoes, but I don't know if the money ever came because I remember having to go to school in summer with wellingtons on.

"Evacuees were very frowned on and if you were a Scouse you were doubly scorned. Everything, according to them, had to be nailed down otherwise it would go. There was a terrible stigma then to being an evacuee from Liverpool.

"I don't know how it happened but Mrs Williams got rid of us and we went back to grandmother's; she must have been in her seventies by then and had two other evacuees. I never wet the bed again and grandmother didn't care if we never got washed from one weekend to the next. The older children reared the younger ones. My mother never got any affection from her which is probably why she was able to leave us like she did.

"Grandmother was a hard woman: she had a long, thin cane and always made sure she whipped the top of your bare legs where it would hurt most. They used to come up in welts that bled. We were made to play outside in hail, rain or snow; we wandered round the village in all weathers. We got dirty heads which gave us another anxiety. I used to pray, 'please God, don t let the nit nurse come today', because then you would be pointed out in class and the other kids would run away from you.

"When we were teenagers we used to go back to see grandmother and we often remarked on how we must have looked back then, three little things wandering about in the rain. The Williams family was not there. We heard the eldest girl married an American soldier and someone said they had all emigrated.

"Grandma's house was up a mountain from where you could see the sea and the road. A bus used to come every hour and I'd look out of the window and watch buses come and go with no sign of mother. We were the last evacuees to go home and I think my mother only collected us in the end out of embarrassment. She was working in a munitions factory and no doubt had admirers so was too busy to worry about us. I can't remember feeling elated on going home. When we arrived mother and father were not getting on and there were rows.

"When I was a teenager I was always frightened of men, I thought they were only after one thing. I don't like anyone to touch me, if I don't show it physically I am feeling it mentally. If anyone talks to me and touches my arm I flinch and if anyone is talking to me from the back and they come close I really don't like it.

"I don't trust men at all. I would never leave my daughter alone with a man, even her father and he is the simplest soul. He didn't know any of this until last year. He didn't say a lot, just 'How awful'. I hadn't wanted him to know because I thought 'He is going to think I am dirty'.

"When I wrote the essay for my college course I could feel the anger going down my arm into my hand and I was pressing harder and harder with the pen until I made holes in the paper. I could feel all my anger and tension going out through my fingers into the words on the page. The tutor was amazed at what had happened to me and was pleased I was able to write about it. I don't know when I started to change, not to feel so inferior to other people, perhaps when I went back to college and got a starred A for my English Literature GCSE. I had taken the language exam the year before.

"My elder sister Joyce went very introverted, she hurt before she was hurt. I told her it would do her good to get it down on paper but she won't hear of it. She is married with four children but I think she has difficult relationships with them. She is still ashamed of what happened to us.

"I have suffered from depression all my life, or at least since those days. I was unhappy all the time. I went to work but always felt so inferior. I acted like a doormat so I was treated like a doormat. At work I never thought I was good enough for promotion, always at the back of my mind were worries like, are they going to blame me for something, anything. Even if nothing was going wrong I expected it to. I've led a life of anxiety. It's ridiculous, I did get promotion eventually and that gave me confidence. I started thinking, 'I'm not as bad as I think'.

"I got more confidence with marriage and these last few years are the happiest I have ever had. Because I have learned to assert myself, I get respect.

"My daughter is 41 now and she only found out last year about what happened to me but she didn't really want to read about it. I had bad post-natal depression after she was born: I didn't think I was good enough to be a mother. I would not leave her until she was 11 and she started at the grammar school, then I went back to work full-time. I found it difficult to show her love, I never cuddled her yet I was very protective of her.

"We three sisters never got any love from our mother and I found myself behaving the same way to my daughter. I have a guilt complex about that. My daughter is just the opposite with my granddaughter. She is marvellous with her: I like to see it, they hug one another. The little one is 13 and she says to me 'give us a cuddle' and I can do it with her, I don't know why. My daughter has managed to break the vicious circle."

Chapter Fifteen
Murder in her heart

Revenge is sweet, forgiveness even sweeter if you can bring yourself to cross the Rubicon. Few evacuees have had the chance to exact any revenge although some harbour a burning desire to do so. The majority just wish they had had the opportunity to confront the people who were supposed to have been "caring" for them so they could give them a piece of their mind. For most it is too late, although not for Peggy whose threat of getting her revenge one day is here.

There is a fascinating story about harbouring a desire for revenge in Graham Greene's autobiography. He carried this boyhood bitterness around with him until he was an adult and may even have obtained a double revenge if his antagonist lived long enough to read the book in which he is featured because they met, years later, when Greene was much more successful than his former enemy.

There was a boy called Carter at Greene's school "who perfected a system of mental torture" based on his difficult situation: Greene's father was the headmaster. "The sneering nicknames were inserted like splinters under the nails," Greene writes. But it wasn't Carter he came to loathe and detest, it was another boy, Watson, who was one of his few friends and who deserted him for Carter.

"Carter continually tempted me with offers of friendship snatched away like a sweet, but leaving the impression that somewhere some time the torture would end, while Watson imitated him only at a blundering unimaginative level. Alone he would have had no power to hurt. Nonetheless, it was on Watson that I swore revenge, for with his defection my isolation had become almost complete.

"For many years after leaving school, when I thought back to that period, I found the desire for revenge alive like a creature under a stone. The only change was that I looked under the stone less and less often. I began to write and the past lost some of its power - I wrote it out of me. But still every few years a scent, a stretch of wall, a book on a shelf, a name in a newspaper, would remind me to lift the stone and watch the creature move its head towards the light."

Years later Greene met a "foxy-faced man with a small moustache" who turned out to be his old enemy. Greene describes the meeting as an anti-climax because he had forgotten Watson so, instead of the humiliations he had years ago dreamed of making Watson suffer, the author was lost for words. But the encounter did make him wonder if he would ever have written a book had it not been for Watson and those years of humiliation. "Had they given me an excessive desire to prove that I was good at something, however long the effort might prove? Was that a reason to be grateful to Watson or the reverse?"

But the sting is in the tail. At their chance meeting Greene had agreed to ring Watson to make a date to watch the latter play polo. "It was only many months later, after I had left Malaya, as I thought, for good, that I remembered I had never rung him up, had never watched him play polo, nor exchanged memories of the three inseparables. Perhaps, unconsciously, that was my revenge - to have forgotten him so easily. Now that I had raised the stone again, I knew that nothing lived beneath it."

Apparently Carter was already dead by the time this episode took place but it would be sweet revenge if Watson read what Greene wrote about him.

Few evacuees have managed to get their revenge on their

tormentors because mostly the foster carers were so much older, except Frank, whose story comes later in this chapter. He managed to get some of his own back. Those evacuees who returned to the scene of the crime and confronted the people who had treated them so badly were faced, usually, either with a terrified old person they could hardly attack physically or even verbally, or a gravestone. There are some, though, such as Helen in the Opportunistic Pederasts chapter, or Peggy Stockbridge, whose story is here, who still harbour thoughts of revenge and whose need could be met since the perpetrators are still very much alive.

In the Bible (Matthew 18: 21-35) Peter went up to Jesus and said, "Lord, how often must I forgive my brother if he wrongs me? As often as seven times?" Jesus answered, "Not seven, I tell you, but seventy-seven times." I believe that forgiving is probably more healing in the long run than thinking about revenge, which keeps bitterness burning bright. But it is an extremely hard doctrine to preach to someone who has been seriously sexually abused. They may not even have the capacity to forgive, and who can blame them?

The consequences of sexual abuse are not restricted to problems in people's sexual life; they impair the development of a self-confident personality. There are several reasons for this. One is that to have your helplessness and dependency taken advantage of at an early age produces an interlinking of love and hate. Many people cannot imagine love without suffering and sacrifice, without being hurt and humiliated. Another is that the evil experience must be repressed which ultimately leads to depression. The consequences of a trauma are not eliminated by repressing it but are actually reinforced. Children have no choice but to repress the experience, because the pain caused by their fear, isolation, betrayed expectation of receiving love, helplessness and feelings of shame and guilt is unbearable. Further, the puzzling silence on the part of the adult and the contradiction between his deeds and the moral principles and prohibitions he proclaims by light of day create an intolerable confusion that must be eliminated with by means of repression.

The notepaper Peggy Stockbridge of Dagenham, Essex, writes on has this at the top: "ME: How beautiful it is to do nothing and then to sit down again afterwards and rest..." which sums up her humour. "I was sexually abused and raped repeatedly at the tender age of nine by the son of the family I lived with," she writes. "I am now 64 and have kept this secret for over 50 years. Since returning home, my health suffered enormously and I have never been well.

"As to the heading on my letter, I've realised I've had ME for more than 20 years, maybe since coming back at ten, who knows? Two previous marriages have failed, two sons let me down - because of being an evacuee - who knows? I came back hating men and although I've tried desperately to live a normal life, I've looked back many times and I am now reliving my past in a book I am writing. This starts when I was four and will travel in time until the present day."

This was the first letter Peggy wrote to me and since then we have spoken many times. Her story is sad, not just because of what happened to her, but also because if only she had been helped at the time, or even since, she could have lived a less self-destructive life. Like many evacuees I have interviewed, she has resorted to a love of animals because "they are the only things you can trust." Peggy has five Yorkshire terriers, and adds another two reasons for preferring them to humans, "They don't answer you back and don't ask you for much."

Peggy is a feisty woman who has a kind heart and is fiercely loyal and protective as well as intelligent and forceful. The sort of person you would like to have on your side. Yet she has been on an emotional roller coaster for half a century with this horrendous secret of sexual abuse hidden away inside her. How much more sympathetic her sons may have been if they had known what torment she suffered when she was a small child. How much more free of her inner devil would she have been if she could have told someone, if her father could have gone to Norwich and given her tormentor a pasting. If only she had been allowed to let the anger flow out of her so that she could put this terrible past behind her, surely her life would have been less filled with bitterness.

Now she is locking horns with her past, going through a cathartic experience by writing it all down. At least she knows that the end will be happier than the beginning and much of the middle. I am full of admiration for Peggy's determination in spite of what it is costing her and I don't believe she will carry out her threat to murder the man who ruined her life. She is understandably angry but I can't imagine she really believes the warped teenager who took advantage of her is worth going to gaol for.

"I want to confront the man who raped me, who robbed me of my life," Peggy says. "I don't know what I will do when I find him. I always promised myself I would find him. I once advertised in *Loot* magazine, for someone by the name of K–, Blank Street, Norwich, and I just said, 'Someone wants to talk to you'.

"I was petrified by just doing that, that checking, so I took the ad out after two insertions. I'm not ready to confront him yet. It's something I will have to do on my own, I haven't got anyone to go with me, to push me. I have made a lot of inquiries to try and find out where the family moved to, the house is now pulled down. Even now I am 64, I can remember as if it was yesterday and one day I will find him. I will walk up his path. It is something I have to do. I know he will never come out alive. I will have something in my pocket. In the back of my mind I will find him and take the consequences.

"I have been so depressed sometimes I feel as if I have literally fallen down this black hole. It is shiny inside and I think to myself, 'I can't get out of this'. There was a time when I didn't know what day it was, when I could neither eat nor sleep. At the moment I am on an even keel but if anything goes wrong, I go back down again.

"I was born in 1935 and was first evacuated to Oxford but, like most evacuees at the time, I returned home for a little while. Next I went to Norwich with three of my sisters but no one would take four children all at once so we were dragged around the streets and we were more or less left until last. It was getting dark and eventually these two women neighbours took us in. So two sisters lived next door and my sister Violet and I went into one house. For a long while afterwards they didn't want to talk about what happened to us there. They all had a better time than me yet they would start moaning they never had this and they never had that. As if that mattered.

"When one of these women opened the door she exclaimed, 'Oh, no, I wanted someone older who could do the washing up and cooking'. I remember the house distinctly, it was detached and had an alleyway down the side. Some steps went up to a sloping garden, I don't remember the husband although I vaguely remember he was a headmaster. There was one room we were never allowed in because it was his study.

"There was a son, Stanley, a teenager of about 17 or 18, who I don't remember going to school. They also had a lodger who was good to us, my saviour, he had to pass through our room to get to his room. When he was at home we were never attacked. Stanley used to threaten me that if I didn't do what he wanted, he would do the same to Violet. At first I had no idea what was going on. I was skinny, just six stone, and only nine and I don't think at that age you are old enough to understand. He used to come into our bedroom, after we were undressed and in our nighties and suggest we play piggy backs. This game somehow tore the sheets which I got a beating for afterwards from his mother.

"I can't remember how soon after the piggy-back game started he began to rape me but Violet used to be asleep or at least she pretended to be. He used to put his hand over my mouth to stop me screaming. I think she woke up a couple of times though afterwards she said she knew nothing about it. Maybe the memory is there but she has repressed it, I don't know. She does get depressed. She married a good husband who gave her everything she wanted whereas I had to pull myself up all the time. Now she is divorced from him.

"Anyway, that's how it started. I used to dread him coming up the stairs. Life was full of mucking about at home, I had brothers and a father, but their playing was nothing like this. I knew it was wrong but I didn't know what to do to stop it. He used to say, 'I will see you tonight' and I knew exactly what it meant. He raped me almost every night. If it hadn't been for the lodger it would have been more often.

"His mother was always drinking so Stanley was supposed to be looking after us. What always puzzled me was, did she know he was coming into our bedroom? Did she just turn a blind eye? He used to say to me he would tell his mother and she would never let me go home again. I can remember being very, very frightened.

"The lodger knew something was going on and must have said something to her, I don't know what, but Stanley got a bashing and stopped coming into my bedroom for a little while. But that didn't last because the lodger was not always there. She decided to lock us in but while she was boozing, so her son could do what he liked. Our bedroom was over the kitchen and he climbed onto the roof and got in through the window. It was easy for him. I don't remember anyone coming to the house to talk to us – we were just evacuees, why would they bother?

"Mrs K was really bad to us. She used to make us spend an hour every evening combing her straggly, greasy hair. Once she even brought her sister round and we had to comb hers too. She told us that our mother had given us up and she never let us read any of her letters so we believed her, we thought our mother was not writing to us. My sister, Violet, was going through a bad patch, she had a swollen leg and she kept crying in pain.

"Eventually I decided I had to do something about it, so I pinched a pushchair from somewhere and walked the three miles to a hospital. She had water on the knee which had to be drained out. I got a terrific beating for that even though we returned with Violet's leg still in plaster.

"I came back from the evacuation hating my brothers and hating my father; even when I had children, if one of them had a male teacher I would go to the school and upset their teacher. I'd go for the teacher like a raging bull. I don't seem to be able to help myself, I just get so angry with men. Psychologically I think there was something wrong with me. I always had a feeling of guilt and shame at the back of my mind. My two sons have not spoken to me for years. I don't know the reason, I gave them everything I could. I was strict with them, if they weren't in by 11.30pm they would get a tongue lashing. There must be something in me they resented, they never bothered to come to see me after they got married. We did have a loving relationship when they were younger, but when they married they went.

"I returned after the war a rebel and I've been a rebel all my life. My mother was always shouting at me and my father hit me with a belt. I just could not settle, could not trust anybody. I blamed my mother for letting us go in the first place and I blamed my father for different things. He bought me a watch for my 14th birthday but I must have done something wrong in his eyes and he said, 'when you behave yourself, you will get this watch'. I never got it. It stayed in the drawer until my eldest brother's daughter was born and she got the watch.

"I married when I was seventeen and a half because I wanted to get away from home and I couldn't think of any other way to get out. I was married to my first husband for about ten years and had two sons. I do all the running after men but when I have them, I don't want them, I don't know why. I can't really explain, I lose interest I suppose. He was quite a nice person but we always rowed - over the children, never over money.

"I fell head over heels in love with someone else and had my eldest daughter by him. He lived next door but he was a mother's boy. I had to spend 13 weeks in hospital when I was pregnant with my daughter and this man apologised to me, but he said he could not marry me or anybody. He has still not married to this day.

"After that I started writing to pen friends, because I thought that way I would not have to meet them. I could put the nice part of myself into letters and didn't have to let them know what I was really like. I suppose they did the self-same thing. I married my second husband out of spite to the man next door who would not marry me but whom I still loved. We had a daughter who lives with me now. He was a soldier who went back to Germany and I wrote to tell him there was no point in his coming back.

"When we moved to where we live now I met my third husband. He lived in the next street and is a good bloke. He has two sons he never sees and I have two sons I never see so we have that in common. He is good with my two daughters and we are making a go of it. I used to get jealous if any of my men spoke to another woman or even if they looked at nudes in the paper, I used to get livid. I was very insecure and hot-headed. I had a terrible temper, it's a wonder I am still alive the number of men I have taunted with sex. I have had knives held at my throat. You can get quite a lot of self-respect by not having sex even when you are married. So you can use it both ways, by giving sex, or withdrawing it, by saying yes or by saying no.

"I once went on holiday with my present husband and he was driving, I wasn't paying much attention, when suddenly he stopped at this siding. I said, 'where on earth are we?' and when he said 'Norwich' I went ballistic. I said take me home. That is when I told him what had happened to me. I would not go through Norwich, I'd rather drive an extra 100 miles to go round it. I still feel the same way now.

"I have 50 pen friends all over the world, mostly they are people with ME. I like writing letters and sending them news of what is happening on the medical front. With ME you feel absolutely exhausted all the time and there is fog in your brain so you can't remember what you did yesterday or a month ago. There was a time when I couldn't put one leg in front of the other. I spent seven months on a couch unable to do anything, sleeping most of the time. Then my feet were put in warm water and electric things were put on them which scared the life out of me.

"Another time I had my neck stretched which also frightened the life out of me. If you have ME, none of these things work. I went to see a homeopath for three years but it didn't do any good. I lived on Valium for years and antibiotics but I am determined to get better. And one thing I am even more determined about is that I won't be confined to a wheelchair.

"I belong to a group and we had an American doctor here recently who treated some of us with injections which seem to have helped but he cannot go on giving them to us and they are not available on the National Health. He is going to Harley Street and I told him I felt as if he had stabbed us in the back, starting a course of treatment and then abandoning us again. If there is something inside of me I need to say, I flare up.

"I tried to persuade some of the others to march on Downing Street to lobby for this stuff to be available on the NHS, but they said, 'oh, we couldn't do that. It infuriates me. I would march given half a chance. I need an injection right now but my husband and I have had a row and he is a motor mechanic so I will have to be good to him otherwise he could use me as a dartboard.

"They always say, Peggy will ask, or get Peggy to do it. They know I am always the one who will say her piece. I don't care who I talk to or how. If the Queen came and she said something I didn't agree with I would tell her. It's only Fate that has made us different, we are both human beings. They say I would make a good Margaret Thatcher which I don't consider a nice way to be. I should sit back and let things go over my head.

"I seem to have been ill from the first time I set foot back in Dagenham from being evacuated. I have a big scar down my neck which no one seems to be able to tell me about. All I know is there was a big lump which had to be cut and when I came back my mother bandaged it too tight so instead of healing, it became a scar. So, from the age of 12, I can't remember feeling well. In spite of everything, I have not got a bad life although I often think I would like to be a different person."

Frank Bromhead does not harbour murder in his heart but he did once feel murderous and is one of the few evacuees who managed to give one of his persecutors a taste of his own medicine. It was years later but it gave him great satisfaction. Frank was seven in 1939 and remembers trucks arriving at his school with the gas masks and marching in a crocodile to the local station.

"I had a sister who was 20 months older than me," Frank says. "We were told to hold hands in twos. I always remember the cardboard label stuck to the lapel of my little blue mac. We ended up with a family who kept pigs on an allotment but we were moved on from there because someone was wetting his bed, they weren't sure who. I went to another billet with a Mrs Yates and the first day there I was taken straight into her garden shed and my head was dipped into a bowl of stinging paraffin. Everyone used paraffin for lamps so I knew the smell but I didn't realise what they were doing was delousing me until a lot later. Then I was marched into the bathroom and given a bath. It was a lovely house. Mrs Yates was nice but all I remember after that was me and this other boy were both in the same bed again and again the bed-wetting thing started. We were moved three months later and split up.

"The next woman had two sons and a husband who was away in the Army. This time there were three of us in one bed and we had to be in bed by 7pm. There was an old blind lady living in the sitting room. I remember the day they came to take the railings away for the war effort. I was digging in the garden with her eldest son, who was throwing bits of earth at me. I threw some back at him - that's when I got my first thump. No messing, I was nearly floored by his fist.

"A few days later, I spilt something on the table and he grabbed me and threw me into the corner. I hit the cooker splitting my eye open. From then on, if either of her boys did something to me, and they did so for the slightest excuse, that was OK, but if I retaliated, I'd get it. This went on for quite a while.

"I must have been nine when we were playing out in the garden and I walked a load of dirt back into the kitchen. Mrs Yates gave me the strap and told me to get up to bed and stay there. It was only 4.30pm in the afternoon. I got no tea and I could hear everyone out playing when I was lying there in my pyjamas. That night I thought, 'I've had enough of this.' I got dressed, put my mac over my pyjamas, took my little gas mask, and sneaked downstairs past the kitchen. I had a money box which I'd never had any money out of, but I used a knife and got five pennies out, thinking that would do me to get a bus. I sneaked round the back and crept under the hedge.

"It was about eight or nine o'clock and I suddenly realised that if I went to the bus stop I would be stopped so I started to walk towards Liverpool. I just kept going. I remember sleeping in a hedge that night. The following morning I kept on walking and walked all day. By the evening I'd reached the outskirts of Liverpool and caught a tram car which cost me about two pence. I knew roughly the area where I lived but I wasn't sure where my street was exactly.

"I wandered around until eventually, it was evening time, I got to our house and knocked on the front door but it was all dark and no one answered. So I climbed over a wall into the back yard and knocked on the back door but there was still no answer so I slept in the outside toilet. I can remember the sirens going and everyone rushing into the shelters so I went into a shelter with them.

"I was given a cup of tea and something to eat and slept in a corner. This went on for a couple of days. I'd knock on the front and back doors in case someone had returned and I hadn't noticed. Eventually one of the ladies from up the road saw me and recognised me. 'You are Frank, aren't you?' she said. 'What are you knocking on your door for? Your Mam's away in hospital.' Then a friend of mam's came, a Mrs Fogg, and took me to her house with her son who was about 14. Three days later, the police arrived to cart me back to Orsmkirk and I said to Mrs Fogg, 'Can I come back here when I run away?' 'Course you can, she said. 'Why?' 'Because I'm not going back. Wherever they take me, I am coming home.' The police weren't interested in what I had to say but anyway, my mum came home from the hospital so I was saved. I was back in my own bed. Mum was annoyed with me; she was very naive, if the authorities said something, that is what we had to do.

"Years later I was getting on a boat over the Mersey when I saw one of the sons who had spent so much time beating me up walking down the gangway. He was the same age as me and I recognised him right away as one of my tormentors. Then I got my own back. I hammered him. He ended up crying his eyes out. People had to drag me away. I just said, 'I'll see you one day' and left. It was a lovely feeling.

"People think revenge is not nice but it gave me great satisfaction."

Chapter Sixteen
Boot camps

Although I compared us unfavourably with the Germans earlier because they did not consider children under ten should be evacuated, when they sent their 10 to 14-year-olds away it was often to youth camps. There they received almost military-like training and were indoctrinated with Nazi propaganda. Parents were discouraged, or at some camps, forbidden to visit them. The regime was harsh as it was at some camps in England for many hundreds of evacuees such as Peggy Taylor, whose story follows, who were physically abused on a regular basis. From the research I have done, however, it does not seem that ours were anything like as brutal as theirs.

For most abused evacuees it was the isolation of their billet, where they suffered torment and torture on their own while other evacuees in the same street were happy and comfortable, that contributed to making their abuse so damaging. At least evacuees in camps could share their discomfort and unhappiness with other children and could get consolation from knowing they were not being singled out for some reason they could not fathom.

According to child psychiatrist John Bowlby, "the child who feels unwanted, whether this is really so or only his imagination, will find it very difficult not to interpret his being sent away as his parents' desire to be rid of him. In child guidance work one finds this belief again and again. This fear is behind the great unhappiness which a few small children have suffered during the evacuation. Such emotional experiences, whether justified by his mother's attitude or the result entirely of imagination and misinterpretation, may leave a child miserable and insecure for a long while to come."

Because they were not alone, their banishment was shared, campers were not burdened with that constant apprehension they must have done something wrong but had no idea what. Of course, plenty was going on in the camps that the children were unaware of which was to their detriment, such as the selling of their sugar, meat or fat rations but, besides a regimented lifestyle, what they suffered from most was food deprivation in the form of such unappetising offerings as custard made with water, uncooked porridge, maggots found in food, mouldy bread or simply not enough of anything edible to satisfy a growing child, at least not one growing into a healthy adult.

Six months before the war began it was agreed to construct a limited number of camps. They had to be 20 or 30 miles from big industrial centres and be readily distinguishable from military encampments, otherwise they would provide the enemy with yet another prime arget. Many authorities argued against them on the grounds that the Germans would dearly like to take out a few hundred children in one go but the Government decided camps would be useful for schools; to provide accommodation for difficult billeting cases; and for refugees fleeing from the cities who would need some rough and ready accommodation to run to.

A year earlier the London County Council had argued against camps, saying thousands of acres of land would be required for camp sites and would thus be unavailable for other purposes. They pointed out that materials more urgently required under the general re-armament programme would have to be withdrawn and that armies of labourers would have to be diverted from more essential or more productive work to build them.

The question of the organisation of food supplies, cooking, sanitation and medical services would have to be faced and a demand would arise for the provision of much more elaborate school and recreational accommodation than would be justified by their temporary occupation for some months of emergency. Moreover, the teachers, most of whom only had experience of acting *in loco parentis* to relatively small groups of children on school journeys, would probably oppose from the start any scheme which assumed that they should shoulder day and night responsibility for groups of 40 or 50 children per teacher.

At one of the many committee meetings to discuss camps versus private billets, the cost versus the convenience, one civil servant wrote on behalf of his boss, "There has been a tendency in some quarters, in the face of the very real difficulties of finding sufficient billets for every child, to suggest the provision of hostels as if it were a solution to the whole problem. Experience has shown that this is far from being the case.

The difficulties of running a successful hostel, though different in character, may be as great as the difficulty in accommodating children in billets and it must be borne in mind that the evils of a bad hostel, owing to the number of children involved, are much greater than the evils of an occasional bad home. The minister considers it to be of the first importance that hostels established by local authorities should not be allowed to degenerate into dumps in which children whom it is difficult to billet are accommodated without regard either for the individual peculiarities or for the character of the hostel."

And a child psychiatrist also wrote for another committee discussing the camps issue: "Almost all cases where a dozen or more children have been billeted en masse in a big house have been failures, except where a genuine home atmosphere has been created.

The children have become wild, disobedient little hooligans, an attitude quickly changed where they have been billeted with a number of homely foster parents. It is for these reasons that psychological opinion does not favour camps, at any rate for children under 11."

Nevertheless, it was agreed that one hundred camps should be built, a figure which was halved at the insistence of the Treasury. In May 1939 the Camps Act was passed entrusting the work to two non-profit-making public corporations, the National Camps Corporation Ltd (NCC) for England and Wales and the Scottish Special Housing Association (SSHA).

A sum of £1.2million was provided for the construction, maintenance and management of approximately 50 camps, each designed to accommodate about 300 people. They were designed almost entirely with reference to their peacetime use and, consequently, for short periods of occupation when children and adults would be sent for holidays of a few weeks. Considerable alterations were therefore necessary since they were camps that were going to be used for permanent residence, possibly for some years.

It was suggested to evacuating authorities that they produce propaganda, including the exhibition of films illustrating life at a camp, extolling the virtues of sending evacuees there. They should also run advertisements and try to place articles in local newspapers with photographs to persuade parents and children what wonderful places they were.

One of the arguments in favour of camps that was put to parents included the fact that some children would inevitably be evacuated to a village where the educational facilities were not good so they would be better off sending their children to a camp where, of course, the educational facilities were as good as they could be, given there was a war on.

It was planned that children from ten upwards could go to a camp as the Ministry of Health was anxious about younger children who were more liable to fall prey to epidemics. Most camps were in high and exposed positions and had no covered walkways between dormitories, lavatories and all the other camp buildings, so evacuees would be exposed to the elements and consequently liable to catch colds, if not pneumonia. As it cost three times more to keep a child in a camp than in a billet, camps had to be full or they were not viable.

Throughout the war most camps were far from full and the NCC was constantly wringing its hands about the lack of happy campers. For example, by November 1940 the figures for a camp in Bootle were optimistically described as having "improved" to just 174 while another in Hull had a mere 93 inmates. The fall in numbers was symptomatic of the general drift back of evacuee children, although a redeeming feature for camp schools as a whole was that the returns were less rapid than the trickle back home by children billeted in private homes.

Homesickness was one reason why children returned. Also, parents took them back when they heard their children's complaints about the food or the institutionalised life. Or parents refused to send them when they heard about the health risks.

In a letter discussing whether there was a way of regulating parental visits because too many children were taken back home as a consequence, one irritated official commented, "Most of the parents would prefer that their boys should attend the day school and live at home. The boys themselves have been used to living at home and there is no boarding school tradition in the family.

"Boys and parents alike see all the inconveniences of institutional life and very often overlook its advantages. Whereas the parent of a boy at a public school usually discounts his stories of hardships, there is a tendency for parents under the new circumstances of a camp school, used for evacuation purposes, to accept grumbles at their face value."

William Tully of Wanstead, east London remembers his time at the Marchant's Hill Camp School, Surrey when he was ten years old. "My enduring memory is of being hungry all the time and cold in the winter," he says. "The type of hunger I am describing is not missing the odd meal but being really hungry day after day. A favourite story my grandmother used to tell after the war was about visiting me and giving me some money.

"She expected me to buy sweets but I went straight into a baker's and got a loaf of bread and then next door for some onions and ate most of it in the street. When you got a food parcel from home you were immediately surrounded by children and the contents rapidly disappeared."

Each camp normally had five dormitory huts and each hut had double-decker beds for 58 children. There was a sick bay, some had amenities such as playing fields while others had rabbit hutches, hen pens, pig sties and a pets' cemetery; many allotted a plot to each child where they were encouraged to grow vegetables and offer parents the results of their labours. They were often set in acres of beautiful wooded countryside far from the sound of wailing sirens, the scream of falling bombs and the bark of anti-aircraft guns.

Not that that was always appreciated at first by the townie kids sent there. The laws of trespass in the country, a social institution which local children had been trained to regard as sacrosanct, were rules with which evacuees were totally unfamiliar. Consequently they tended to ignore the usual Keep Out signs and their behaviour in other respects caused anguish to country people.

An inspector visiting a camp at Marton, Cheshire remarked, "At first that unfortunate tendency of town-bred children to destroy every living thing in sight in the country predominated. A horse or a cow took the place of the street light as a target for stones and, greatly to the annoyance of the local hunting gentry, the boys would gather together in bunches and raise the most blood-curdling shouts on the approach of the local hunt."

Parents who could afford to paid six shillings a week for their child to go to a camp and supplied the same clothing all evacuees were expected to take with them: trousers, jumper, shirt, vest, stockings, handkerchiefs, pyjamas, towel, strong shoes or boots, plimsolls, mackintosh or overcoat, toothbrush.

On the application form parents had to sign it stated: "Anyone found to give false information in reply to these questions will be liable to a fine not exceeding £100 or to imprisonment not exceeding three months." That was to deter parents fraudulently claiming they were on benefits so they would not have to provide all the extra clothing.

City children often went around in plimsolls summer and winter and had no warm coat, as Alderman Edwin Smith told a conference of local authorities in London. He added, "Purchase Tax has pressed unduly heavily on the widow or pensioner and parents find it difficult to provide their children with clothing during an arduous winter.

If parents of camp children are in real difficulty, though not on benefits, boots and clothing can be provided out of charitable funds, including the £8 per month received from the USA relief fund." Many generous gifts came from across the Atlantic. A note of appreciation was recorded at the Pateley Bridge camp in the West Riding of Yorkshire for a gift of £200 from the Foster Parents Plan for War Children, New York.

A typical camp day would go something like this: 7am get up and make bed; 8-8.30am breakfast; 9am prayers; 9.30am-12.15pm lessons, with a break of 15 minutes at 11.30am; 12.30-1pm lunch; 2.15-4.15pm activity, for example, crafts, woodwork, rambles etc;

4.30-5pm tea; 5.45-7pm homework; 7pm prayers; 7.30pm supper; 8.30pm prepare for bed (two teachers per dormitory); 9pm lights out. Weekends: Friday evening was given up to recreational activities, for example cinema shows or a sing-song in lieu of homework. On Saturdays the boys and girls were allowed to visit the local cinema under supervision. Sunday: a parents' visiting day or tea with friends in the local village.

At the Amber Valley Camp, Woolley Moor, Derby there were 254 boys aged between eight and 11 in September 1940. A typical day's menu consisted of: Breakfast: smoked haddock, bread and butter, cup of coffee. Lunch: steak pie, mashed potatoes, peas, mince tart, custard; cup of tea; tea: jelly, bread and butter, cup of tea; supper: bread and milk.

There was a notice on the bottom of a week's menu saying though lettuce was not included it was given at least every other day. Oranges consisted of one half orange on two days a week. Each child, in theory though not always in practice, received one third of a pint of pasteurised milk daily; milk for cooking was raw.

The weekly menu does not sound too bad until you realise that from lunchtime until breakfast the next morning these growing children had next to nothing: tea and supper were fairly meagre meals consisting of little more than thin slices of bread with a scrape of margarine. The serious implications of this were set out in a letter on December 11, 1942, to the headmaster by the doctor whose job it was to give the boys regular check-ups.

Dr W. H. Mosbery wrote, "When treating the boys of Derby School at Amber Valley camp I have formed the opinion that the boys take somewhat longer to recover from various, mostly minor, ailments such as inflamed throats, common colds, etc, than would be reasonably expected. I think the nursing care and attention is excellent so I wonder if the boys' diet is adequate and properly balanced. A diet deficient in protective foods such as butter and vitamin enriched fats might explain the situation.

"I trust that I am not obtruding unduly on the school affairs but I feel that a difference exists between the response to treatment of your boys and other boys in a similar situations (ie evacuated) in the district."

Winnie Struthers who now lives in Waitakere, New Zealand, has many vivid memories of her time at at a hostel in Westington, Chipping Campden, Gloucestershire. "It is not easy for me to talk about this," she says, "And I suppose, like many others, the tears are streaming down my face when I recall my time as an evacuee. Thinking or reading about the war years has that effect on me.

"My worst experience was when I was sent to the hostel. There were quite a lot of children there and I think I was about nine at the time and considered one of the big girls. It was our job to look after the younger ones, bathe them at night before bed, get them up in the morning and change any wet sheets and put them into soak in the bath. We also had to wash and dry the breakfast dishes before going to school so we were invariably late and consequently got hit with the ruler across our hand. I don't think the schools liked having evacuees.

"Once I didn't eat all my breakfast because I didn't like it so I scraped what remained into a small rusty tin that I had and hid it in my locker next to my bed. It was found by one of the women who was supposed to be looking after us and when I arrived home from school that afternoon I was forced to sit at the table and eat the remains out of the tin. All our letters home were censored so I couldn't tell Mum what was happening."

At another camp His Majesty's Inspector (HMI) Sir Roger Curtis accused someone of trafficking in rations because they did not reach the children. He also pointed out that the tuck shop was run by the camp manager's sister. He said there was so much uneasiness about the camp and in view of the rumours which were rampant in the vicinity, he recommended an investigation by the Minister of Food.

Complaints about the children's diet in the camps came from many quarters. The chairman of one parents' association who had obviously been paying over the odds for some reason, wrote to a headmaster, "In future I shall be obliged if you will kindly reduce my subscription to the six shillings usually required. The extra that I have been paying will be added again when the catering arrangements at the camp are improved to what they should be. I hope you will enter this as a protest in the correct quarter. The feeding lately has been an absolute disgrace."

At another camp two HM inspectors found an "objectionable" smell in the fridge, crockery and cutlery not washed hygienically, porridge that tasted bitter, tea that was stewed and with very little milk and breakfast, teas and suppers prepared by kitchen staff, none of whom were cooks.

At another camp milk was not bought from an accredited supplier and there were reports of sour milk, possibly due to dirty churns left uncovered; meat generally re-cooked and cabbage served in a water-logged condition. It was pointed out at one camp that masters were given ham, cold beef, cold meat and cheese for supper yet it is a fact that growing boys eat more than adults. Children had to rely on considerable quantities of tuck sent by their parents.

In November 1940 it was estimated that the cost of feeding a child for a week was seven 7s 6d per week but three years later this amount had dropped by sixpence to one shilling a day. Another medical officer reported that between 20 and 40 children at the camp he had to inspect had not gained as much as 5lb in a year, the weight which he considered was desirable.

So distraught were some parents that the secretary of the Leeds Evacuees Parents' Association wrote direct to Walter Elliot, the

Minister of Health, "In consequence of the prevalence of skin trouble among the evacuee children at the camp we appeal to you direct before this becomes a public scandal in Leeds. Several children came home at Easter full of this complaint, scabies, given it to their parents and in one case a whole family, including a baby.

"For many months this trouble has persisted and we feel now only your intervention can stamp it out before the summer months aggravate it. We feel some compulsory inspection is needed. Also, the parents complain that there is not suitable bathing accommodation, showers not being enough to cleanse the body. We suggest their sleeping bags need fumigating as the children often change beds and their hand towels hang too close together.

"We do not intend to disparage the wonderful efforts of Mr and Mrs Walmsley on behalf of all our children but rather to ask you to come to their aid and rid the camp of this bogey, which is undermining our children's happiness in what is otherwise a paradise for city children."

The education committee of Derby Council minuted the information that "it is impossible to ignore the fact that a considerable portion of parents have expressed themselves dissatisfied with the feeding arrangements at the camp and that when boys go home they take diseases back with them."

It is surprising that the children were not kept clean considering one of the many stipulations about running a camp for evacuees was that when boys had a communal bath it should be half filled with 300 gallons of water to which 3oz of Jeyes fluid or 10oz of Dettol had to be added. Needless to say, standards varied from camp to camp. William Tully remembers one hot summer day when he went swimming in a lake some miles away from his camp. "By the time I got back I felt very ill," he says. "I kept falling over. I realise now I had either sun or heat stroke. We had long since learnt not to go near the medical centre for anything less than the Black Death. The nurse or matron in charge had very basic ways of dealing with complaints and was not a pleasant personality. I simply spent the weekend in bed and apart from friends no one was any the wiser."

One of the joys of being an evacuee, which goes some way to offsetting all the horrors and deprivations, was the relative freedom we all enjoyed through lack of supervision on the part people who did not care too much what happened to us. William, who stayed at the camp for 18 months, remembers an incident at his camp which illustrates how this lack of supervision, fine when you can roam around the countryside enjoying innocent play, can have fatal repercussions for children not old enough to understand the consequences of their actions.

"There was an army camp and training ground in the vicinity of our camp and in 1943 a boy brought a mortar bomb back to the dormitory next to mine," he says. "Of course, it exploded. Three boys were killed and about eight injured. I remember walking into the dormitory and the first thing I saw was a human leg."

For Margaret Taylor of Hinckley, Leicester, known to everyone as Peggy, the camp for evacuees she stayed at was the saving of her, in spite of the deprivations and the brutality. Not only did Peggy survive what today would probably be described as a boot camp, she went on to be a star of stage, screen and side shows as Tina Robbins.

Now a fit and ebullient grandmother of 72, Peggy is proof that a brutalised childhood does not automatically produce a brutal adult. On the contrary, she never hit any of her four sons and insisted, when they went to school, that no corporal punishment was meted out to them there either.

Like many others who have reason to be grateful for their wartime experience, Peggy thinks her evacuation to Colmendy camp in Wales proved her salvation. In spite of the harsh regime and the cruelty –

the place was run like a prison – she considers it not only saved her life physically from the bombs, but also gave her a far better start than she could ever have expected had she stayed behind at home.

"I remember the day war broke out," Peggy says. "I was skipping in the street with two friends. They were holding the rope and I was the one in the middle. People used to leave their front doors open in those days and the old women were sitting on the step with shawls over their shoulders when we heard the announcement on the radio."

Peggy lived in Liverpool, attending Aspen Grove Primary School until 1942 in a state, as she describes it, of abject poverty. Even if she survived the war without being sent to a camp, she would still have been a victim of a different kind – of her background and environment.

Her father was a tram driver who, if he happened to arrive late for work, even for a good reason, could be laid off for a week. In the mornings she says she had to knock cockroaches out of her shoes and she used to go to shoe shops to ask for empty boxes to play with because toys and dolls were unknown to her.

When she was eight Peggy contracted impetigo which quickly spread, including into her eyes, and she was sent to a clinic where they swathed her face in bandages soaked in starch. She was always starving, her main diet consisting of "fades" as the bad fruit she was given to eat was called then.

But, worse than the extreme poverty were her mother's feelings for her. Peggy says, "My mother loathed and detested me. She often told me she hated the sight of me, that I was a mistake, that she loved my little brother's little finger more than me. She used to make me tremble because she was such an evil woman. I once told her, when I was a little girl, 'one day I will have rings on every finger, I will never be like you'. And I carried it out. I was never out of a job.

"Although the camp was harsh and they were cruel and it was run like a prison, it was the making of me. First of all, it was spotlessly clean. We had baths once a week and hair washing once a week. It was the first time in my life I had a pair of new shoes on my feet and any new clothing. Until then everything I wore came from second hand shops. If I had stayed in Liverpool I would have been wrecked, like all the others, they are all dead now and I am very fit.

"I received harsh treatment right up to the age of 14 but the discipline, hygiene and religion taught me to have initiative and it made me into a doer rather than a watcher. That kind of regime teaches you self-control and self-respect. Today I don't drink, I don't smoke, I don't drive a car, I don't go on holidays, I live a simple life and I am content.

"We slept in dormitories, each one named after one of the hills in Snowdonia, and we had to get up at 5.30am and go to the ablutions block in hail, rain, frost, ice or snow. It was a good distance away from the dormitory and there we had a shower. We dressed, lined up and were marched to the food hall. After breakfast we marched back up to the dormitory to make our beds, folding our blankets prison style, then we'd stand by our beds for inspection.

"After that we had another march to school. We had a break at noon for lunch and at two o'clock set off to climb one of the mountains in the Snowdonia range. We arrived back in time for tea, lined up for evening school back in the classroom until 6.30pm. Then it was ablutions again and ready for bed at 7.30pm. We said prayers before lights out.

"The 'prison' chief warder was a Scot called Mrs MacDonald, who had an evil temper. She was cold and big, like a giant, with a red face and silver-rimmed glasses. She gave us the cane or belted us across the face with her hand. There were no rules or regulations about that sort of thing then. She was the boss and could do what she liked with us.

"But then, in Liverpool schools, a teacher in a boys' class would think nothing of flinging an ink well across at a boy, or anything else he could pick up in his hands. I was caned constantly from the age of five by a teacher called Mrs Hughes. I can still see her now, stuffing chocolates into her big mouth, chewing away. She used to give the boxes with big ribbons on them to her pet, a girl called Olive. Mrs Hughes loathed and detested me. Everybody did, I wonder why?"

Here Peggy, who has been entertaining audiences since she was 16, singing, dancing and being a queen of spiel, roars with delighted laughter. "My father adored me so he made up for everyone else. He was a wonderful dad who was put away in a home when he was eight for stealing a can of condensed milk.

"I also had a best friend called Dottie, we were in prams together, and her mother loved me. She often used to say 'I wish you were my daughter' because I used to do shopping for her. I'd have run my legs off for her. Dottie and I were friends until she died a couple of years ago."

The mother of four sons and a grandmother, Peggy looks back on the way she was treated with equanimity. Happily married and with a successful career in the entertainment business behind her, the demons of her past have been vanquished. That she survived such a tough regime so well says a lot for her spirit, but that she survived so well when her own mother treated her badly is remarkable. She talks about her now not with bitterness but with incomprehension.

"My mother never once sent me a letter or a parcel when I was away in that camp. I had no sweets all the time I was evacuated and she never came to visit me.

"Yet when she was dying it was me who looked after her, not her favourite son, the boy who could do no wrong, and I made sure she had a good burial. She said to me as she lay dying, 'Peggy, I love you.

Kiss me.' But I just said, 'Mam, when I was a little girl all I wanted was your love, it's too late now'."

Chapter Seventeen
The Crafty Hag

Now, in the 21st century, mention the word epidemic and Aids springs to mind. But for the greater part of the century, it was polio that spread panic through the populations of the Western world. It was not a killer but specialised in maiming people and was often nicknamed the Crippler. Polio is a virus that attacks the nerves in the spine, cutting off the impulse from the brain to the muscles and causing the affected muscle fibres to shrivel and die. An unpredictable element of the disease came through not knowing how much of the initial damage was temporary, the nerves, as it were, merely stunned, rather than taken out by the virus, and how much was permanent. It was largely cured by the invention of the Salk vaccine.

Franklin Delano Roosevelt, the American president during the Second World War, suffered from polio and so did Doreen Ingram who was stricken when she was a baby and spent 18 months in Queen Mary's Hospital, London. By the time the war started she was four years old and was sent away to be evacuated at three convalescent homes, the third one in Tarporley, Cheshire.

She believes that the abuse she suffered there set a pattern of brutality which led her into a violent marriage. "We children were given no encouragement, no love. You go through life like a ship without a sail," she says. "I grew up with no self-esteem. I thought I had done something wrong and was being punished for it. That is why I assumed my marriage was destined to be bad. My husband once threw a plate at me in such a way that if it had hit me, it would have killed me. I just ducked but it was the last straw. I had ample grounds to get a divorce. I think, subconsciously, children who have been physically abused attract abusers."

Although Doreen talks about a pattern of abuse repeating itself she made sure that pattern was not repeated with her own three children. She loved them and did everything she could for them and is proud of the way they have grown up. She now has six grandchildren and lives happily alone, close to her family.

"It is not until you are older and have children of your own and have to do something for them that you realise how neglected and cruelly treated you were yourself and begin to understand fully what happened to you. These memories are extremely painful and they have made me angry.

I have written about my own experiences because I want it to go on record. So many accounts of evacuation have glossed over what really happened and I am determined to get it all out into the open. To this day I can't bear to read any stories in the paper about child cruelty. They make me cry, I pity the child so much and I know that it is also myself as a child I am crying for."

A few years ago Doreen went to a reunion at Peckforten Castle organised for a television programme, and she met, once again, the woman who was matron there, Mrs Jessica Thomas who wrote a book in 1967, Hope for the Handicapped.

"There was nothing in her book about the terrible things that went on at the castle, everything was glossed over, it all sounded rosy and nice. There was no mention of the bad times which is why I want to speak out," Doreen says.

Redressing the balance is one of the reasons my book has come about, because history has a way of being rewritten, often to paint a pleasanter picture than the ugly reality.

"There are people who insist evacuation was a good thing because their experience was happy, as if only they count and the awful things that happened to other children should be discounted. Why? Why should our misery be swept under the carpet? Unhappy experiences are just as valid as the others' positive experiences and I think Doreen's own story, written with the help of a friend, are a fitting testament to the need for evacuees who were persecuted to have a voice at last.

"I was four years of age, living at Yeldom Road with my mum and dad. My mother told me I was a little horror, defiant, self-willed. Despite being a victim of polio and my right leg encased in a hideous calliper, I would fly up and down the street with a funny, stiff leg, snatching other children's prams or balls and taking them off, much to the tears and upsets of my little victims and their irate parents - and my mum.

"Throughout my first two previous evacuations I had never cried, not since that day I boarded the coach. I had not seen my mother or any member of my family since. But at my third place an overwhelming feeling of sadness and depression came over me. The tears just fell. There was a whole new routine in this cold, stone building. Gone was the easy, carefree routine of the earlier convalescent homes. Here we were met with a harsh, unloving, Dickensian orphanage way of life. There was one reason, one culprit, for this air of harshness, I named her the Lancashire Hag. Her name was Miss Smith.

"She was a white, leatherish-skinned woman with steel-grey hair done in a wartime hairdo that rolled tightly all the way round her head. She had thin lips and cold, snake eyes. There was no hint of kindness or affection in that face, a cruel face to match a cruel heart.

"Miss Smith had previously looked after boys and she made it quite clear she did not like girls. We stood no chance when the mood took her. She often made a bee-line for me and though I was afraid of her, I developed a defiant attitude towards her. One thing I do have to give her credit for, even though it was brought about through cruelty, was that she taught me to learn to walk without my calliper.

"This is how it happened. I had done nothing, said nothing to her but she would wait until I had my calliper off and was sitting on the edge of my bed, putting my nightdress on. She would stalk up to me and whack me round the head. Inevitably I fell to the floor, I had no balance without my calliper on. It was a tremendous struggle to get back onto my feet and it made me realise that if I didn't learn to do without the calliper I was always going to be vulnerable. So eventually I learned to walk without it.

"One day, while attending church, I had a nose bleed. I was sent back to the dormitory with another girl but who was there to meet me but the Lancashire Hag herself, delighted at my plight. Perhaps it was the sight of blood which excited her. She grabbed my long hair and pushed me towards the basin. 'Got a nose bleed, have you? We'll soon get rid of that for you'.

"With that, she pushed my head into the basin and nearly drowned me. Both taps were on full force. She harshly ducked me again and again into the flow of water. I cried and spluttered, trying to get my breath and can still feel that sense of nearly drowning today.

"Eventually she yanked my head out, flung a towel round my face and shoved me onto a bed. She jeered at me in front of the other girl, attempting to get he girl to agree with her that I was a pitiful wimp.

"Mrs Thomas who was the headmistress, was not seen very often, only on special occasions. There was a Miss Bottomley who, like the Hag, dealt with us children on a day-to-day basis but she must have been part-time or lived outside the castle. Needless to say, the Hag was live-in staff. She was constantly there with never a kind word or deed for us.

"I remember one occasion which made me hate her forever and is the reason I feel so much anger today. One of my friends was Audrey Fairfull, a thin little girl whose disability had to do with her chest or lungs. Each morning we all had to line up in our navy blue knickers and wait our turn for the sink. God help us if we got out of turn or didn't follow the girl in front in time. That is what happened to Audrey one day.

"For whatever reason, she didn't follow quickly enough for the Hag and the Hag pushed Audrey so hard the poor girl fell against a cast iron bed, the type with ball-shaped casters on. I can remember the thud Audrey's little chest made as she fell against the iron frame. It left her gasping for breath.

"She sank to the floor, white-faced and with her eyes closed. The children stood around, frozen with horror and fear. How the Hag got away with that incident, I will never know. Audrey was badly bruised for weeks. I vowed from that day that somehow, someway, I would bring the Hag down.

"Whatever disability we kids had, she would ridicule and laugh at us and scorn us. If some poor kid had a deformed back with a hump, she would mimic the child's action. One little girl had rather large front teeth which protruded. She called her George Formby and gave her a whack around the head at the same time.

"One of the daily tortures she relished administering was combing our hair. She used a steel comb and as I had curly hair, you can imagine how painful it was for me. There was no stopping for tangles, she used to just scrape it from my forehead to the back of my head. That went on day after day, year after year. I can still see her sardonic smirk as she must have known we were gritting our teeth, holding back tears of pain. Whatever she did for us, or whatever she had to do for us, was done in a spiteful or cruel way.

CHAPTER SEVENTEEN

"Good occasions were rare but I especially remember when the Americans came in a convoy of lorries to visit the castle which had a lot of historic interest. The Americans put on shows for us and brought goodies which we had never seen before. Some of the lucky kids received Shirley Temple dolls. I never did. I never had visits from anyone except Mum who could only make it now and then, perhaps because it was wartime and we were quite a distance from London.

"The occasional parcel came. Mail and parcels were given to us at morning assembly and it was hard to control the excitement as we were not allowed to open them ourselves, or any letters for that matter. Incoming letters were read to us by the staff and any letters we wrote were read, or intercepted.

"Once I received a parcel from home and all the longing for the unobtainable was too much for me, and I began to make a hole with my finger through the brown wrapping paper. Bit by bit my little fingers burrowed deeper until I came across something hard. I was too excited to stop. I could see two candy fishes, pink and yellow so I had scratched and then licked them. That is as far as got. It was taken from me and I never saw the fish or anything else that was in it again.

"After that I began to wonder about the sweets the Yanks brought but which we children rarely received. Where were all these sweets? It did not add up: the American soldiers often brought sweets but we received only a handful. They were so rare in fact that I had a little tin I used to put my precious sweets into. Every now and then I would open it up to look at them and allow myself a few licks. Eventually my craving for sweets became so bad that I could not look at my candy store without feeling sick with longing. This love of sweets led to my downfall in the Castle, but what a lovely downfall it was.

"I am not sure for what reason, but I was moved into another dormitory and my bed was facing a cupboard. I noticed that before lights out the Hag would often open this cupboard and take things out and put them into a bag. Then one night she left the key in the lock. Making sure plenty of time had gone by since the Hag was round, I crept out of bed and skipped over to the cupboard.

"I felt about inside and there were lots of bags of different shapes and sizes. I pulled out a rather large shape and realised it was the biggest bar of chocolate I had ever seen in my life. I couldn't believe it. My hand began to tremble with excitement as I discovered other goodies, lots of toffee and sweets of all kinds. It was like an Aladdin's Cave and I became a Fairy Godmother, dishing out chocolates and sweets to all the other kids in my dormitory.

"'When you have finished with your wrappers,' I told them, 'hide them in your gas mask cases and toss them away when we go out to air-raid drill'. They agreed to do this but by this time the next door dormitory had heard the commotion and were scampering in. So I dished out more lovely goodies to them.

"With all the noise of rustling, I'm amazed the Hag didn't hear and come storming in. But my naughty deed was soon discovered anyway because of poor Betty Fish who slept in the next bed to me. Betty had a weak bladder and had to get up many times during the night to go to the bathroom. The Hag came back to the dorms with her old torch flashing and got Betty up for the loo. As she arranged Betty's pillow, whoops, there lay a bar of toffee.

"Then the questions started. Inevitably she managed to find out who the culprit was who had raided their store cupboard and I was dragged out of bed, by my hair, naturally, and made to stand in the corner of the room. With my calliper off, it was difficult for me but I stood there in the dark for hours. I was cold but at least I was full up with sweets. Next morning at assembly I was put on trial for my confectionery party by Mrs Thomas who told all the children what I had done, rather unnecessary since most of them had shared in the sweetie bonanza.

"The last days of the Hag began one evening when we were all lined up for a bath. When it came to my turn she put the boiling water tap on, filled the bath, but, unbeknown to me, did not run the cold tap. I stepped into the tub and immediately tried to get out. She pushed me back down into the scalding, half-filled bath and I screamed. My legs and backside were scalded. I just stood, holding onto the side of the bathtub, screaming with pain.

"I must have made a helluva noise because Mrs Thomas came rushing in. By the time she got to where I was, the crafty Hag had turned on the cold tap. However, my bright red backside and legs were sufficient evidence for Mrs Thomas to know that I was not screaming for nothing. The result of that incident, when I was six years old, is that I cannot get into a hot bath to this day, it has to be just lukewarm.

"There must have been other complaints about that cruel woman who put such fear and misery in our young lives during the time we were at Pekforton Castle because peace was to reign eventually. Several months later, the Hag walked in, wearing a black coat which was unusual, she was normally in a white uniform. Her parting shot was directed at me: 'I suppose you are satisfied now'. And with that she turned and walked out of the room, never to be seen again.

"As I mentioned before, our letter-writing was monitored and any critical messages were censored and intercepted. A Miss Webster was in charge of our group one day and while her mind was busy on another matter, she told me to seal the envelope myself. I seized the opportunity to quickly scribble a message on the inside of the envelope to my mother 'PLEASE MUM, TAKE ME HOME. WE ARE BEING CRUELLY TREATED'.

"Thank heaven the message got through and she came to the home to see the headteacher and demand my return."

Chapter Eighteen
Dear Mum

Receiving letters was considered crucially important during the war. Getting the mail through was almost as urgent as delivering rations and ammunition. Letters are a tremendous morale booster. During the Second World War the Post Office delivered 20 million letters or postcards on average every day, in spite of the bombs. In his book *The Post Office Went to War*, Ian Hay writes, "The first thing that happens in war time from the Post Office point of view is that, with the population dispersed throughout the country to military centres and munitions factories, millions of people change their address and, having changed it, embark upon an orgy of affectionate correspondence with those left at home."

If letters were important for civilians working for the war effort, if they were a lifeline for soldiers in the field, imagine how much more precious they would be to a young evacuee, alone, away from home and unhappy. All the more cruel, then, that one of the commonest ways for host families to show their resentment at having to take in children was to tear up or confiscate the letters, parcels and money their parents sent to them. Many also refused to allow them to write letters or postcards home, not surprisingly perhaps, fearing their evacuees would spill the beans.

Fearful and uncertain, what evacuees needed most at that time was to hear from home. They needed reassurance they were loved and not forgotten. There were no telephones in those days so, for those old enough to write, a letter was their only way of communicating. Not hearing from their mothers and fathers must have made evacuees feel even more isolated, even more rejected.

It has been said that the people who organised the evacuation were used to sending their own children to boarding school, so they thought there was nothing strange about sending young children away from home. But at least at boarding school children were encouraged to write and receive letters. For evacuees there was no such luxury or comfort.

Dorothy Harmsworth of Cosham, Portsmouth, was one of the abused evacuees who was not able to tell her mother what was going on because her foster mother tore up the postcards she was going to send. But luckily for Dorothy, another foster mother wrote instead.

"War broke out the day before my eighth birthday and I was evacuated to Parkstone, near Poole with my brother, Dan, who was three years older, and other children from Northam School in Southampton," she says. "Like so many other siblings, Dan and I were parted, he went to a family that only wanted boys and I was billeted with an old couple called Mr and Mrs Hamilton and their middle-aged daughter, whom I was instructed to address as Miss Hamilton.

"My brother lived in a huge house across the road which had lots of ground and animals and he was happy there. The lady had lots of sons and she let them all run wild, they lived like pigs in muck and Dan was as happy as a sandboy. I was in a big house, too, which was dark and dreary. The Hamiltons were house-proud and the punishment for being untidy or dropping crumbs on the table, let alone the floor, were harsh. One was to be made to get down on my knees and pick up every crumb and then I was not allowed to finish my meal.

"I was a nervous child and had never slept in a room on my own.

My bedroom was large with big Victorian furniture, all dark and gloomy. In one corner was a pedestal upon which there was an alabaster statue of Jesus on the cross, arms outstretched - and it glowed. I was terrified and cried out the first night when I first saw it but was told to be silent. I wet the bed and next day my pyjamas were hung round my neck and I was given no breakfast. After that my punishment for still crying was to be dragged down the garden and made to stand between the wall and the shed. It was alive with spiders, of which I am terrified.

"I was physically abused many times, being beaten and punched, and was made to wear dresses with long sleeves to cover the marks of bruises on my arms. The verbal abuse was dreadful; they called my parents names, saying things like my mother was a slut, which I did not understand at the time, and they said I would end up in a home for bad girls. But I had not done anything bad and I cried yet again. So, with my arm twisted behind my back, I was marched down the garden and put with the spiders. I fainted on more than one occasion but then I'd wake up with spiders crawling over me which would make me faint yet again.

"They used to call us snotty-nosed little urchins from the slums and we did come from Northam, which was the slum part of Southampton, but my mother always kept us spotlessly clean and I resented the way they talked to me but I could not do anything about it. I can laugh about it now but at the time it was traumatic.

"I used to write a card to my mother every week begging to be taken home but the Hamiltons never posted them. My brother also used to send a card saying we are fine so I guess my parents thought that meant me too.

"Once, when I went to visit my brother the lady there asked if I was happy and I burst into tears. I told her what was happening and she contacted my mother who came and took me away. The

Hamiltons threatened to call the police but my mother just said to them 'go ahead'. She said she would report them to the authorities, so nothing more was said and I returned to my own home in Southampton.

"My mother went across the road to see Dan and was horrified at the state he was in. She thought he was too dirty to take on the train so next day my father went down with a truck to bring him back and Dan was brokenhearted. He loved living there because he never had to wash and could please himself what he did.

"The Hamiltons were cruel people who should never have had a child in the house. I am now 67 years old but those memories are still fresh in my mind and are one of the reasons I suffer from nervous problems. I shall never forget those days and I shall never forgive the people who should have checked to see if we were being well-treated. They didn't check what sort of houses they were sending children into, my brother's house was an absolute tip. If it happened now the Government would be sued for compensation."

Elsie Hewitt from Manchester was extraordinarily lucky, as she acknowledges. She was 12 years old, quite mature compared to many evacuees, and grown up enough to be cunning in the face of imminent danger when it came to the survival of herself and her sister. What might have happened if she had not managed to get round the censorship placed by the foster parents on her and her younger sister does not bear thinking about. In the spirit of the best Enid Blyton heroine stories, Elsie managed to out-fox her prospective persecutors. Here is how she remembers the ordeal of her evacuation which, thanks to her determination, was over almost before it began.

"My sister and I were evacuated to Clayton-Le-Moors, near Blackburn," she says. "I was 12 and my sister was eight. We went to this family, they were a mum, dad and two sons in their thirties. The father was a builder. I never got any letters from home. I found out later this lady read them and threw them away. When it was bedtime, the elder son wanted to bath us but I said 'No, I can do it and my sister as well'. I always kept my eye on her. We did not like it there, we were frightened. The younger son was always playing with himself and I had to sit next to him at meal times.

"I wrote and told my mam and dad but they didn't get my letters. The foster mother held them back but one day I arranged for a friend to wait near the bedroom window and I threw a letter to her to post and thank God my mam came to our billet and it all came out.

"The woman called me a liar and said she was sorry she took us in but mam told her she believed me. We told the evacuee organiser all about it and said we wanted to go home. It was a happy day when we left there. It's the first time I've written about this and I'm nearly 72. I think we were two lucky girls."

Sheila Caddick, who now has a son and daughter and three grandchildren, was 11 when she was evacuated from Caterham in Surrey to Yeovil, Devon, with her two sisters, Margaret, seven and Joyce, four. She went with their mother's last words ringing in her ears: "Mind you look after them two."

"We were taken from school to a bus station and put on buses which were going to take us to the railway station,"she says. On the way, branches from overhanging trees broke some of the windows and the children were showered with glass. Not a good start.

"We ended up in a big hall and I was hanging onto Margaret and Joyce but no one wanted to take the three of us and they took those two off to stay with a Mrs Penny. Me and another girl from my school who was about 6ft were the only ones left. Eventually we were taken in by a Mrs Lane, a nice-looking lady in her mid-thirties.

"Mrs Lane had three small children of her own, one who was just school age, a toddler, and a baby and she may have been nice looking but she did not have a pleasant nature as I soon discovered. We were put into a box room with just a mattress on the floor and one blanket each to cover us. There were no pillow cases or sheets, it was awful. We used to have to get up and do all the housework and wash the kids every day. Then we'd go to school in our filthy frocks and because we were so dirty no one would play with us.

"She used to beat us with a copper stick all the time. I can't remember why, except I used to give her some lip sometimes. I'd say something like, 'My mum never makes me do this at home' but you soon learn to keep your mouth shut. Joan never said anything, she was the quiet type.

"My worst memory was the day my mum came down for a visit. Mrs Lane had threatened me that if I ever said anything she would kill me and, of course, I believed her. My mum said, 'You're quiet, are you alright?' but I was too frightened to say anything. Then, when she left, Margaret and Joyce were jumping up and down, waving at the train and I collapsed on the station sobbing. I was thinking, 'She's gone and I haven't told her'. That is the time I remember most about being evacuated, that sobbing on the station. I have never cried so much in my life before - or since - as that day. I was broken hearted to think I let her go.

"On Saturdays and Sundays I used to have to entertain Mrs Lane's three children all day. There was a big, old-fashioned pram which I had to push around the town, return for lunch, and do more pushing in the afternoons. I hated the sight of the children and taking three children out all day is not what a girl of that age wanted to do. It was boring.

"Mrs Lane used to go to a place in the town called Nine Springs where she'd meet American servicemen. Joan sometimes went with her and I'd ask her 'What do they do?' but Joan had no idea. She was sent off to go for a walk and we couldn't imagine what Mrs Lane could find so entertaining about going to this place where the

American soldiers were.

"The particular chore I remember which was the last straw happened over the family's children who never ate their crusts. When their mother wasn't looking, they used to run into the front room and stuff them down the side of the sofa. One day she told me I had to give the lounge a good clean, vacuum clean the floor and brush the cushions. When I lifted them up the sofa was crawling with maggots.

"We were not allowed to write home but I managed to tear a piece of paper from an exercise book at school and somehow borrowed a stamp from another girl in my class - we were not given any pocket money by Mrs Lane and certainly would not have been allowed to buy stamps - and I posted a letter to my mother, telling her how horrible it was and saying that I wanted to come home.

"The girl I'd borrowed the stamp from lived next door and she told Mrs Lane I had written a letter to my mother so out came the stick again and she gave me a beating. But this time it was worth it. My mum sent the money for my train fare home. She was horrified when I told her what had been happening to me. I don't know what happened to Joan. I heard her mother had gone to Taunton with the younger children so perhaps she joined her there for the rest of the war. I know the family never came back to Caterham.

"Or perhaps, when she was left on her own with Mrs Lane, she killed her."

John Gough and his brother Tony, who were 11 and six, had two sisters who were evacuated to the same village but they were never allowed to see them. When the girls, Jean, then 12, and Beryl, eight, tried to pay them a visit, they were told to go away and the boys were locked in their bedrooms. Being locked up was a regular feature of the torment that went on for years while they were in the so-called "care" of a Mr and Mrs Lomas in Lypstone, Devon. For any misdemeanour, or more likely a contrived misdemeanour, the two boys were banished to their bedroom with no supper. Like all the evacuees who have written their accounts of what happened to them all those years ago, the hurt, frustration and feeling of unfairness, runs through his prose.

Sadly, the Goughs is not an isolated case of foster parents being spiteful even at Christmas. "The Lomases had two sons of about the same age as us and for the first two weeks everything was fine," says John. "We thought it was great at first; they couldn't do enough for us. Having come from a big city, Bristol, to a small hamlet, it seemed great to us. Mr Lomas was the gardener and he had a house on this estate.

"But after about two weeks things got rough. We were always starving. We used to steal swedes and sugar beet from the fields to eat and he used to grow prize dessert apples so we would eat the backs of them and leave the fronts so he didn't notice. They used to lock us in our bedroom from around six until eight the next day. It was like an imprisonment. If we said anything about what was happening to us, we would get a beating.

"When Christmas came we had no toys but their boys had an enormous wooden soldiers' fort set. We found out afterwards that the fort was sent by our parents. Dad had had it made for us but we never got it back They took us to Exmouth once to her parents' house. We were in the kitchen, starving of hunger as usual, so we ate a bit of chicken. Mrs Lomas's brother, who was in the Army, aged around 19, punched me on my nose. It started to pour with blood.

"When I grew up and did my National Service, I was a big strong man then, and I went back to look for them. I was going to give them a good bashing but when I got there they had all gone.

"There was some sort of Army set up in the grounds of the house at the time and some of the soldiers used to give us chocolate which kept us going. One of them was so upset about the way they treated us, he wanted to sort Mr Lomas out but we just told him they'd make it worse for us later. I remember one Sunday when Tony left a bit of fat on his plate. It was served to him for the next meal, nothing else, just the bit of fat, and the next and the next. Eventually we managed to smuggle it out in our pockets.

"I don't think they wanted us. We were just bunged on them and these people felt obligated to take us but they resented it and were never going to let us forget it. No one ever came to check up to see if we were all right. I don't think I went to school more than twice, I used to spend my days just looking for shrapnel and after the war I didn't go at all.

"Later on our heads became full of lice and scabs. After about a year our father came down to visit us and Mrs Lomas locked us in our room and told him we were out. But we started screaming and banging on the window and luckily he heard us and took us home.

"I used to help a farmer while I was evacuated and I don't know why he didn't do something about the way we were treated. I might have stopped him because of the repercussions but I think Mr and Mrs Lomas would have denied it anyway, they would have accused us of lying because we wanted to go home. In those days people never believed children.

"My two sisters had their own evacuation story to tell: not of abuse but an adventure. They were evacuated with a policeman who had a German helmet so they thought he was really a German and they tried to escape - by "borrowing" a rowing boat and rowing back to Bristol. They were caught and eventually sent back to a different billet. This time they ended up in Looe, Cornwall, presumably on the grounds that it would be too far for them to row back home."

John has never married. After the war his parents went on to have five more children and when his father died he stayed at home and help to bring them up. He has spent 40 years as leader of youth football clubs. "After what I went through, it made me want to make life better for children," he says.

Chapter Nineteen
Children v children

Children never feel friendly towards new born additions to their family. They sometimes pretend to do so; at other times they are mollified by the smallness and complete helplessness of the newcomer. The newly billeted foster brother or sister, on the other hand, is often neither small nor helpless. He usurps rights which the other child is unwilling to give up. The billeted newcomer, for his part, is deeply conscious of his second-rate position and is embittered by it. There are certainly all the elements for jealousy, discomfort and competition in the circumstances.

It was a situation in which the host family's children had the upper hand and they exploited it to the full, sometimes with the blatant connivance of their parents. Looking back, I wonder what sort of people those children became when they grew up.

Evacuees may have harboured a sense of grievance but our sense of fair play was surely honed by these injustices whereas, for children to be encouraged to be sly, thieves or bullies by their parents would surely do them more lasting harm. According to a recent survey the British have more bullies in the workplace than any other European country. Perhaps the experience of evacuees gives us a hint of why: it is something that is passed down from one generation to the next.

A survey conducted in London at the time of children entering nurseries with a sibling showed that they cried less and showed fewer outbursts or marked hostility. During the early days especially, siblings constantly sought each other out.

There was no sympathy, however, for evacuated siblings needing each other once they reached the end of their train journey: the billeting officer split them up according to the needs of the people he was only too grateful to for taking the evacuees off his hands. The last thing he was going to worry about was pandering to the whimpering of a younger brother or sister. This act of tearing them apart from their loved ones was the first hint evacuees had of the flint-hearted treatment they would often receive.

Ruth Newark of Edgware, Middlesex is one of dozens of evacuees who have written to me about the cruelty they were subjected to at the hands of the host family's own children.

"I was an evacuee aged four, the youngest in the school to be evacuated. I was with my brother, seven, who had been told we must not be separated and we had to wait to be 'chosen'. The first family we stayed with was keen to 'do their bit' but only for a short time. The next 'family' was a widow with a daughter of about 16. It was absolutely horrendous living there.

"My mother and father used to come down bringing food and sweets which friends had given them but, after they had gone, we never received any of it. I had to sleep in a room with no light and no heating. The toilet was outdoors and we had no running water. We had to get water from the well across the road and I had to break the ice on an outside tub to wash my hair.

"All these things were tolerable - just. However, there was no warmth or affection offered and I changed from an outgoing little girl to a shy pale child. The daughter once locked me in and chased me round with a red hot poker, finally burning me on the arm - I still have the scar.

"When her mother saw my arm and asked her daugher about it she said I had been playing with the fire and burned my arm on the oven door.

"Anita, the daughter, threatened to tell her mother I had not been eating my school dinners if I told the truth about the burn and I would be punished for this as well as playing with the fire. Another time I had been to the school dentist, by myself, by bus and had a tooth extracted by gas. When I got home at lunch time I was sick and the mother made me clean up my own vomit.

"Like others I never told anyone at the time thinking it was how it was supposed to be. Of course years later, when I told my mother about some of the things, I am sure she felt guilty and I often wonder how anyone could leave a child as young as I was with total strangers."

There was, not surprisingly, much rivalry between local children and the evacuees which led to numerous playground fights. This is the normal stuff of growing up, especially among boys.

Macdonald Coventry of Wootton Bassett, Wiltshire, who shared a double desk with a boy called Colin Birmingham, remembers an inter-school fight "after the local kids had handed out more than their fair share of insults".

He says, "One dinner time an assault party of we evacuees set off for a school about a mile or so away, close to St Albans railway station, to do battle. Not only did we arrive back well after 3pm, but evidently the headmaster of their school had telephoned our head, a Mr Clayton, who was ready, cane in hand, to greet our return."

Jim Taphouse of Andover, Hampshire, was born in a workhouse in the Walworth Road, Peckham, south east London and he was sent to a babies' home in Hastings, so he had experience of being away from his family before being evacuated. "At first I was evacuated with my mother, elder sister and younger brother in Yeovil, Somerset. We lived in a house where the lady used to make kid gloves and she had a son who had a car which we went out in once or twice. How he managed to get the petrol, I don't know. At that time I suppose it was the phoney war and shortly we were to return to London.

"Then we were issued with gas masks, my younger brother being given one known at the time as a Mickey Mouse gas mask. Then the bombing started so my brother, sister and I were put on a train to St Neots, Cambridgeshire. My sister and brother, though they probably would not admit it, fell lucky.

"Three spinsters whose father once owned a brewery, now deceased, took them. I waited in the hall, people came in, picked up children and went out. It was dark and I was the only one left. Why I was last I can only put down to my obvious poverty.

"A reluctant woman was encouraged to come in to pick me up and take me to her home. But she was not happy about it and the next day she took me to her mother saying 'I am stuck with him and I don't want to look after him. Will you take him on?' So I finished up at No 2 The Crescent, St Neots.

"It was quite a large family, about six. I don't really remember but she did have a son called Don, Don Smith who was quite a bit older and stronger than I. One day, for no reason that I can remember, he beat me up. I complained to his mother and her reply was, 'So what?' Then I knew that I was in for it. He was a bully. He used to make me steal from shops and if I didn't he would beat me up.

"The school I went to was dedicated to evacuees, there was no such thing as integration, and my classmates were supportive. They offered to duff him up if ever he touched me but I declined their offer even though I carried around for a long time broken teeth and physical scars. He once tied a piece of string to my penis and pulled me along, something I didn't even talk to my wife about until now.

"He once had a milk round or more properly helped the milkman. I suppose it must have been a Saturday when the milkman collected his money. Don sent me to the various houses, saying that I was collecting the money for the milkman and that he would be along later. Instead I had to give the money to him. Of course we were caught. I was met by a plain clothes policeman outside the school and taken to the police station. I know I cried.

"Funny, when I was caned at school one thing that you must never do is to cry and in playtime, if someone asked 'Did it hurt?' you always said no. But I cried that day. I suppose it was the injustice of it that made me cry, being forced to do something by that bully and then getting into trouble for it."

Bullying is not something that is confined to boys on boys: girls are equally capable of being spiteful and vicious. Kathleen Wenburn, from Dagenham, Essex, is one of the few evacuees who was rescued by someone in authority but before that she had to run the gauntlet of evacuee-baiting.

"I was evacuated on September 2 from Ford's motor works jetty in Dagenham with my younger sister and two brothers," she says. "Pat was six, David was four and Bill was ten; I was eight.

"We sailed on the Queen of the Channel up to Great Yarmouth, then went by coach to Norwich where we spent the night in St Andrew's Hall, sleeping on straw-stuffed sacks. The next day we went to East Dereham, Norfolk, where we all got billets. My brothers were together in one house, my sister was next door with an elderly couple. I was sent to live with a family at the end of the road, the parents had two daughters older than me and they made my life a misery. They used to hit me and take the food off my plate so I was always hungry.

"Their favourite way of tormenting me was at bedtime when they used to roll me in a blanket and sit on me. I can still recall the feeling of suffocation I suffered. I told their mother but she would just say I was being silly and they were only playing. Then I would be beaten for telling tales.

"After a few months I was moved to stay with another family, about two miles away from my brothers and sister. They were lucky being with good people. My new family had a mother and four children. I don't remember a man being in the house. The mother was quite strict. She told me I would have jobs to do in the house like making beds and peeling vegetables, also scrubbing the kitchen floor every Saturday.

"The mother wasn't happy with me though. I can recall hearing her saying to her children how she wished I had never gone to live there. Then the children started called me names. It wasn't just them but their friends as well used to shout at me in the street. Names like dirty stinking Londoner and rotten flea head. I can remember being upset enough to shout back at them that I didn't come from London anyway, I came from Dagenham.

"I started wetting the bed, which the mother told all the neighbours about. She always used to say 'as if I haven't got enough to do without this'. She used to drape the mattress over the garden wall at the side of the house so anyone walking along the road could see it, especially the other children. I was so humiliated and felt so alone and unhappy. As we lived in a corner house everyone used the back door, even callers to the house.

"One Saturday I was scrubbing the kitchen floor as usual, when I saw a lady watching me from the doorway. Everyone else had gone out. I think she must have been some kind of social worker. She asked me about my life in the house and did I often clean the kitchen. I told her it was my job to do it on a Saturday. Also, to blacklead the Victorian range and whitestone the hearth. She wrote it all down and told me one of the neighbours was worried about me as I had grown so thin and pale.

"I can remember all this as though it had happened yesterday. For years I never thought or talked about my life as an evacuee but I have been thinking about it lately. I am sure a lot of children suffered much more than I did. There were so many other incidents with the families I was with but writing some of it down has helped, even though it made me cry.

"Soon after the visit from the social worker my mum came and took us all home. It was one year after we left so we returned in time for the Blitz."

Chapter Twenty
Mother knows best

Many eminent psychologists and psychiatrists thought sending children away to be evacuated was a worse fate than letting them stay at home and taking a risk with the bombs. Anna Freud and Dorothy Burlingham's 1943 reports on children exposed to trauma during the Second World War presents this latter view. "The fact is," they wrote, "children survive danger and some may even overcome its challenges in ways that enhance their development. Children in the care of their own mothers or a familiar mother substitute were not psychologically devastated by wartime experiences, principally because parents could maintain day-to-day care routines and project high morale."

A senior psychiatric social worker at Guy's Hospital, London, wrote early in 1941, "Before the Blitz it had been anticipated that many children who had remained in London would need special care after suffering the experience of being bombed, whether or not actual physical injury had been sustained. Arrangements were therefore made by the social worker, both within the hospital and in cooperation with outside social agencies, for all such children coming within the purview of the hospital to be followed up with a view to treatment and disposal to suitable convalescent homes in safe areas.

"To this end, night raids being the deadliest, and immediate contact important, the social worker obtained permission to remain in the hospital for the first few months of the Blitz. The relatively few casualties, compared with the numbers anticipated and considering the numbers of shattered homes, was one of the remarkable features of this period of the war on the home front.

"The percentage of children suffering psychologically through their air raid experiences has yet to be computed for, surprising though it may seem, the number passing through the hands of the clinic has been negligible."

It is extraordinary how much evidence there was at the time that children were not in such grave danger in the inner cities - not, anyway, compared to the dangers some of them faced as evacuees. Mary Childs from Newcastle is one of many who eventually managed to get herself back to the safer environment of the bombing.

"At last," she says, "Someone has written that the evacuation wasn't wonderful. I've always thought my brother and I were the only ones who suffered. I was about six and my brother, Robert, was eight when we were evacuated. I knew nothing about it. I went to school one day was taken to Central Station, Newcastle, and put on a train. We were given a packed lunch and all the other children started to eat theirs as soon as the train left but Robert said they would get into trouble so I, being a timid little thing, followed his advice and didn't touch mine. Consequently we didn't have anything to eat because it was taken off us.

"We all went to Creswell, Derbyshire; most of the children went to a camp but we were sent to a couple who had no children whom we were told to call Aunty Tizzy and Uncle Walter. Aunty Tizzy couldn't stand dirt, we had to be spotless, or the belt. They hated boys but I would not be parted from Robert. They were strict and horrible to him but wanted to adopt me and they were so nice to me. This, I think, was so cruel as I adored my big brother.

"I remember listening to him crying upstairs while downstairs they were giving me sweets. They would say 'Don't take any notice of him, he is wicked but you are a lovely little girl'. I remember feeling devastated. I don't know how long we stayed there although I remember spending a Christmas with them. I think it was about a year and we would probably have stayed longer but they wrote to my mother asking if they could adopt me. My father, who was in the fire service, came down straightaway to take us back home.

"Next we were sent to Whitehaven on the Cumbrian coast to a large family who were supposedly Christian where, once again, it was misery. I never saw any seaside. We didn't fit in and were often beaten. About five of us used to share a bed, she could not officially have had enough spare room to take in evacuees so I suppose she was doing it for the money.

"You couldn't write home to tell your parents about what was happening because your letters were censored so we just had to put up with it. I remember once soiling myself and carrying my knickers home then having to wash them in cold water. The woman was screaming at me at the top of her voice, 'Dirty, stupid evacuees'. I was terrified and stood there crying, not knowing what to say to her. I think I spent a lot of my childhood shivering and crying.

"We, like a lot of evacuee children, got scabies. We were sent to a Dickensian hostel, somewhere in Cumberland, where we were mistreated. My brother and another boy ran away, with me tagging along. The police found us and took us back in a police car. They questioned us closely together and separately to try and find out what was the reason for us running away because a hostel is an official place so it should have been run properly but, of course, it wasn't. But I don't know if anything good happened as a result of their inquiries.

"My brother was locked in an attic because he wouldn't say sorry. He was a typical Geordie boy, cheeky and tough. He wouldn't be put down by anyone. Eventually he managed to smuggle a letter out, I've no idea how, and my Dad, who was by now in the Army but was home on leave, came for us. He made us walk home from the Central Station to our home in Byker because he thought we were in too bad a state to take on a bus or a tram car. For years afterwards my Mam talked about the state of us when we arrived home.

"My cousins were evacuated and they had a wonderful time and I had never heard of anyone having a terrible time. Robert and I thought it was just us. War was a terrible thing to happen to children anyway but to have people who were supposed to be protecting you from it being cruel to you on top of that defies description. I often wonder how these people lived with themselves.

"After we went back home, my mother took in her brother's children because their mother had died so there were five of us and when the sirens went we used to have to dress in the dark to go to the air raid shelter at the top of the street. I can remember always having either one shoe belonging to one of the other's on or my shoes on the wrong feet.

"This went on for months then my mother said, 'Right, all of you into my bed. If a bomb drops we'll all get it' and so that's what we did for the rest of the war. To this day, if I am passing a factory and I hear a siren I go absolutely cold. I was with one of my daughters in the South of France on Bastille Day and was absolutely terrified of the fireworks, I was really shaking.

"Now, at the age of 65, my brother is dead and all I can say is no child should have had the childhood we did. I was protective of him, our experience together created a bond that lasted all our lives. I'm sure, after reading about others, it does help, because I have never heard anything but what a fantastic time we all had. Not true. I'm so sorry for any other children who suffered."

Chapter Twenty-one
Happy ever after

Kathy and Ron Hill of Romford, Essex, are so typical of evacuees that I wanted to include both their letters because they illustrate so clearly much of what this book is about: abuse from adults who should have known better, bullying from the foster family's own children, the humiliation of bed-wetting; being moved from billet to billet; being rescued; overcoming the mistreatment to grow up into well-adjusted adults and finally going back to the scene of their torment to confront the perpetrators. Kathy and Ron are also typical of the majority of evacuees who are not bitter but who feel it is about time the world listened and understood what they went through.

After she read an article of mine in the Evacuees' Reunion newsletter, Kathy wrote: "When I read your article I was quite relieved because all I had heard up until then were people on the radio and television saying things like, 'Oh, we had a wonderful time' or 'They were the best years of my life'. Well, not so for my sister and me.

"We were evacuated three times and each time our mother brought us back. I don't remember very much about the first two visits, but the third one, when we were sent to Flint in North Wales, I do remember. I was about eight years old, my sister two years older. We went first to a couple who lived in a condemned cottage and soon we were rehoused with them into a small shop. I don't know why but we were moved on. I must say, they were not too bad, giving us a lot of freedom, though thinking about it now, perhaps that was why we were moved on, because we were running wild.

"We were next sent to a person called Mrs Evans. I can see her now: she was tall and thin, with her hair scraped back. There was no Mr Evans in sight, I expect he must have been in the Forces.

"Her home was uninviting, a dreadful place. It was so cold, she had no mats or carpets anywhere. She was houseproud and had no children of her own and she certainly did not want us.

"Mrs Evans decided to give my sister the money the Government gave her for our keep, minus our board. Can you imagine? She got the food and we bought it from her. The first two or three days we ate well, but when the money ran out, we lived on cow cake we picked up in the field, or turnips and apples we scrumped. We were both thin and my sister caught scabies. She was covered in sores. We worked in the field potato picking after school but never saw the money.

"You'd have thought someone would have noticed our condition but if they did, they chose to ignore it. Next door lived Mrs Jones, Mrs Evans's sister. She must have seen what was going on but, because it was her sister, it must have been difficult for her. However, eventually she took us in to her overcrowded home. (She had three children of her own and was a sick lady.) She must have had an argument with Mrs Evans because she never had her in her house again while we lived there. The funny thing is how resilient children are because, while living with Mrs Jones, I remember being happy, never thinking of the horror of next door.

"Talk nowadays about moving your children to a new school and everyone is up in arms saying things like, 'Oh, it will have a bad effect on them, it will make them insecure'. It makes me smile to myself when I think of my childhood.

"But I grew up to marry a wonderful man at 17, had four children who are our pride and joy and we have five grandchildren. I think the lasting effect my childhood had on me was to make me an overprotective mother but my children who are between 32 and 46 years old always tell us their childhood was full of love and happiness. When my youngest son was old enough, I went to college, always making sure I was there for him after school, and became a nursery nurse and looked after small children and cared for them as I did for my own.

"I have ended up a happy woman, surrounded by the love of my husband, children and grandchildren. So that dreadful woman did not crush me, I'm glad to say."

And her husband, Ron Hill says, "I was evacuated with my brother when I was six years old and he was ten. We travelled by sea from Dagenham Dock to Great Yarmouth and eventually ended up in Dereham, Norfolk. Our first billet was in a small house, the owners being a soldier and his wife who had no children and their idea of a joke was to place a plateful of bones on the table in front of us and say 'This is your tea'.

"Now, because I wet the bed, the big brave soldier thought he would teach me a lesson. He took the cane to me. My brother said, 'Leave him alone' so he gave him the same treatment. One night when we were in bed and we were talking about running away they must have overheard because from then on we were locked in.

"Our next billet you would have thought might have been an improvement but unfortunately it wasn't. There are many ways of making a child unhappy. This lady had four children of her own and should have known motherless children needed more consideration.

"For example, in December her sons who were older than my brother and I, called to us that a parcel we expected from home had arrived. We rushed in to see a large brown, wrapped box on the table. We quickly pulled the string and paper off and, on opening the box, we found it was full of snow. To this day I can still feel that disappointment. Some people might think that this was a childish prank but what kind of a woman stands by and allows her children to play a trick like that?

"I continued to wet the bed and dreaded coming home from school on Mondays, washdays, because she would wait for me and I would get a good hiding, and I remember my head hitting the wall. Our mother sent us parcels but we never received them. One day my father came to see us and decided to take us home. We never left home again, spending the rest of the wartime nights in the air raid shelter.

"A few years ago my wife and I went to Dereham and I decided to make a call at the house. When one of Mrs B's daughters answered the door she recognised me immediately and took me in to see her mother who said, 'You have to remember, Ron, that in those days we did not have washing machines'.

"So seeing me must have pricked her conscience. I did not feel that I could say anything to her because I am 6ft 2in and weigh 16 stone; she was about 80 years old, 4ft 10in and about six stone. I must say, though, I still feel angry about it all."

Chapter Twenty-two
A lucky escape

Exerting control over children by using blackmail and threats in order to elicit compliance was common. The evacuee would be so fearful of the consequences of what was being threatened he or she was obedient. They were often subjected to a constant drip, drip, drip of abuse and criticism. This form of psychological abuse was overwhelmingly carried out by women, whereas physical and sexual abuse was carried out by men, though not always. But women could be fierce hitters too.

Psychological abuse tends to be unrecognised by society at large because of its complex definition and subtle, multi-faceted expression. It also leaves no visible marks. This is often why children fail to alert the outside world but at the time of the Second World War, even when children did tell adults what they were going through, they were not believed, as Barbara Charlton of Waterlooville, Hants, confirms in her recollections.

Holding onto a sense of reality and retaining any sense of self-worth can be extraordinarily difficult when faced with extreme psychological maltreatment. Children who experience such ill-treatment often grow up with a sense of inferiority and low self-esteem which, thankfully, was not the outcome in Barbara's case. Such abuse can also make children angry and serve to motivate an abused child to seek ways of rescuing her or himself from the abusive situation, which is exactly what some of the evacuees in this chapter did.

Barbara celebrated her golden wedding last year yet, even at the age of 72, and after a full life, she says, "My memories of the time I spent in one particular billet are still vivid. They tormented me, and I'll never forget the humiliation, accusing me of trouble-making. Eventually I ran away and - it must be the homing instinct because there were no sign posts on any of the roads, they had all been taken down - I managed to find my way.

"We all shot off together to be evacuated and I had two billets first that didn't work out. One was with a young couple who didn't know how to cope with a youngster my age. The next one went bad because I caught head lice so my mother would not let me go back.

"At the age of fourteen I was allocated a new billet in Salisbury - I was at the Southern Secondary School for Girls, Portsmouth - which I was to share with a classmate, Katie. I had no choice in the matter. My form mistress took me to the house and I was introduced to a Mr and Mrs Meech, their two children, John and Anne, who were ten and eight years old. Mrs Meech's father also lived with them; we were told to call him Granddad. I was welcomed in and Katie showed me to the bedroom with its double bed which I was to share with her. She helped me to unpack and put away my belongings and then we went downstairs for a meal.

"I felt strange and shy but everyone appeared to be friendly and I soon forgot my shyness. The following day I was alone in the room with Mrs Meech and Granddad and she said to me, 'I have some chocolate here for you and, Barbara, and there will be more treats if you are good.' I thanked her, thinking how kind she was and then went out into the garden and said to Katie, 'Have you eaten your chocolate Katie?' She said, 'What chocolate? I haven't got any.'

"Suddenly, I realised that it was only me who had received it. I couldn't understand this favouritism as, being one of four siblings, at home we were always used to sharing everything.

"It didn't take me long to find out what type of woman Mrs Meech was. Within a week I was suddenly out of favour and Katie could do no wrong. Everything I said or did in school and outside was reported back to Mrs Meech. I couldn't even write a letter home without Katie sidling up to me to read what I was writing and if I covered up my letter to hide it from her she would call out, 'Mrs Meech, she's covering up her letter. I wonder what she's writing?' On those occasions Mrs Meech would come into the room and snatch the letter from me and read it. Even when I tried to write a letter in class it was reported back and I was accused of writing things I shouldn't.

"As I shared a bed with Katie I noticed that she was continually scratching which eventually transferred to me as well. When I went home for my Easter holiday my mother was appalled at the state of my skin and took me to see a doctor who diagnosed scabies. I was not allowed to return to school until it was cleared up. Meanwhile, my mother wrote to my head mistress and it was consequently checked out at my billet.

"On my return I was in for it. Mrs Meech said they had all been examined which had caused embarrassment and denied that any of them had had scabies and I was accused of lying and causing trouble. I wrote to my mother as I was upset and she wrote a nasty letter to Mrs Meech and my head mistress and a teacher was sent to see Mrs Meech.

"What she told this teacher I never knew but I was summoned to see the head on my return to school and severely reprimanded for telling lies and causing trouble. She wouldn't listen to me and I went back to the classroom in tears which again was reported back.

"We were expected to help with the housework and my job was to polish the bedroom floors each day. Most days I only buffed them up but on this particular day I thought I had better do the job properly or it might be discovered that I hadn't done any proper polishing. I was upstairs for longer than usual. 'Why have you been so long today?' I was asked on going downstairs. "I've been polishing all the time," I answered. 'Most probably she's been turning out the drawers,' Katie piped in spitefully, which prompted the dragon to accuse me of being nosey. She reprimanded me for delving through other people's belongings which I hadn't and strongly denied, only to be accused of lying, once again.

"Katie and I had to look after John and Anne when the Meeches went out at night. Almost as soon as they were gone Katie and the children would gang up on me until I retaliated, which was reported to Mrs Meech on her return so she had an excuse to deliver the usual tirade. This constant treatment went on for several months, always in the same vein.

"One evening I felt I could stand it no longer. Suddenly I felt very calm and knew what I had to do. I looked at everyone and said, 'I'm going to bed now.' 'Best thing you can do and get out of our way' was the response from Mrs Meech. I was awake at six o'clock the following morning and as I crept out of bed Katie stirred and I said to her, 'I'm just going to the toilet Katie'. Fortunately she believed me and went back to sleep. I knew I would never achieve my aim if she woke up properly.

"I picked up my clothes and crept downstairs, then dressed over my pyjamas. I cut two slices of bread from the loaf on the table in case I felt hungry on the way, then had the major feat to perform - of unlocking the back door silently. It was beneath the Meech's bedroom.

"On entering the garden I grabbed my bicycle, opened the noisy back gate without being apprehended and reached the street. I had to walk for about the first mile as I had a flat tyre. I eventually met a paper boy who pumped up both tyres for me and I was on my way.

"I pedalled furiously and every time I heard a car behind me I thought it was our gym mistress chasing me. Once I was on the Portsmouth Road, after reaching Southampton and crossing the ferry, I felt safe.

"After six hours of pedalling I arrived home, much to my mother's amazement when she heard me at the back gate. After a meal my mother wanted to hear the whole story and I don't think she had ever realised how bad it had been for me. Whenever I managed to write a letter to her I think she thought I was exaggerating and only now did she comprehend the mental abuse I had had to tolerate in that billet.

"She sent a telegram to my head mistress to let her know I was safe and then followed that up with a letter. I saw Katie afterwards and she said to me 'Why didn't you wake me up?' Apparently she had trouble after I left. But if I had, I know I would never have escaped."

The reason many evacuees are not more traumatised by their experience is that the abuse was not committed by their parents, but by strangers whom it was easy for them to hate; a healthy reaction. Also, most eventually went home to loving mothers and fathers and although few ever talked about what had happened to them, they put it behind them, leaving it locked inside their minds until now. For yet others, the abuse did not last long enough to damage them to the extent of inflicting on them personality complexes.

Yet short-lived and relatively painless though some of their experiences were, they were nevertheless traumatic at the time and still live on as memories that hurt. Iris Bruns was subjected to the sort of deprivations, locked away in a room with only bread and water to eat and no comforts in the form of toys, that are commonly associated with prisoners.

Iris is 66 now but she still remembers the injustice meted out to her 59 years ago by the woman who was in charge of St Ruan Manor,

Helston, where she was evacuated with her older brother Ivor, and some other children. "I was put to sleep with a little girl of about three years old and one night she wet the bed and I got the blame for it," Iris says.

"The Scottish lady in charge, I don't remember her name, told her housekeeper to put me on bread and water for a week. But this kind lady whose name was Mrs Freshwater - funny how you remember people who are kind to you - would feed me when the other woman was out."

Iris, from Hartcliffe, Bristol, was seven years old when she had a label tied to her coat and was put on a train for Cornwall. "I don't remember anything about the journey but when we arrived those of us who weren't well off were supplied with coats and shoes and the only things left when it came to my turn was a pair of wellingtons. I can still remember the marks on my legs from wearing those wellingtons all the time."

She and the other children tried to rescue themselves by running away from St Ruan's but were stopped by a man in a car. "We thought he was going to help us but instead he took us back there. We were then sent to another place in Redruth that was just as bad. As soon as we came home from school we were fed and put to bed with the blackout blinds down so we couldn't see the daylight. Then one day my Mum came to visit and found the toilet in a filthy state so she took us home.

"She even took another girl home who lived in our street. She didn't have enough money for all the train fares so she negotiated with the train company to pay them back so much a week. I have been back to see the house but it is in disrepair. I suppose I wanted to lay the ghost.

"What happened to me might not be so bad compared with what happened to other kids but I will never forget it and I often wonder what happened to the children who tried to run away with us.'

One former evacuee wrote to tell me I should not write this book, that what happened happened and that we should not rake up past memories. There are also people who accuse some adults of "false memory syndrome", in other words, what they remember about events in their childhood did not actually happen. Both suggestions are nonsense. The first because, as I stated earlier, it is about time evacuees who were treated badly had their say about the war, and the second because these memories are not the product of someone's imagination, nor were they planted there by over-zealous therapists. It is an insult to even suggest such a possibility. When you have first-hand evidence such as these, they resonate with the truth of genuine childhood memories.

Vivienne Stamp, who now lives with her brother George in south east London, was six years and two months old - she remembers almost to the day how old she was - when she was evacuated to Bell's Farm, St Neots, Cambridgeshire, with her sister, Gracie, who was just four years old.

"I was a happy-go-lucky child before being evacuated but the cruelty I was subjected to made me withdrawn and quiet," she says. "No child should be subjected to that. The man there was a sadist and seemed to take an instant dislike to me. He used to beat me with a bridle until I was black and blue from my neck downwards. He also had water tanks to catch the rain water and he used to grip me by the neck and half drown me in the water. That left scars on my neck I can still feel to this day.

"The woman my brother was billeted with must have been worried about me because I can remember being asked to lift up my gym slip to show her my bruises. She wrote to my mother, 'Come and take your little girls away from that farm', and my mother came for us soon after that. She told me afterwards she saw this little mite walking towards her and didn't realise it was me. I was so starved and downtrodden with the beatings she didn't recognise her own daughter. If that neighbour had not told her what was going on, I doubt I would have been alive today."

Two sisters, Joan and Peggy Waite, were rescued by their father although you wonder how on earth two children could have been evacuated to this basement flat in the first place. "We were evacuated from Brixton, south London, to Brighton," says Joan. "I was ten years of age and my sister three years younger. My dad saw us off as mum was too upset and had our one-year-old sister at home. Dad's final words on that awful day were 'hold Peggy's hand all the time and go nowhere without her'.

"Nobody seemed to want two girls but eventually we were taken to a basement flat near the seafront and handed over to a couple of spinster sisters and their bachelor brother.

"The place was dark and dirty and we were put in a small room with a single bed. All our belongings were taken from us, including the rations we had been given and we were starving that night having had just a drink of lemonade since we left London.

"Next morning, there was a lot of shouting and we found the three fighting and throwing things at each other. We dressed and someone called to take us to 'school' which, after a very long trek, we went to for only half a day.

"We had some bread and jam when we returned and were absolutely starving. My sister kept crying and I tried hard not to as I had to be 'grown up' being the older one. I asked for paper to write home as our parents didn't know where we were for a few days and to tell them we were hungry, cold and very unhappy, frightened children.

"One of the spinsters, however, dictated what I was to say. On the first Sunday morning there, we were taken to church and the first hymn was 'Bread of Heaven'. My sister started sobbing, looking up at the ceiling. 'I wish some bread would fall down on us Joanie she said.

"There were two happy incidents that I recall: when a woman heard us crying she opened the front window of her house and gave us some carrots, and another time when a girl's guardian gave us a halfpenny each to buy an apple. We ate them so slowly 'to make them last forever' as my little sister remarked.

"We had been in this awful place six weeks and had become thin, ill, we had head lice, and nobody cared at all. Then, one day, we heard my father's voice shouting at the front door. One of the women had just dragged us to the table for dinner and when my dad stormed in and saw the state we were in, he went berserk.

"There was one sardine and a small piece of potato on our plates and dad threw these 'dinners' into the backyard for the birds, grabbed our hands and literally ran to a café where we had mugs of tea and huge slices of bread pudding. As we approached our home, we could smell lamb stew and dumplings cooking ready for us. My favourite meal to this day.

"My parents had a feeling something was wrong when they got 'my' letters without a stamp and not in my handwriting. They sent us money (sixpence each a week) and it wasn't mentioned. It had been taken, of course.

"It was horrific and, all these years later, I still feel the pain as did my sister who, unfortunately, died seven years ago. I believe people who took in evacuees received a certificate from the King and Queen.

"I didn't know about this until recently when an old lady showed me hers. She had taken in three evacuees and, quite openly, told me she did it purely for the money. One child was only four and started wetting the bed. This woman's husband said 'we're not wasting the money on soap to wash a sheet out every morning, she'll have to do it herself'.

"This woman didn't seem to understand that the little girl was fretting and, as she told me, they 'got rid of her'. I was so upset and cross I told her in no uncertain terms what I thought of her. I wonder how many others received those certificates?"

What evacuation did for many children, incredibly young as they were, was make them spectacularly resilient and resourceful. If they were not going to be rescued by the authorities, and time and time again appeals to them proved fruitless, then, by hook or by crook, they were going to get themselves out of the dreadful situation.

Tommy Thompson of Wallasey, Merseyside, was six when he was evacuated to Anglesey, north Wales. "It was a February morning in 1940. My school, St Pauls, and Daisy Street School had to meet at Sandhills Station at 10am. Neither my mother nor any of my family were there to see me off. As a six-year-old, you can imagine how traumatic it must have been. Like most evacuees, I will never forget that day," he says.

"On the station there were tables with cups of cocoa and a bunloaf but I didn't have any money. As I was boarding the train, my friend asked me if I'd had any cake and cocoa. I said I had no money. He said, 'Oh, it's free.' I ran back but a teacher stopped me and pushed me onto the train.

"It seemed a long journey and I was travel sick. We arrived at about 2.30pm and were all ushered into a school hall. There was food and drinks laid out on tables. As you can imagine, I was even hungrier by then. There were lots of people, all looking at us. A teacher took my hand and another boy and led us over to a lady who tried to pull us out and we started crying because we didn't want to go. All the children were crying, especially the girls who were screaming.

"I arrived at the lady's house, it was a little cottage with two bedrooms. She was 24 years old, married to a man of 65. My little friend was called Freddie Sloan who I've never seen since. Some evacuees went to nice homes but the majority didn't do so well. My experience of the Welsh people was that they were very mean to us. The lady I lived with didn't feed us very well and every weekend she would go off to Rhyl with her husband and stay on a farm with his sons, leaving us on our own with no food. We used to dig up raw potatoes and eat them.

"I tried to run away but was brought back. Then one day the lady I was staying with wanted to see Liverpool so she took me with her and I made sure, when it was time to go back with her, I hid in the docks area. She couldn't find me so she had to go back alone.

"Twenty years after the war she wrote to me and asked could she come and meet me. I refused because of the bad memories I still have of her and that place. I have been back in the last five years with my wife to show her where I was living. It is now derelict and as I looked at it, I realised how unhappy I had been there.

"So many children went through the same and sometimes worse. The evacuation took our childhood away."

Anne Wheeler, 64, of New Malden, Surrey, was shunted backwards and forwards for most of the war. Evacuated here, returned home, evacuated there, returned home. Hers is a forlorn tale of good billets and bad billets, of loneliness and despair interspersed with short periods of life at home. Lately her daughter advised Anne to write about her experiences as an evacuee. "She said if I wrote it all down I would finally get it out of my system and that is just what happened," says Anne. "After I wrote it all out I couldn't look at the final paper for six months. Then I found that going through it all again was therapeutic.

"For the first five years of my life I led a very sheltered existence. Being a sensitive child, I cried a great deal, but rarely heard my mother raise her voice in anger. My father, ten years older than my mother, doted on me.

"Seven days before my fifth birthday, Adolf Hitler and his Nazi Stormtroopers marched into Poland and the Second World War began. "Reluctantly, when the bombs started dropping on Camberwell, south-east London, where we were living at the time, my mother arranged that I should be evacuated to the country for my own safety.

"I believe my father was becoming ill at that time with the first of several nervous breakdowns, due in some part to the stress he had endured during the First World War. He joined the Army as a young man and his regiment had almost immediately been captured by the enemy. He then spent the whole of the four-year war in a German prisoner of war camp, living mostly on potato peelings.

"Sometimes, he became maudlin and recalled his own mother who had died while he was a prisoner of war. What upset him most of all was the fact that, as a careless young man, he had sauntered off to war saying 'Cheerio' in an offhand manner, without even kissing his mother goodbye and he never saw her again.

"My first recollection of being evacuated was with a family called Pronger. The husband was a soldier and away in the war. his wife was trying to cope on her own with several young children who seemed to me to be all my age or younger. She was taking in evacuees for extra money to help with her large young family. As I was only five years old at the time, my main recollection during my short stay with this family is of being constantly hungry and sitting round the table with all the other children waiting for this small portion of porridge, made with water and no sugar; there did not seem to be anything else to eat.

"I could not have been with that family for more than a few weeks before my mother came to take me home. She must have had to find another billet for me almost immediately and my next recollection of evacuation was with a Mrs Brockhurst whose husband was also away in the war. She lived in Pease Pottage, near Crawley, Sussex, and had children of her own, a boy and a girl, both slightly older than myself. I was now about five and a half years old and to me she seemed to be the exact opposite of my mother. She had a piercing gaze, glasses and sharp features.

"Mrs Brockhurst had no patience with a timid child who was forever weeping and I just could do nothing to please her. After I had been living with the family for a few weeks, she began whipping me across the tops of my bare legs with a switch, mostly because it annoyed her so much that I cried every time she shouted at me, for not eating my food, for walking too slowly, for not swinging my arms as I walked, just about everything about me made her cross.

"I remember writing letters to my mother asking her to come and take me home. However, unbeknown to me, my father had become ill again with yet another nervous breakdown and my mother was working all hours under the sun to keep our home together. Mrs Brockhurst read the letters I had written to mother and threatened to 'put my head in the copper', the huge pan used in those days to boil dirty clothes.

"I endured the misery for a while longer but I was so terrified of Mrs Brockhurst that I began to wet myself. This made her even more furious and she would often degrade me when talking to a neighbour about me, by suddenly grabbing me by the crotch of my knickers and showing a neighbour where they were wet. I can't recall how many miserable months I spent with that family. Time and time again I counted the rows and rows of brick-red chimney pots that could be seen through the attic bedroom window, trying not to sob in case Mrs Brockhurst could hear me. It seemed like an eternity until the day when my mother came and rescued me.

CHAPTER TWENTY-TWO

"By this time she had moved to Madora Road, Brixton. My nerves were in a bad state and the weals on the top part of my legs were still red and angry. I believe my mother was advised to take me to a doctor and to take Mrs Brockhurst to court for ill-treatment of an evacuee. However, the thought of having to see her again filled me with such terror my mother thought it best to let me get over my ordeal gradually with lots of love and kindness that only she could give me.

"Sometime during this period we moved again. The lady downstairs 'Aunt Lil' was married to a tailor who worked from home. They had a baby boy, Brian, who was only a few weeks old. By this time I must have been around seven Other than getting nits my memory of school life at that time was keeping a library book about a frog. I think the story of this poor frog was so similar to my life of misery with Mrs Brockhurst that I wanted to hang onto the book.

"During 1941 the bombs were dropping almost all day and all night and we spent most nights sleeping in the Anderson shelter. Aunt Lil and my mother discussed my evacuation - again. Aunt Lil suggested that I stay with her brother, in High Wycombe, Buckinghamshire.

"He was lodging with a Spanish lady, and her five children. So began another year or so of my evacuation story. However, this was a happy time. She was a kindly lady who wore a fold-over apron. Much later I discovered my father had asked them to treat me as one of the family because he was worried about my timidity and tendency for tears. He thought that being part of a large family would help me to gain trust and confidence. I have vague and happy memories of that evacuation, a feeling of being free and happy. But it was not to last.

"Around my eighth birthday my father came to take me home because he missed me so much. The Spanish lady cried because she was genuinely fond of me and didn't want me to go home. I was old enough to realise there was something wrong with my father and was secretly a little scared of him. He doted on me and was always buying me presents but he always seemed to be ill and when he was unwell he used to say peculiar things and I was forever asking my mother, 'Is Dad alright?'

"By now we had moved again to a Victorian house that had two large cellars leading off from the kitchen in the basement. In the upstairs part of the house lived a Mrs Dibdon with her two sons, Reggie and Freddie. Reggie was thin and wriggly and Freddie was fat and the elder by about a year or so. His nickname became Fatty Arbuckle which made him unhappy. In one of the cellars was a corrugated iron air raid shelter and the next year or so of my life was to be spent sleeping there with Reggie and Freddie.

"The four bunks were tiered and narrow. Freddie, Reggie and I had a bunk each with one of the lower bunks left for the grown ups to sit on and drink tea together while we three tried to sleep during the air raids. Suddenly, I had to make a choice of where I would like to be evacuated. Again.

"Aunt Lil wanted me to go with her and Brian, who was now walking and talking, to Wales but Mrs Dibdon enticed me to go to Glasgow with her boys. She made it sound wonderful and exciting...I can remember the scared, unhappy feeling on the train journey to Glasgow. My mother was working so could not come with us. Mrs Dibdon was forever fussing over Reggie. Freddie and I were told to sit on the cases in the corridor.

"This 'wonderful place' was a flat in a dismal block in the Gorbals. I would be sleeping with this big girl in a cupboard in the wall. We slept on a mattress and most of the time she hogged all the covers and left me shivering. When we first arrived at this so-called "wonderful place" I remember gazing from the window and looking down onto the shelters, my eyes filling with tears. I wanted to go home but Reggie, Freddie and I were to stay with the Holts for the next three months. In fact, just after we left, Glasgow was heavily bombed so it was no safer than London. A regular game for us was jumping the dykes. The shelters were in rows and each one stood about ten feet high and about 12 feet long. The gap, dyke, between each shelter was about three feet and often a girl or boy would fall through the gap with horrendous results."

Anne's tale of being shunted from one billet to another, some OK, some dismal, ended when she was rescued for the final time: by Hitler. When he surrendered.

Chapter Twenty-three
An indomitable soul

Some evacuees had a terrible life before they were sent away - and afterwards - so it is impossible to blame everything that happened to them later on the war years. Peggy Taylor, whose story is in the Boot Camps chapter, is one and Christine Morris of Hemel Hempstead is another. In Peggy's case her evacuation to a camp was the making of her. For Christine, who eventually went to seven different billets, the evacuation added to her many woes. Her last billet could have given her life a happy-ever-after twist but sadly her mother, who had her own problems, stepped in and, instead of the fairytale that could have been, Christine was condemned to inhabit the real world, the one she had the misfortune to be born into.

Hers is an incredible story which she tells with honesty and humour, her indomitable spirit keeping her head bobbing above the swell of bad luck that would have drowned most people long ago. She calls to mind George Bernard Shaw's comment on his mother, "Misfortunes that would have crushed ten untrained women, broke on her like waves on granite."

Christine has a remarkable memory and in spite of crippling arthritis in her hands, managed to write her story in great detail. One of her letters to me covered 19 A4-size sheets of paper.

"I was born on Christmas Eve, 1927 and I have many long and unhappy memories of my childhood before being evacuated in October 1939 and ever since..." she says. "My mother drank, my father knocked her about – to 'knock' some sense into her. I was neglected while he was at work, and they had two legal separations so I was deprived of my Dad for extended periods. We moved in with my Mum's parents but Grandma died in 1931 so I lost out again. Grandad did his best for us until he was compulsorily sacked at the age of nearly 70 in September 1938. I think his age became apparent during a merger and after £8 weekly and a monthly bonus, he was reduced to the ten shillings weekly pension.

"Mum had to go out to work to make money for booze, consequently her rages were terrible and so was our poverty. I was not allowed to take up either of the two scholarships I won. I guess I cried a lot. With my upbringing I was described as highly-strung and then I was fretting and melancholy. My mother got me a week's holiday at the Sunday School Convalescent Home near Bournemouth a week before the war broke out but I was frantic being so far from home. While a nurse wasn't looking, I peeled off the stamp from a postcard and stuck it onto a new one and wrote to plead with my Mum to let me go home. Somehow I got it into a postbox without being seen and it must have reached her because I was put on a train to Waterloo.

"That was on September 9, 1939. However, soon afterwards my mother soon informed me I was being evacuated and I think I cried for the rest of that month and the next but I was made to go. No billets were really available, I was a nuisance as I had missed the general evacuation that happened on the 3rd but somehow I was sent to Farncombe, near Guildford, Surrey.

"My first billet lasted for two weeks with a Mr and Mrs Elliot whom I adored. It was bliss, they gave me lots of tender loving care but their daughter, who was 21, did not want to share her bedroom with me, she had recently lost her fiancé in a motor cycle accident and I was having noisy nightmares which upset her even more.

"My second billet lasted three or four weeks and I was not wanted. There was a funny iron bed about two feet wide which I had to share with their two daughters. We only had one thin sheet and one thin blanket and it was getting cold by then. At my third billet which I went to just before Christmas in 1939 we lived on threepenny 'pieces' from the butcher. I think they just wanted the 10s 6d they received from the Government for taking me in, they didn't want me. I got ill there with an abscess on one of my front teeth which was taken out by the school dentist and I had a gap there until I was 17 or 18.

"Mum sent me the return fare so I could go home for the Christmas holidays - and so I could do her housework. We visited relatives who told me they had sent presents and money to me but when I returned the presents were undone and given to the two daughters of the house and the money was gone.

"My fourth billet was a two-up-two-down house where they already had two other youngsters with their mother and their father who came for weekends during the Blitz. I slept in a chair and caught head lice from one of the older children and so was moved on. Also, I needed a bed.

"My fifth billet was with an old couple who were not married. When I went home on holiday once I received a letter accusing me of stealing her silver and a brooch which I did not. I have
never, ever been a thief. But it stuck, and I was moved again.

"By the time I reached my sixth billet I was getting older and bathing in front of the kitchen fire with the father watching (why was he watching? I have no idea...) was embarrassing and I was moved again and so my evacuation nightmare continued. My seventh billet was with a Mr and Mrs Woods, who had lost their son, Michael, at the age of five from pneumonia. They also adopted a baby of eight months called Jennifer who was a war orphan.

"This was the happiest billet, I had my own bedroom and they encouraged me to go to evening school at 14. I was there for 15 months. Suddenly, the atmosphere changed and I did not understand why until much later.

"My mother insisted I go home to go out to work and earn money in an office. Eventually she told me the couple had written to her to ask if they could adopt me. That would have drawn my mother's fire and rage and they received a rotten letter back which I suppose is when I sensed the change in the atmosphere. I was my mother's possession and no one was getting their hands on me.

"I was upset when she told me about the adoption proposal but I had no one to talk to about it. I kept my hurt inside.

"All of this has not helped in relationships and friendships yet somehow I stayed married for 39 years until my husband died of cancer. He constantly berated me, calling me 'stupid', until one day I finally flipped. He looked astounded and said he didn't mean it like that, to which I replied 'Don't tell me – it's a form of endearment...'

"I don't think he ever called me stupid again, he just sent me to Coventry, in bed also. I don't think my three sons would have been aware of anything untoward in our marriage, and I know deep down I did the best I could bringing them up.

"As a child and a teenager I was always frightened, putting on a brave front, but all the time mainly being a doormat, a dogsbody, always eager to please. I have all sorts of health problems, including depression which dogs me. After my husband died I went to college and passed exams in maths, English and French. I also studied creative writing, poetry and the guitar but unfortunately have had to stop everything because of my severe arthritis.

"Most of my evacuation was sheer unhappiness and getting home to earn what I could was the beginning of years of more unhappiness. It was inhuman to part us, well, most of us, from our families but I am surviving, I always have. And I somehow have a great sense of humour and cheer other folks up. Who knows what sort of life I might have had if I had not been shunted around like that? Or if I had stayed with one of the good families?”

Chapter Twenty-four
Where's my teddy?

Although the slight reprimand Helen Codd received for not knowing the place in a book her class was reading does not even register on the scale of abuse recounted in this book, what she and many other evacuees suffered during the war when they were banished from their home and parents is years of emotional neglect. Uprooted from family life, their existence was without warmth, without cuddles, without any of the security and comforts of home which children should be able to take for granted and need for their wellbeing.

Left in a limbo of uncertainty and rejection, their feelings of loneliness were sometimes compounded by spiteful relatives or carers who seemed to relish their power to inflict even more psychological pain. It is unbelievably unkind but true that some children - like Helen - who were evacuated were frequently told "Your mother doesn't want you" or even "Your mother is dead." Because these children were away from home they had no way of knowing whether what was being said to them was true or not. Letters, birthday cards and Christmas cards were intercepted so Helen never knew as she grew up if any had been sent.

Helen suffered from extremely bad allergic asthma when she was a child and, when she was eight years old, was evacuated, on April 10, 1942, to a convalescent home in Bournemouth called the House Beautiful, something of a misnomer. It was owned and run by a

Methodist organisation, The Sunday School Union. Helen has a photograph, taken on her second birthday, of herself with a huge teddy bear.

"When I arrived there I had my big teddy with me," she says now, nearly three score years later and still wistful. "It was put on the piano in the playroom and I was not allowed to touch it. Eventually it disappeared and I never saw it again. The more I see and hear about child abuse, the more I realise how cruel they were in this home."

Helen's father was in the RAF and her mother carried on his garage business but then she met someone else and divorced Helen's father before the war ended. "My sister Anna, who was evacuated to the same place, and I occasionally saw our grandparents at weekends when we went to his hotel for lunch before Sunday school in the afternoon. We had to write letters home every Sunday and were made to start them with the words, 'I am well and happy'. One day I wrote 'I am unhappy' under the tissue lining of an envelope and sent it to my mother but she didn't see it.

"I found out a long time after the war that my mother used to come down to see us but the matron always told my grandparents and we were taken away for the day with gran and grandpa. Because of the divorce they wanted to cut her off and did everything they could to keep her away from us.

"Apparently, sometimes our mother watched us play from the bushes as she was stopped from seeing us. The matron told me once that my mother was no good and I should forget her. Eventually, grandpa said she had been killed in the bombing in London. I didn't find out until I was grown up that this was a lie and that my mother was still alive.

"My sister Anna, who suffered from infected ears, came to the home a few months after me. Children usually only came for a few weeks, a lot of them from London, but the matron was a friend of my grandparents and took Anna and I on an indefinite basis. She also took a brother and sister, Patrick and Maureen Connolly long term. The four of us used to go to St Paul's School where Asda is now, next to the railway station.

"It was a good school and I learnt a great deal there but one day the children were taking it in turns to read the book *What Katie Did*. I was reading further on than I should have been so when it came to my turn I didn't know the place in the book so I was rapped on the knuckles with a ruler for being naughty. That was the only time I ever suffered corporal punishment.

"The home was run on strictly Christian lines. I was in a dormitory with about 12 beds and the window was so high up, looking over the back of the hotel next door, that we had to stand on the back of our beds to see out. The matron had a parrot in a cage which used to sing songs it heard the children sing. It used to squawk 'I will make you fishers of men'. The parrot seemed to get much better treatment than all of the children put together and seemed to have better food and I hated it very much. My diaries usually say that matron was even nastier when grandpa was away.

"There was a monkey puzzle tree in the garden and a sun house where children would sit out in warm weather. Anna was made to sit out on the grounds the sunshine would help to cure the infection. We all sat in the sun a lot, it's a wonder we don't have skin cancer.

"Children were bathed together and if you were naughty, you had to sit outside matron's room on a wooden bench in the cold, sometimes until 10pm. At that time, all children were woken up to go on the potty which was placed in the middle of the room. If you were one of the last on the potty, it was so full that your bottom would get wet with cold urine and it would spill out on the floor.

"I don't remember much about the war for we were never informed of any news but I do remember the only bomb I heard. In the home there were Morrison shelters for the boys in the dining room and shelters for the girls in the playroom at the other end of the building. Morrison shelters were like metal boxes with mesh wire round the sides.

"On Sunday lunchtime on May 23, 1943, when we were having lunch in the dining room, I know this because I kept a diary, we heard the whistle of a bomb coming down. We were so well-trained to be apart from the boys that the boys all went into their shelters in the playroom and we scuttled off to ours. Had we received a direct hit, the boys may have survived but the girls would have been killed. The shelters had no blankets in them so on the few other occasions when we went into them due to air raids, they were not at all comfortable especially for children who were convalescing.

"One day American soldiers appeared with their vehicles and as we walked to and from school each day they talked to us and gave us sweets, the sort we did not get at that time. There was severe rationing and the only sweets I remember were Fry's creams which I never ate again after the war.

"We used to go out walking two by two. A favourite place was Boscombe Gardens and halfway down was a pool called Giant's Foot. It has now been filled in and is a garden. The sea front was blocked with barbed wire and we never went on the beach at all for the whole of the war. There were also other places we went to and the main occupation I remember seemed to be climbing trees. The fir trees were great for climbing as you could be lost on your own up in the branches. Once I got a piece of barbed wire stuck in my leg and my terrible screaming brought everyone out from their homes and someone tried to get the wire out. It was stuck so I had to hobble back to the Home with it sticking out of my leg. The matron was cross and stuck my leg in a bucket of hot water and just yanked it out. It was incredibly painful and I still have a scar. I was not sent to hospital for a tetanus injection, they were not freely given in those days.

"Christmas was the only enjoyable time at the Home. The superintendent of the National Sunday School Union would come down. We usually did a pantomime. One year we did a play with one of the boys pretending to be an uncle to three girls, of which I was one. We were supposed to kiss him goodbye and I absolutely refused to kiss him. We were so indoctrinated into not going near boys that I could not bring myself to kiss him even though it was only acting.

"The nurses used to bring the stockings to the beds before they went to bed at night and one Christmas I was awake and had the most lovely doll with curly hair like Shirley Temple. I opened the stocking before I went to sleep so had nothing exciting to look at next morning.

"I once caught chicken pox and to prevent infection spreading in the Home, matron asked grandpa to have me at the hotel. I was put in a room which is above the stained glass window on the right of the main front door. I seemed to be in there for weeks and weeks. No one wanted to come in in case they caught chickenpox and my food was placed just inside the door for me. I was very bored so did an embroidery of a cloth that had a pattern of spots on it...

"I also made butter. The top of the milk was sent up in a glass jar and I tied a piece of string round the top, then tie it to the edge of the bed springs and, reading a book with one hand, pulled the string with the other to shake the bottle. Eventually butter appeared on the top of the liquid and I had this on bread and it was the best butter I have ever tasted.

"The boys' bedrooms were on the second floor and the girls were not allowed to go up there. The nurses were not at all kind, I can't remember a nice one. When we were in the playroom, we had to learn short religious songs such as *I Am Saved* or *I Am Happy* etc and one day a friend and I counted up how many we knew and it came to more than a hundred. Every week we had to learn some verses from the Bible and on Sunday each child had to stand up and recite what had been learned.

"I was still suffering from asthma a great deal and was often in bed. We had our belongings in big baskets under our beds, not in drawers. When I was ill I was not allowed to read or do anything but had to just lie there and get better. I hated this as it nearly sent me mad not doing anything to take my mind off the asthma attack so I got the other children to smuggle books to me.

"I used to be reading then hear a nurse coming, her shoes making a noise on the lino as she approached, so then I put the book in my basket but she inevitably heard the basket being slid under the bed so found the book and confiscated it. Sometimes I moulded pieces of bread into letters or took threads from the blanket and played games. To this day I always take something to do or read whenever I go out anywhere; I cannot sit for a moment without having something to do.

"The treatment for asthma included adrenaline and ephedrine tablets. There was also some powder called Potters' Asthma Cure which would be ignited and the smoke had to be inhaled. One day a girl came from Birmingham with some injections for her to have for asthma so my doctor decided to try them out on me. became seriously ill and had a strange experience. I felt I was going up a hill towards a bright light and over the top but then turned and came down and this coincided with getting better.

"The matron and deputy matron used to take it in turns to sit by my bed so I must have been quite ill. I once slept in the matron's bedroom and was, for the first time, allowed to read a book without fear of a reprimand. I remember crying my eyes out: It was *Uncle Tom's Cabin*.

"Because of the total unhappiness at the Home, I used to

sleep-walk and one night found myself over the other side of the dormitory with my hands over another girl's eyes. She was screaming so much matron came in and was, needless to say, not understanding but very cross."

After the war Helen and her sister lived in the hotel with her grandparents. "You never knew where your bedroom was because always it had to be guests first," she remembers. She was still asthmatic and could not go upstairs easily or play games. She was sent to boarding school where she remembers being teased because she was so modest, always having a bath wearing her vest, not wearing shorts because her grandparents did not approve of them. There was some normality, though, when she went to Devon to spend the summer holidays with her father.

"It was glorious and I have many happy memories of those holidays," she says. "He was normal, he drank, smoked, laughed. When he died in '63 I could not bear to go back until recently. I was tearful, on my own in the churchyard, but then I went to the local pub and people remembered him and that was nice."

From the age of eight until she was 18, Helen did not see her mother and when she did, they never regained a proper mother-daughter relationship. Helen was going to London for an interview at a secretarial college when she got in touch with her mother again. She was living with Walter, her second husband, in a tied cottage at Lambeth Palace where he was a gardener.

"They had two children, a boy and girl aged four and five. I began to stay with them occasionally but then they moved on to another tied cottage. When my grandfather retired he decided to forgive my mother and wanted her back in his life in his old age so he bought her a house in Bournemouth. Eventually my mother moved into the family home and when she died she left everything to my half-sister (her son died of a brain tumour when he was 19). Anna and I and our children were not even mentioned in her will. It hurts, not because of the money, but because I feel as if I never existed in her mind."

When evacuees talk about their past they often speak with the voice of the child they once were, not as adults. It is sad to hear them describe their childhood years, not because of the physical punishments but because of the emotional deprivation they suffered. Helen's relationship with her mother was disrupted because of the war and made worse by the attitude to divorce of her grandparents. And then, after being reunited in adulthood with her mother, to be cast adrift once again by her mother's will.

Even in establishments like a convalescent home in a beautiful country house, where they looked after a mixed bag of evacuees and stray animals, the so-called carers could be cruel. Lamentably, the child care officer who did not know what was going on at Don Page's home has echoes of today's social workers whose children on the at-risk register get battered in spite of frequent home visits.

Ferne House in Wiltshire was first built in 1582. It was rebuilt and added to over the years and in 1939 Nina, Duchess of Hamilton, established an animal sanctuary there. It was to this picturesque country estate, surrounded by woods and plantations and approached by two carriage drives, that foundling Don was taken when he was three months old.

"I was born in London on March 1, 1940 and for whatever reason was given up at three months old to the local social services and duly evacuated to the Duchess of Hamilton's country estate in Wiltshire," says Don.

"She was caring for the waifs and strays of the war zones and built accommodation for the cats and dogs that suffered in the Blitz. She opened her mansion to children from all over and sometimes there were a hundred infants being looked after by nurses in uniforms supplied and paid for by someone. I remember they had tall headgear with a white flap down the back.

"The duchess was a big, scrawny old girl but she obviously had a kind heart. She had all the land in the world and also used to save horses, rescued from circuses. But like most aristocrats, she had strange ways of behaving. At bath time, if anyone opened their mouth, they would get a bar of soap stuffed into it.

"I don't remember any meals but there was a big bay window in the dining room where we used to sit and watch the birds and listen to the wood pigeons. We slept in dormitories and I can remember the nurses putting up beds of hessian sacking, a bit like deckchairs without legs, for us to sleep on in the garden in the afternoons.

"I was chief mouse catcher. Mice used to get into the pedal bins and while the nurses and girls squealed with terror, I used to put my hand in and catch them by the tail and throw them out of the window. There was a sand pit where we were allowed to play and eat sandwiches and in the garden there was a lawn with two levels where we used to play roly-poly, tumbling from one level to the other. That was great fun on a sunny day.

When the war ended there were three children left unclaimed at Ferne House. Don, Leonard Freelander and Maureen Bailey. Don was offered a home by the man who ran the estate, Mr Bill Birt, and his wife. They had two daughters who were by that time in their teens, working in the Land Army on the estate, which was a working farm. Don was under the care of Wiltshire County Council and boarded out with the Birts, no adoption could be processed as parental consent could not be obtained.

"All through my childhood I was told on the one hand my mother had died yet when I did something wrong, was threatened to be put in a boys' home as 'your mother didn't want you'. That was said by Mrs Birt, the woman I had to call 'mother'. This so confused me, begging more questions from me, such as, 'You said she was dead, so how could she not want me?' etc. Well, climbing trees, tearing trousers, doing boyish things, all used to set her off and she would call the Child Care Officer to come and have a severe talk to me.

"This went on until my adolescent years and it wasn't until I was leaving school that the truth came to the knowledge of the Care Officer. He asked me why I hadn't told him sooner, but when he used to come, they used to talk in secret before I was called in to be chastised for my so-called misdemeanour. And I was just a small boy and was so afraid of this ghastly boys' home I didn't dare say anything.

"I never had hugs or kisses or a feeling of family warmth so that today I feel embarrassed and even soppy when someone - even my wife - shows affection or wants me to hold her hand while out in public. Yet I have loads of compassion for the needy, the downtrodden, for deprived children and animals and those poor little children who lose their lives through brutality."

Chapter Twenty-five
The happiness principle

Utilitarianism is a philosophy based on the Greatest Happiness Principle which argues that an action that is considered in the best interests of the majority is the correct or moral one. It is probably the most famous ethical doctrine in the English-speaking tradition of moral philosophy, designed to explain why some actions are right and some are wrong. It was propounded in this country by two famous philosophers, John Stewart Mill and Jeremy Bentham. The Government of 1939 who decided on the evacuation of schoolchildren were obviously Mills and Bentham followers.

Many misguided people, especially those in authority, often are and on the face of it, the Greatest Happiness Principle does sound sensible. Utilitarianism does not, however, take into account the effect the happiness of the majority may have on the minority. Take slavery: that may have been perfectly acceptable for the majority at the time but it was manifestly unjust for the minority.

In the case of evacuees, it may have suited the Government, the army, the air raid protection wardens, the fire service, the police and so on to get children out of the way to what they deemed to be safe areas away from the bombing (one of the minutes of the Evacuation Committee before the war records a civil servant admitting "from the standpoint of wartime efficiency, children are a liability and not an asset").

Their motives were good in the sense they meant to make children safe from harm, although that did not always happen as, for instance, on Sunday, June 28, 1941 when the Germans bombed Weston-super-Mare where hundreds of evacuees had been sent. What utilitarianism did not allow for was the price some evacuees would have to pay for the safety of the majority: those children who were sent into an exile that was dangerous and sometimes evil.

Those innocents were sacrificed to serve the majority and ever since the war it is the majority's view of the evacuation which has held sway, they have had the loudest voice. We are well aware that no one likes to listen to whingers and I hope that is not how the people in this book have come across. All they want, as I never tire of repeating, is that their suffering should not go unacknowledged.

In this chapter there are two contrasting stories with contradictory outcomes. For one boy his evacuation experience was, at times, horrendous and yet he grew up to live a fulfilled and carefree life. For the other his evacuation experience was fairly pleasant yet the constant psychological placing of him as an inferior person and his post-evacuation depression have left him with bitter memories.

Joe Chesters has been married for 45 years and has five children who are all now married. He promised himself that his children would never suffer the brutality he did. He managed to bring up his family to be good, law-abiding citizens without lifting a finger in anger. Perversely, his feelings about what happened to him as an evacuee will give succour to all those who still believe in "Spare the rod and spoil the child". For Joe, in spite of all his memories of the woman who beat him so viciously, credits her with giving him a start in life that he would not have had without the war.

"I was evacuated at the age of five with my older brother and sister," he says. "Although we did not travel together, we arrived at a small village in north Wales midway between the towns of Wrexham and Mold, where we were all assembled in the local school hall. I was taken by a man named Mr Williams to his home and met his wife, his son, who would be about ten years of age, and his sister, who was about eight years old.

"Although I was young I could recognise love when it was offered, but also I could recognise resentment. The love and friendliness came from Mrs Williams, the resentment came from Mr Williams who was the local coal merchant, of whom I was terrified. He absolutely forbade me to play with any of the children's toys and when he bought a pony for his son he gave strict instructions 'do not let him have a ride on the pony'. Small things, maybe, but he made it quite clear that he did not like me and these hurts stay with you for life.

"I was with the Williams family for about four months when I was suddenly passed over the garden fence to live with the family next door, a Mr and Mrs Salisbury and their teenage daughter Irene. And, strange to say, the same format continued, with Mrs Salisbury and Irene friendly and caring and the husband, a coal miner and rather a small man, who made it quite clear that he did not want me in his house.

"He would not allow me to sit on any chairs. I had to sit on the floor for meals and on the rare occasions that custard was made, I never received mine in a dish, I was given the saucepan to scrape out. I had never seen plants before and when I picked the flowers from the top of his potato plants he threatened to take me to jail.

"Although I suffered no physical abuse from either family my mental state was in tatters. I never knew when to stand or when to sit. During my time there, I think it was about 18 months, this man never spoke one word to me unless it was to threaten me.

"I was finally moved to another village called Bradley, about 11 miles away. It was about three miles from Wrexham and I was placed with a lady of about 50 years of age called Miss Dodd who was the owner of a small shop. She was a strict disciplinarian and I can still hear her words thundering in my ears, 'What I say is law, not what other people say, what I say is law'.

"It was not too long before the beatings began. She had a thick leather belt that hung on the wooden clothes line above the kitchen table, apparently it was a horse's belly band and if I was a few minutes late in getting home from school I would be beaten mercilessly. If I got my socks or shoes wet I would receive the same treatment and for any small mistake the same thing. Mostly I would be beaten on the bottom and the back where my clothes would hide the marks and she appeared to be completely out of control at these times. The number of instances these beatings occurred are too many to detail.

"My young brother who joined me towards the end of the war never received the abuse I did. Although I must say that in other ways she was good to me, she taught me good values in life, to respect other people and their property, to be well-mannered and responsible. I consider myself to be a gentleman, and it is due to the upbringing I received from Miss Dodd.

"I stayed in Bradley until 1953 because my father, who was a soldier, decided he was not coming home to his family and my mother and father divorced. On a visit to my mother in 1953 – I had not seen her since 1940 – I met my future wife and I made a happy life for myself, even if it did start off badly."

There is no uniform "beatings equals sad life," "good food and fresh air equals good life" outcomes. The subtlety with which many foster parents meted out their cruelty is legion; the stoicism of the children who put up with their punishments is equally remarkable. For some, though, their vulnerability, their very youth, made it impossible for them to get over their experience without it gnawing away at a corner of their psyche for the rest of their lives.

Donald Winnicott, a child psychiatrist who devoted his career to the study of children, wrote, "Why is it that if I stand up here and say that I had a good start it sounds like boasting? All I am in fact saying is that nothing I am capable of is just me; it was either inherited, or else somebody enabled me to get to the place where I am. From my point of view, what you teach can only be implanted on what capacity is already present in the individual child, based on the early experiences and on the continuation of reliable holding in terms of the ever-widening circle of family and school and social life.

"Psychoanalysis tends to show that the basis of mental health is not only hereditary and is not only a matter of chance events; the basis of mental health is being actively laid down in the course of every infancy when the mother is good enough at her job, and in the span of every childhood that is being lived in a functioning family."

Sadly, for many evacuees, living in a functioning family when they were small was not an option. Peter Hares of Rainham, Essex, had to retire early because he had angina - and depression. "Some parts of my experience are pretty vague and other parts are crystal clear," he says. "Certainly the evacuation did affect me mentally and even today at the age of 64 I cannot be at ease in certain situations.

"The Somerset people I was evacuated with I feel let me down badly, especially after I returned home. After six years there with deep affection for some of them I thought they would feel the same for me; I waited for them to write and ask me back for visits. I received a few letters but never an offer to visit. I was upset by this and it made me feel unwanted.

"Psychologically my treatment by them left me sensitive, I was forever concerned about being rejected.

"I was evacuated with my brother Patrick, who was five years older than me, and a girl called Jean Neal. We were taken in by a Mrs Redler and her family who were the top people of the small village.

Her father had been mayor of South Molton in Devon three times running and her husband was a director of a big company and a magistrate. So, there we were, miles away from home in this seemingly grand house called the Poplars with a cobbled back yard that I often had to weed till my fingers got sore.

"Mrs Redler was a good cook but she also made some awful dishes which she forced me to eat. She was also very strict. I had to address her as Madam, almost Victorian it was. The other evacuees used to call their foster parents "uncle" and "aunty" but I was never allowed to call the Redlers that.

"Her daughter was the kindest and would try to ease my crying. She had a twisted foot and used to say 'Nobody will want to marry me'. I tried to cheer her up by saying she had a lovely face and smile. The son was at training college learning to be a farmer and he often goaded us by saying the Government didn't pay enough for our keep.

"I was undersized and got the nickname of Giant. I was also boss-eyed after whooping cough and sometimes wore a patch over the worst eye. It was rare to see kids in glasses then so I was also called Four Eyes. To build me up, at school I was prescribed cod liver oil and malt. The headmaster was strict but sometimes we were allowed to see a film and that was marvellous. Most of the local Somerset school kids did not like us Londoners and made no bones about it. I did make one firm friend, though, he was called Stanley Wiltshire. He lived on the top of the beautiful Quantock Hills. There were stunning views up there. Stanley came from a poor agricultural working family and he had a long walk to school, mostly downhill but going home it was all uphill. The local council gave him a bike so he would not be late so often. He ended up in hospital with severe nervous trouble. I sent him money but he stopped writing to me after that. I was upset that he turned out to be so unreliable. I often think of him today and wonder if he is still alive.

"There was a Land Army girl there and later on two prisoners of war, an Italian and a German. I got on well with both of them. The German gave me a beautifully-written scroll before I left. Sadly, I never found it when I arrived home and I wonder now if they took it. I often worked hard and I had my meals apart from them. I also often waited on them at table, like a servant. There were Americans near us in about 1944 and we used to run after their vehicles shouting and they threw out gum, candy, soup and things. At the chapel at harvest festival, the local baker make a magnificent loaf in the shape of a sheaf of wheat and sometimes an American priest officer led the service of thanksgiving.

"Mum, who stayed in Plaistow, endured a lot of the bombing and was once fired at by an aeroplane's machine gun. She used to send me a parcel of comics once a fortnight and visited Somerset once a year. My grandma came once also. Dad did not come often but I do remember him being put up in the summer house in the garden although I am sure there was probably room in the house.

"I wanted a bike and Mrs Redler made me save for it with six pence a week, the pocket money mum sent. I had to pray every night for this bike and it took over three and a half years to get it, almost too late to use in Somerset. I took it home with me and outgrew it eventually. The one good thing Mrs Redler teach me was thrift and the good handling of money.

"Once I fell through the ice in a pond. Luckily it wasn't too deep because I could not swim. I went to the house of the nearest farmer who knew me well. He was a Sunday school teacher yet he showed me no Christian charity. He would not take me in to dry me off, but sent me home a mile away in soaking wet clothes and there was snow on the ground. I was always made to dress in short trousers even in winter and my knees and legs would get red raw and sore with frost cuts.

CHAPTER TWENTY-FIVE

"After about one and a half years my brother Patrick was transferred to another billet as he was more trouble than me. I heard that his new foster parent beat him with a walking stick but I was too young at the time to do anything about it and it is sketchy now. In later years poor Pat became a chronic schizophrenic. How much the move to Somerset and his ill-treatment contributed to his illness we can only guess at but I would imagine it had a fair impact on his mental health. Pat died in 1980, aged just 51.

"Evacuation was a great upheaval for such young and impressionable minds. Some were lucky others were not so lucky. When I went back to Plaistow I thought 'they will write to ask me back', not just the Redlers but all the others I held in such high regard. However, I was to be disappointed. I suppose it was a case of "out of sight, out of mind".

"The letters inviting me to return never came and although I made a few trips back for the day, I was clearly not welcome. Once I had travelled 140-odd miles and was greeted by a neighbour I had considered a friend barking at me, 'I can't put you up overnight'. 'Nobody asked you to,' I replied. He was another Sunday school teacher though his Christianity obviously didn't extend to us evacuees. My illusions that they liked me were certainly shattered."

Chapter Twenty-six
What the war was like

This account of her evacuation and subsequent life during the war by Sylvia Rogan, née Chesser, should be required reading for everyone but especially for school children sitting their GCSEs. They study the war for their exams and I don't think they will come across a more vivid account than this; one that includes some of the horrors of what evacuees went through plus all the minutiae of ordinary daily life in those days. All of you who are of a similar age will recognise many of the things Sylvia describes: the poss tub, the day-long rambles over the countryside with a couple of jam sandwiches and a bottle of water, the local bobby you were afraid of, the eccentrics you were not afraid of, the rationing, the gas masks.

Sweet rationing began on Sunday, July 26, 1941, to be followed soon by a ban on ice cream though it probably did not mean all that much to most of us: what you never have you never miss. Children were allowed two ounces of sweets per week.

George Murray, a writer in the Daily Mail, said at the time he thought children should get more sweeties. He argued that children had no toys to speak of and they weren't allowed to go to the seaside because the beaches all had barbed wire across them, whereas grown-ups had cinemas, concert halls and pubs. But he was inundated with letters from people disagreeing with him. No doubt they were more of those "kindly folk" who felt so warmly towards children.

We never had bananas either and if a shop had oranges there was a queue round the block within minutes.

Sylvia writes about the toys her brother managed to cobble together and that is the sort of makeshift plaything children had in those days, nothing like the incredible toys they have now. Soldiers used to make toys out of Spam and sardine tins; scraps of black-out material and bits of wood were converted into a wide assortment of railway engines, lorries, tanks, dolls and animals. Evacuees were over the moon if they managed to get their hands on one of those.

The Government started discussing gas masks in the early 1930s. A Wing Cdr Hodsoll pointed out on January 10, 1934, that on the outbreak of war there would be such a clamour on the part of the civilian population that it would be impossible to limit the supply of masks to the defence services or those engaged in essential services. I should say so. He suggested the Government had better get its act together and make sure enough were being manufactured to go round. Ironically, someone proposed paying £140,000 for a German patent, the property of a Doctor Hugo Stoltzenberg.

Some of the early trials of new gas masks were conducted at a Dr Barnardo's home and at the Girls High School, Sutton, Surrey. Of particular concern were contraptions for babies and small children; one suggestion for toddlers was that they should have brightly coloured face pieces so they didn't look so frightening. The original designs also had to be altered to make them smaller and lighter.

One boffin suggested that prams could become a mobile gas-tight box until someone suggested that that could look like protection for the rich and not for the poor, because most of the poor did not have a pram. "If they don't have prams, what do they take their children out in?" one of the civil servants, who was charged with the care and protection of the next generation, asked. "Do they cart them about in their arms or what happens?"

Wing Cdr Hodsoll, in a letter dated March 16, 1937, was worried:

"The question of the protection of babies is a very big and important gap in our protection proposals and it has been dragging on for so long I am really getting very concerned," he wrote.

A gas mask, if properly put on, protected the eyes, nose, mouth and lungs and ensured a supply of pure air for breathing, by means of filters which were able to absorb any known war gas. They consisted of a rubber facepiece with a transparent window and a container which held the gas filters. Gas masks had two filters, one of which consisted of specially prepared charcoal and the other of a specially prepared pad or pads.

People were advised to walk with extreme care, to avoid all damp splashes and, if they had to go outside, to always keep their gas masks on. "Though the hostile aircraft may have gone, there may be gas drifting about or splashed on the ground," a leaflet warned. The facepiece, which fitted closely round the face, prevented any air from getting inside the respirator except what passed through the filters. It was held in position by adjustable straps behind the head. They made you look extraordinarily ugly and frightening.

It would have been interesting to read a first-hand explanation of a parent struggling to fit a gas mask on a baby in extreme circumstances, when bombs were falling, but my research failed to uncover any such account.

Sylvia's is a traumatic story in the beginning when she was first separated from her brother, as they inevitably did separate siblings in that cattle market at the end of the train journey. She was beaten, she was made to stand in an outside toilet riddled with spiders and constantly tormented, but eventually she was reunited with her mother, brother and baby sister then finally her father when he was demobbed. She wrote her story so her own children and grandchildren would know what the evacuation was really like, and I reproduce it here because it illustrates so well both the good and the bad parts of our shared childhood.

"I would like everyone to know what happened in those dark harrowing years," says Sylvia. "When war was declared we were living in Hoxton, Shoreditch, in the east end of London. I was five and my brother Ron was ten and there was Shirley, just a baby. Ron and I, complete with a gas mask in a cardboard box over one shoulder and a label with our names on attached to the lapels of our coat, gathered at the railway station along with hundreds of other nervous and crying children. I remember Mum saying to Ron 'Look after your little sister' and I clung to him desperately, completely unaware of what was in store for us.

"Our destination was to be Cambridge, and we duly arrived in a little village, were herded into the institute hall and sat on benches and waited. Men and women (mainly women, though) came and walked along the benches and picked out the child, or children, they would take into their homes. Ron kept hold of me, fiercely announcing that we were not to be separated.

"As it happened we were billeted out to a farm some two and a half miles away. Ron was to stay with the farmer and I with the farm labourer's family in a cottage attached to the farm. So I came to lodge with Mr and Mrs Cater and their daughter Jean who was a bit older than me. They never wanted to take me in and every day I lived there they never missed an opportunity of letting me know what a nuisance I was.

"Mind you, very few of the evacuees wherever they were sent were ever wanted. A lucky few had a great time with smashing foster parents, but a great majority were treated terribly, even though the people who did take them in got an allowance, but because of the war they got away with it, and who would believe the children against the word of the 'nice' foster parents? Even after all these years there are still some who remember us as 'those London evacuees'.

"We had to walk to school, a distance of two and a half miles, whatever the weather. In winter it was still dark when we left home and dark when we returned. There were no lights to guide our way and our walk was mainly through country lanes. School was held in the institute hall, a curtain divided the village children from the London children. We had two teachers who came with us from London, Miss Bubbles and Mrs Scott. Mrs Scott was a retired lady and she lived in a house on the edge of the green which was in front of the institute. I remember her with great affection as she often befriended me, and many others who missed their Mums and their homes. Many times we would sit by the fireside as she comforted us. Sadly, one day she got terribly mauled by a dog and her injuries made it impossible for us to call on her again.

"There was also another family in the village who were very kind to us. They owned a large house called The Spinney and were related to the family where Ron was billeted. Mrs Cater, my foster mother, cleaned for them and so during school holidays I had to go along with her and her daughter Jean and we were allowed to play in the sun house at the bottom of the garden. I also remember they had a well in the garden with a roof over it.

"After Ron had been at the farm for a few months, the wife of the farmer became pregnant. Unfortunately, she was poorly on and off so Ron was taken away to stay with some people near the Fens, a marshy area, who made their living making cane baskets. So then I was on my own and even though Mum wrote letters to us and sent us a postal order when she could spare the money, I never once ever saw them. I was just told, 'Your mother has wrote (sic), she is safe and well'.

"In the meantime bombing had got worse in London. Our Dad was in the Civil Defence and they were having a terrible time digging people out from the ruins of their homes and rescuing people where they could.

Grandma Chesser lived opposite the Gainsborough Film Studios where many of the early English films were made. Will Hay starred in many, along with other classic stars of the pre-war era. I remember Dad once telling us that they were paid one shilling to be extras in the films and once they were part of a crowd supposedly beating up a politician making a speech, but things got rather out of hand and the poor man landed up in hospital.

"Anyway, for a time the studio served as an air raid shelter and Mum and Shirley went there, but Mum was scared of all the scenery stored there and the big marble columns and statues. She felt if they did get hit they would certainly be buried under all that lot. Grandma's house got hit twice in the bombing and once Dad and his brother had to rescue her through the roof. Remarkably, she survived to live nearly seven years after the war.

"Then the Germans started to send over the flying bombs, named V1s and V2s. They were a pilotless bomb that you could hear whistling along and then it would go silent and that's when it dropped to the earth below and exploded. The order was given for mothers with young children still in London to be evacuated and that included Mum and Shirley. They were first sent to Norfolk and then on to Yorkshire, arriving in a little village called Embsay.

"Meanwhile, life for me was very hard with the Cater family. My diet consisted of soup every day except Sunday when I was allowed the treat of two sandwiches for my tea. It was no good complaining and to leave anything meant instant punishment. Almost every day without exception after tea, Mr Cater would take off his belt, a thick leather one, and spank my bottom for something I had, or hadn't done, it didn't matter either way to him. Inevitably I would wet myself through fright and then I would be locked up in the outside lavatory until I had 'calmed down'.

"Even to this day I still go cold when I see creepy crawlies for they horrified me in that outside hut. This went on almost every day that I was with them, two and a half years in all. Today Mr Cater would have been imprisoned for being a pervert, but it happened to many children, and they just got away with it because of the war.

"Although he meted out the punishment, his wife and daughter were always there to watch. I shared a bedroom with the daughter, Jean, who just seemed to take pleasure in getting me into trouble, blaming me for silly little things which would annoy her mother who in turn related them to her husband, and so the cycle went on.

"The only time it didn't happen was when I had an accident at school. We stayed at school for midday lunch and had our dinner sitting at our desks. Beside my desk were all the milk bottles for the class and one lunchtime someone came and sat beside me and pushed me off the end of the seat right on top of the bottles. My left leg was gashed open from just above the knee to the thigh.

"I can vaguely remember a young doctor coming in, scrubbing down the table top, placing me on top and sewing up my leg, there was no anaesthetic, just me screaming my head off.

"I was then six years old. Next day my leg had swollen to twice its size and I was very ill. Another doctor came to see me and gave me some 'sweets' to eat. I remember nothing more until I woke up and found my leg in plaster from top to bottom. I was in that plaster for about three months and I didn't mind one bit as I was out of the way of Mr Cater, but I still have the scars on my leg to this day.

"In Cambridge we knew very little of war events, apart from being told that London and other places were being bombed; life in the village slowly went on. I saw Ron at school and after school we would walk part of the way home together, talking of Mum and Dad and Shirley and wishing we were home. Ron had a flair for writing and putting on little shows, something he did on a much larger scale later in life while in the Army. The longer we were in Cambridge, the more the evacuees got fed up. Many tried to run away, some made it, others were brought back. Ron and I talked many times of running away, but to where?

"We just clung to the hope that one day soon we would be re-united with our Mum, Dad and baby sister. So Ron had the idea to put on a show to cheer us all up and, with the help of our teachers, it gave us all something to do.

"One day, when we were out in the fields, a German aeroplane came down and the pilot surrendered himself to the local air raid wardens. It caused great excitement but that was about as much of the enemy as we ever saw. We could hear the planes going over at night and you could tell which were our planes and which were the Germans by the sound of the engines. I used to cover myself up with the sheets and keep saying 'Please God let them pass over' and then when it was all quiet again, 'Thank you very much God'.

"Mum was determined to save up the train fare to enable Ron and me to join her in Yorkshire. Any parents who wanted their children to join them had to pay the fare themselves and it was a lot of money to find from the small allowance Mum had. So she almost starved herself, did as many cleaning jobs at the large houses in as it was possible to fit in in one day, and even scrubbed the grave stones in the churchyard for two shillings and six pence. It was to be a mammoth task, but Mum finally made it and we were re-united after two- and-a-half years apart.

"I can vividly recall that morning. Up to that date I had not been allowed to see any letters from Mum and Dad, I was merely told that they were alright, that Mum and Shirley had been evacuated to Yorkshire and that my Dad was still in London. Our letters home were only copies of what we were told to say and then posted by our foster parents.

"So, on that morning, when an official letter arrived saying that someone would be taking me to the station I was so excited, but Mrs Cater and Mrs Elsie Good, her neighbour, had other ideas. They taunted me right up until the moment when the car arrived, saying that I would not be allowed to leave. I just didn't know what to do and it was a great relief when I joined Ron and we were finally on the train.

"We arrived on a bitterly cold winter's day. The stationmaster's wife, Mrs Fisher, whom Mum had done some cleaning for, asked us into her house and warmed us up with some soup. That was one thing I really could have done without after enduring it every day, but we were so cold I ate it up.

"After Mum had arrived in Yembsay she was given an old house, 39 Main Street. It had been an old coaching inn, built in 1693, and still had stone flags on the floor and was bitterly cold, with a stone staircase and no carpeting. She shared the house with another London family at first, but they hated it and took their chances and went back home. Furniture consisted of boxes and any odd bits and pieces that people would have thrown out, but 'donated' instead to the evacuees.

"One night the one bed we had which slept Mum, Shirley and I - Ron had a camp bed - collapsed, it was so worm-eaten in the legs. It went straight through the floor boards and finished up on top of the sideboard down below. The floor boards had woodworm in them, too. We thought a bomb had hit us, but we all had a good laugh after we got over the initial shock.

"Even though there wasn't much in the house in terms of furniture or food we were all together and never again would I endure the assaults and mental cruelty I had at the hands of my foster parents and their daughter. It felt so good that night cuddled up to Mum and Shirley, safe at last, and listening to Mum telling us a bedtime story, she was quite an expert at making up stories, each night adding a bit more on to the original tale.

"I'm sure that my mother was totally devastated at the thought of what I had gone through, but there was little she could do situated as we were, miles from anywhere and no one concerned enough to do anything about it.

"After a few days when we had got used to our new surroundings, we enrolled into the local village school. The headmaster was Mr Albert Williams, known by the schoolchildren as 'Pop Williams'. He wasn't really a teacher, just a stand-in because most of the male teachers had been called up for the Forces.

"The other teachers were three maidenly ladies called Miss Graham, Miss Hurst and Miss Lister. I was in Miss Lister's class to begin with. She was a nice grey-haired old lady who treated me well. Sadly, that was not the case with many people in the village for they tended to look upon the evacuees as rowdy uncouth people from London invading their village. At that time they didn't really know us and it was an opinion formed by gossip and rumours.

"One person who really hated the evacuees was the headmaster, Mr Williams, and whenever he could have a dig or humiliate Ron he would do so. Ron tried to stand up to him as much as he could, but one day he just couldn't take any more and told 'Pop' what he thought of him and then ran out of school. When he got home of course Mum wanted to know what he was doing home at that time of day, so Ron told her of all that had been going on. Well, that was good enough for her. She marched Ron back up to the school; it was a church school and had a big wooden door with a heavy knocker and Mum banged on that door with all the anger welling up inside her.

"We were later told by other children that old 'Pop' had fairly quaked in his shoes as he guessed who it was at the door. When Mum confronted him and gave him more than a piece of her mind, he had little to say but she reminded him of how safe he was in his nice easy job while other men were out fighting for their country and the likes of him. She also told him that we were not scum from the slums of London, but decent ordinary folk who should be treated accordingly. Next day Ron was made a monitor which gave us all a good laugh.

"After we had been in Embsay for a while Dad came up to see us, it was his embarkation leave. He had been called up for the Forces and had 14 days leave before being sent to North Africa and later Italy. That was to be the last time we saw him until the end of the war.

"So we settled down to life in the village, making new friends along the way. Mum kept busy doing what work she could, for the Army allowance from Dad was pitifully small, but as there was little to buy in the shops due to rationing, we didn't crave luxuries. The shops never knew what goods were going to be delivered; they would get a few boxes in and when word got round that the Co-op had had a delivery everyone would just queue up, whatever you got was welcome and a great treat.

"One day we were able to buy a small tin of red salmon - now that really was a luxury, but Mum said we would save it until the day Dad came home and then we would have a feast.

"Well, that tin of salmon stood on the pantry shelf and many, many times we looked longingly at it just imagining the taste of salmon, but no, Mum was adamant that tin was to be saved until the war was over. Came the day when Dad finally returned home and we opened the tin of salmon and spread it thinly on sandwiches so we could all have a taste. But when Dad saw it he said he didn't want any as they had thrown tins of the stuff away, so much had been sent to the Forces from Canada and America, they were fed up to the teeth with it. We just couldn't believe it as it had taken so much willpower never to open it until that day.

"Whenever there was a concert at the village institute, and that was, basically, the main entertainment, Mum would offer to play the piano. She had never been taught to play but could just sit down and play most of the songs and tunes of the day. Ron would play his banjo and Mum encouraged the people to sing along. She would always keep saying how much the village needed livening up and she loved nothing more than having a good sing-song.

"Many more evacuees kept arriving, being moved on from place to place and Mum couldn't turn any away even though we hardly had room, but she thought of us and how we had felt away from home, and she did her best to make them feel welcome. During those war years Mum took in a total of 17 evacuees. Someone in the village donated an old piano, it didn't have much tune to it but Mum managed and it got to be a regular occurrence for the other Londoners staying in the village to come to our house for a sing-song of the old London tunes.

"If Mum could manage it, she would make a bread pudding, every Cockney's favourite dish and a reminder of home. When the parents of the evacuees came to visit their children they would beg to stay at our house, even though it meant sleeping on the couch or armchair, but they felt so much at home with Mum and many of those friendships lasted until long after the war.

"Mum took in several boys from a large private school in Brighton, they became known as the Brighton Boys. One of those boys, Johnny Ames, kept up his friendship with Mum right until her death in 1981. He brought his family up for them to meet her and nicknamed her 'his wartime Mum'. After her death he wrote a lovely letter to us all saying how fond he was of her and how she had done her best to be a second mother to them all.

"Most of the evacuees returned to their homes down south when it was sufficiently safe to do so, but Mum had already decided that we would stay where we were as we had no home in London to go back to and conditions in Shoreditch where we came from would be far worse as many, many streets of houses had been completely wiped out.

"It was a struggle to keep going but it was better to stay put and make the most of what we had. Living in Yorkshire surrounded by the countryside you could take advantage of picking wild fruits or plants to help out with the daily rations. There were many well-off people who paid handsomely for extras, known as the Black Market.

"For us it was the other way round. Mum would save up our butter and sugar rations to sell so that we could buy much more needed items and as much as I hated stew, it was our mainstay as there were very few alternatives we could get for a meal. Indeed, a pan of stew could last for a few days by just adding another potato or carrot each day, depending on the generosity of someone with a garden who would sell or give you a few vegetables.

"Ron and I would get up early when the time was right to go and pick mushrooms which we could either sell or exchange for vegetables. We didn't have coal for the fire so we used to go 'sticking', that was picking up bits of twigs or branches that had fallen off the trees. We had an old pram and walked up to the woods and fill the pram up with as much wood as we could. We had a black stove and everything was cooked on the fire, including the big black kettle, or in the oven at the side of the stove. We hated the job of raking out the stove, cleaning out all the old ash and then shining it up with Zebra polish and a lot of hard brushing.

"We had no bathroom, indeed we didn't have any hot water system. In the kitchen we just had a deep brown sink and a cold water tap. Bath night meant bringing in the big zinc bath from where it hung on a nail in the back yard and filling it up with pans of hot water which were boiled up on the stove. It was lovely, though, on cold winter nights to have the bath in front of the fire.

"The house next door, No 41, became vacant after another London family returned home and Mum applied for the tenancy and got it. It felt like moving into a palace after the old, cold house of No 39, but we still had no electricity, only lighting by gas mantles and that just downstairs. At night we had to have a candle to see our way to bed.

"Washing clothes was done in an old boiler in the wash house in the back yard. It was an old copper boiler encased into the wall. We filled it with water, then lit the fire underneath. When it was hot enough Mum scrubbed the clothes with a block of Fairy soap or Sunlight on a tin scrubbing board, then put the clothes into the boiler and let them boil up.

"Sometimes she put them in a big tub and used a posser, which was like a big plunger. Then the washing was taken out of the boiler with a big pair of wooden tongs and fed through the mangle. One of us would have to turn the handle controlling the rollers on the mangle.

"From there the clothes were put into another tub to be rinsed in cold water, then fed through the mangle again until all the water had been squeezed out, then onto the clothes line. Wash day started early and went on for quite a few hours. Ironing was done with a heavy, solid iron which was warmed up either on the fire or on the stove, cleaned on a cloth before use, then the ironing was done as quickly as possible because the iron soon cooled down and you had to repeat the heating up process all over again.

"When the clothes were ironed they were put on a wooden clothes rail which was on a pulley and hoisted up over the fireplace so the clothes were always warm and nicely aired.

"As you had to have coupons to purchase clothing nobody had

that many clothes anyway, so mainly most of our clothes were kept on the wooden airer. It would be one set of clothes for school and one set for Sunday best, with a few old blouses or shirts to change into for playing out. We would always go to the local jumble sales in the hope of getting a bargain and usually came away with something that we could make do or mend.

"While Dad was serving in Italy he sent home a parcel which included two lemons. Imported fruit was unobtainable and most children born after war was declared did not know what a banana was. The few oranges available were usually sent to hospitals etc for sick children.

"Anyway, two lemons were like gold dust. So Mum took them to the British Legion as a prize in a raffle, the proceeds to go towards the Red Cross Parcels for the Troops and Prisoners of War. They were gratefully received.

"We were encouraged to pick rose hips during the summer holidays and were paid six pence a pound. They were made into rose hip syrup for young children.

"During the war everyone was urged to buy saving stamps as a means of helping to buy equipment and arms for the Forces, and I remember one day when a large replica bomb was delivered to the post office. It stood on a large cart and those who bought a six pence stamp could stick it on the bomb and say 'That's a bit more towards blowing up Hitler'.

"Another wartime slogan was 'Dig for Victory' which was aimed at anyone who had a garden, however small, to grow vegetables instead of flowers and then help neighbours by giving them fresh vegetables. All iron gates and railings were also taken away to be melted down for use in the foundries making ammunition or tanks. You couldn't buy new saucepans so if you got a hole in one you would have to mend it by putting in a washer fixed with a nut and bolt.

"It wasn't all doom and gloom though and indeed most people went out of their way to try and put on a cheerful face and to make the most of what we had. One morning Ron came rushing back home just after nine o'clock shouting, 'Mum, Mum, guess what?' and Mum replied 'Don't tell me, the war is over.' 'No,' said Ron, 'better than that - the school is on fire and we don't have to go in today'. It wasn't a big fire, just the boiler got overheated. It did cause some damage to one of the classrooms and we had a holiday until it was all mended.

"Ron had a friend called Eddie Scott who lived nearby, they used to like making things up out of any old bits and pieces they could find and once they made a bogie cart on wheels which had a box on top to sit on and an old rope to steer it along. I had the privilege of first ride down Main Street, in those days there was very little traffic, and I felt like a queen sitting up there on the wooden box. It seemed we were going very fast, clinging tightly to the rope guiding us along. We had lots of fun on that old bogie until it got smashed up and couldn't be repaired again.

"Another time when it had been snowing heavily and the field behind our house was several feet deep in snow Ron made some skis from bits of tin and two old broom handles. The field sloped down towards the house so it made a good place to ski or sled down with an old tray as a sledge. Unfortunately, one day I came a bit too close to the wall at the end and went over, splitting my head open. Mum had to take me down to the surgery in Skipton with a towel wrapped round my head and the doctor, Mrs Goodall, stitched the gash up for me.

"One thing with living in a village, you knew almost everyone. Certainly as far as Main Street was concerned we could tell anyone who lived at such and such a number of house, and all the schoolchildren living on Main Street mainly stayed and played together. We made up our own games, as well as the old favourites such as marbles or hop scotch, spinning a top or skipping.

"We also did a lot of walking, there being few means of transport in those days due to petrol rationing. So, in the summer holidays, we would go hiking over the moors or gather bluebells on Bluebell Hill in Whitaker Wood. One of our favourite pastimes was going to Rowton Beck on the Bolton Abbey Road.

"We could paddle or catch tiddlers in a jam jar and then we would jump from bank to bank of the beck, some parts were wider than others and we dared each other to see who could jump the furthest. More often than not you landed up missing the bank and finished up in the water but to us it was good fun, and if we got soaked we could always sit on the grass until we had dried out.

"There were many characters among the village folk. Our postman was one. His name was Joe Smith. He didn't have a uniform but wore ragged clothes, his trousers were held up by a bit of string and a big safety pin held together the front of his jacket and he had a big floppy hat. His nose was nearly always sporting a dew drop but for all his appearance you could always rely on him whatever the weather. He said he always ate mustard sandwiches to keep him warm but I think he also got many titbits from the householders.

" If you were ever lucky enough to get a postcard, he read it out to you before handing it over, but no one ever seemed to mind.

"Our village policeman was PC Marsden, a huge man, at least to us he was, and he never stood any nonsense. Any girl or boy up to mischief could expect to be taken home firmly gripped by the ear. We used to run if we saw him but he always managed to be just behind you. There really weren't any crimes committed but we had respect for him as a man of the law.

"In Main Street we had a post office, a Co-op store, a small grocery shop and a pub called the Elm Tree. It was called that because at the top of Main Street was a huge elm tree. On the stone surround enveloping the tree was some lettering relating to the Chippendale family but it was well worn and hard to make out what it said exactly. There was also a little garage on the corner, but as they had very little petrol to sell, they just did odd repair jobs or mended the farm machinery which was essential to the war effort.

"Next door but one to us was the Methodist Chapel. Soon after we arrived in Embsay, the superintendent there asked Mum if Ron and I would like to join the Sunday school. We did and later on when she was old enough, so did Shirley. Although Ron gave it up when he got older, both Shirley and I remained within the Chapel until our twenties, taking part in most of the activities, joining the chapel choir and youth club and becoming Sunday school teachers and guild members.

"Across the road from our house was the recreation ground. It had a slide, two swings and a roundabout, also a tennis court, rather the worse for wear but it was used occasionally. We had lots of fun in the rec as it was known.

"We would hold concerts, dressing up in any old bits of clothing we could find. If you could sing or say a poem, you were in. We also held our gang meetings in the rec. Gangs were mostly made up of about a dozen girls living on Main Street. We had a list of rules which nobody kept but we would pass notes to each other at school and plan what our next 'move' was going to be. Then someone would fall out with one of the gang and we would argue and say we were not going to speak to them again but we would all be mates again a few days later.

"The village institute in the entrance of Main Street was the meeting place for all the villagers. It also had a small billiard hall attached to it. Dances were held there and village concerts made up of local talent. More or less any local event was held there. At Christmas there was a party for all the children and you got a small present from Father Christmas and in the evening there was a dance for the adults. The band consisted of a pianist, a drummer and some other musician depending on who was available. When I was old enough to go it was a great event for me.

"Further down in the village was the newspaper shop. Both Ron and I delivered papers. I took over from him when he was 14. I enjoyed doing it, particularly at Christmas when we got tips, but one winter a lady from Easterby, the next village, walked through the night to the Tannery Dam and threw herself in. It was a lonely part of the village and there was only one house along there that I had to deliver a paper to but I got so frightened by her suicide I gave up the paper round.

"We also had a fish and chip shop. Fish cost six pence and tuppence for the chips, but you could get a pennyworth of scraps which were the bits of batter scooped up from the fat; if we added them to the chips, we had a good meal, as there were often bits of fish sticking to the scraps.

"Some four or five miles further on from Embsay was Bolton Abbey, a beautiful and peaceful village. It had a priory church and ancient ruins and the River Wharfe flowed majestically nearby. You could cross by the bridge or go across the famous stepping stones, which was quite an arduous task, especially in the centre where the stones had wider gaps. We loved to go to Bolton Abbey and spent many happy hours there. If you were to walk further along by the riverside you came to the Strid which was a whirlpool and which had claimed many lives. We rarely walked that far as we knew what a dangerous place it was.

"Embsay was a good place to grow up in, surrounded as it was by moors and lovely countryside. We went walking over the moors a great deal and visited Easby, Halton East and Barden Towers which were all within easy reach. Transport was almost non-existent, at least for us, so if you wanted to go anywhere, you walked but for children it was a great adventure.

"During the school holidays, weather permitting, we set out with sandwiches and a bottle of water and spend the entire day walking over the fields and hills, going through the woods, exploring as we went along, and learning about nature, finding plants and wild strawberries growing along the hedgerows. There seemed so much to do in those days and we were never bored. In winter when we usually had heavy falls of snow we went sledging which was always great fun.

"When I was 11 years old I was able to leave Embsay school and go to the secondary modern school in Skipton. Ron had left school and was working in a cotton mill and Shirley was now going to my old school. I also joined the G.F.S. - Girls' Friendly Society. It was supervised by a Miss Earnshaw, a retired headmistress and the meetings were held in her house. She taught us sewing and embroidery as well as singing and other activities.

"The war was still going on and on land between Embsay and Skipton they built a prisoner of war camp. I think it was only used for Italian prisoners. Many times the Army lorries and tanks would come through Embsay and sometimes the prisoners would offer sweets or chocolates to the children but Mum had forbidden us to accept any as Dad was still out in Italy in the thick of the fighting.

"In May 1945 victory in Europe was declared. Everyone went wild, at last the long war was over, although fighting was still going on in the Far East with the Japanese. Parties were held and everyone talked of when the Forces would be coming home. Actually it was quite some time before the men were demobbed. First to come home were all the wounded and then over many weeks and months the other men and women came home.

"To celebrate the end of the war the parish council invited householders to decorate their houses in suitable red white and blue and there would be a prize. Mum bought as many paper flags as the corner shop could spare and we sewed them onto strips of white tape and strung them from window to window, upstairs and downstairs. We had photographs of the King and Queen, we worked really hard to make it special and we won the first prize of ten shillings. Quite a nice gift for us.

"We saved all the bunting and when Dad finally came home we decorated the house again but this time Ron had painted a large banner with the words Welcome Home Dad on it. What a day that was.

"In August 1945 the Americans dropped an atom bomb on Hiroshima and a couple of days later another bomb on Nagasaki and the Japanese surrendered. The Second World War 1939-1945 was finally over. We went back to see my grandmother and aunts and uncles in London and were able to share the street party in Hoxton in celebration of the end of the war.

"Our cousins thought we spoke funny as by now we had acquired a Yorkshire accent. Although we had all been born within the sound of Bow Bells, as a true Cockney should be, we now counted ourselves Yorkshire bred.

"Ron, Shirley and myself all went on to do well at school and in our chosen careers and for that we owed so much to our Mum who endured so much hardship and loneliness without Dad to bring us safely through the war. We can be eternally grateful that none of our children has ever had to go through the experience of war and evacuation and please God future generations will not have to do so either. I always vowed that if another war ever came – God forbid – none of my children would be taken away from me."